HOLT Handbook

Fifth Course

Developmental Language and Sentence Skills Guided Practice

- ■ **Grammar**
- ■ **Usage**
- ■ **Mechanics**
- ■ **Sentences**

HOLT, RINEHART AND WINSTON

A Harcourt Education Company

Austin • Orlando • Chicago • New York • Toronto • London • San Diego

STAFF CREDITS

EDITORIAL

Executive Editor
Robert R. Hoyt

Senior Editor
Marcia L. Kelley

Project Editor
Eric Estlund

Writing and Editing
Guy Guidici, Amber M. Rigney, *Associate Editors*

Copyediting
Michael Neibergall, *Copyediting Manager;* Mary Malone, *Copyediting Supervisor;* Elizabeth Dickson, *Senior Copyeditor;* Christine Altgelt, Joel Bourgeois, Emily Force, Julie A. Hill, Julia Thomas Hu, Jennifer Kirkland, Millicent Ondras, Dennis Scharnberg, *Copyeditors*

Project Administration
Marie Price, *Managing Editor;* Lori De La Garza, *Editorial Finance Manager;* Tracy DeMont, Jennifer Renteria, Janet Riley, *Project Administration;* Margaret Sanchez, *Word Processing Supervisor;* Casey Kelly, Joie Pickett, *Word Processing*

Editorial Permissions
Janet Harrington, *Permissions Editor*

ART, DESIGN AND PHOTO

Graphic Services
Kristen Darby, *Manager*

Image Acquisitions
Joe London, *Director;* Jeannie Taylor, *Photo Research Supervisor;* Tim Taylor, *Photo Research Supervisor;* Rick Benavides, *Photo Researcher;* Cindy Verheyden, *Senior Photo Researcher;* Elaine Tate, *Supervisor*

Cover Design
Curtis Riker, *Design Director*
Sunday Patterson, *Designer*

PRODUCTION
Belinda Barbosa Lopez, *Senior Production Coordinator*
Carol Trammel, *Production Supervisor*
Beth Prevelige, *Senior Production Manager*

MANUFACTURING/INVENTORY
Shirley Cantrell, *Manufacturing Supervisor*
Amy Borseth, *Manufacturing Coordinator*
Mark McDonald, *Inventory Planner*

ISBN 0-03-066391-1

8 9 10 11 12 13 1410 17 16 15 14 13
4500428783

Contents

Contents

Contents

Using This Workbook

The worksheets in this workbook provide instruction, practice, and reinforcement for the *Holt Handbook* and *Language & Sentence Skills Practice*.

This workbook is designed to supplement *Language & Sentence Skills Practice* by providing additional instruction and practice to students who have not yet mastered the rules and topics covered in *Holt Handbook*.

You will find throughout the workbook several special features, which have been added to aid students' mastery of grammar, usage, and mechanics. The special features include notes, reminders, tips, points of instruction after instructional and exercise examples, and guided practice for the first one or two items in each exercise.

- **Notes** provide students with pertinent information related to the rule or topic covered on a given worksheet.

- **Reminders** review grammatical terms and concepts that were covered on previous worksheets.

- **Tips** provide students with tangible aids for understanding abstract concepts. These tips include mnemonic devices, identification tests, and recognition strategies.

- **Points of Instruction** explain how the rule or topic applies to the instructional and exercise examples provided.

- **Guided Practice** helps students with the first one or two items of each exercise by asking questions that guide students to the correct answer.

Teacher's Notes and an **Answer Key** are provided in a separate booklet titled *Developmental Language & Sentence Skills Guided Practice, Teacher's Notes and Answer Key.*

Symbols for Revising and Proofreading

Symbol	Example	Meaning of Symbol
≡	Fifty-first street	Capitalize a lowercase letter.
/	Jerry's Aunt	Lowercase a capital letter.
∧	differ*e*ant	Change a letter.
∧	the capital *of* Ohio	Insert a missing word, letter, or punctuation mark.
⌐	beside the *lake* river	Replace a word.
℘	Where's the the key?	Leave out a word, letter, or punctuation mark.
℘	an invisibile guest	Leave out and close up.
⌣	a close friend ship	Close up space.
∩	thier	Change the order of letters.
(tr)	Avoid having too many corrections (of your paper) in the final version.	Transfer the circled words. (Write *tr* in nearby margin.)
¶	¶"Hi," he smiled.	Begin a new paragraph.
⊙	Stay well⊙	Add a period.
∧	Of course you may be wrong.	Add a comma.
#	icehockey	Add a space.
⊘	one of the following⊘	Add a colon.
∧	Maria Simmons, M.D.∧ Jim Fiorello, Ph.D.	Add a semicolon.
=	a great=grandmother	Add a hyphen.
∨	Pauls car	Add an apostrophe.
(stet)	On the fifteenth of July	Keep the crossed-out material. (Write *stet* in nearby margin.)

The Noun

1a.   A **noun** names a person, a place, a thing, or an idea.

PERSONS	dentist, cousin, Tiger Woods, Mrs. Mendoza
PLACES	kitchen, Detroit, Grand Canyon, mall
THINGS	notebook, map, Washington Monument, chair
IDEAS	bravery, talent, self-esteem, Buddhism

Common Nouns and Proper Nouns

A **common noun** names any one of a group of persons, places, things, or ideas, and generally is not capitalized unless it begins a sentence or is part of a title. A **proper noun** names a particular person, place, thing, or idea and is generally capitalized.

COMMON NOUNS	poet, city, game, philosophy
PROPER NOUNS	Matthew Arnold, St. Louis, Super Bowl, Zen

EXERCISE A Underline each noun in the following sentences. Then, underline each proper noun a second time.

Example 1. Chris and his brother loaded the projector onto the cart. [*Chris* names a particular person; *brother* names a person, but not a particular one. *Projector* and *cart* name things that belong to a general group.]

1. While in Spain, Kelly and Veronica toured many old castles. [Which nouns are common and which are proper?]

2. These shoelaces are too short for my new shoes!

3. *Gone with the Wind* was the only book that Margaret Mitchell ever wrote.

4. Do temperatures vary widely in this region of the country?

5. The sundial, an early timekeeping device, dates back several thousand years.

Concrete Nouns and Abstract Nouns

A **concrete noun** names a person, place, or thing that can be perceived by one or more of the five senses (sight, hearing, taste, touch, and smell). An **abstract noun** names an idea, a feeling, a quality, or a characteristic that cannot be perceived by the senses.

CONCRETE NOUNS	snow, lemon, birds, cotton, yogurt
ABSTRACT NOUNS	guilt, perseverance, joy, Buddhism, humility

GO ON ➡

EXERCISE B Decide whether each of the following nouns is *concrete* or whether it is *abstract*. Write *C* for *concrete* or *A* for *abstract* on the line next to each noun.

Examples __C__ **1.** balloon [A *balloon* can be perceived by the senses, so it is a concrete noun.]

__A__ **2.** encouragement [*Encouragement* cannot be perceived by the senses, so it is an abstract noun.]

__A__ **6.** promise

__C__ **7.** Shaquille O'Neal

__C__ **8.** bandage

__A__ **9.** self-control

__C__ **10.** pillow

__A__ **11.** humility

__C__ **12.** skateboard

__C__ **13.** microphone

__A__ **14.** urgency

__A__ **15.** hope

Collective Nouns and Compound Nouns

The singular form of a collective noun names a group of people, animals, or things.

COLLECTIVE NOUNS   audience, batch, bunch, cluster, crew, family, flock, group, herd, jury

A compound noun uses two or more words together to name a person, place, thing, or idea. The words of a compound noun may be joined together in one word, written as two or more separate words, or linked together with hyphens.

ONE WORD   hairbrush, roadblock, noisemaker, checkbook
SEPARATE WORDS   baby sitter, White House, high school, King John, San Diego
HYPHENATED WORD   jack-in-the-box, mother-in-law, half-moon, self-assurance

---

EXERCISE C Underline each noun in the following sentences. Then, if the noun is collective, write *COLL* for *collective* above it. If the noun is compound, write *COMP* for *compound* above it.

Example 1. The group put up a flagpole next to the post office. [*Group* is a collective noun.

Flagpole is a compound noun made up of two words written together, *flag* and *pole,* and

post office is a compound noun written as two separate words.]

16. Several couples in the audience rose from their seats and danced a two-step. [Are any of the

nouns in this sentence made up of two words? Do any of the nouns refer to a group?]

17. Will the jury render a verdict by this afternoon?

18. Even the strongest weight lifter could not budge the massive boulder.

19. The crew of the ship went ashore to gather supplies from shops along the shoreline.

20. Has Mariana ever visited Yellowstone National Park?

The Pronoun A: Personal Pronouns, Reflexive and Intensive Pronouns

1b. A *pronoun* is a word used in place of one or more nouns or pronouns.

The noun or pronoun that a pronoun replaces is called the *antecedent* of the pronoun.

EXAMPLES Tourists usually take **their** cameras along with **them.** [*Their* and *them* take the place of *Tourists; Tourists* is the antecedent of *their* and of *them.*]

Arnold has a key, but **he** left **it** at home. [*He* takes the place of *Arnold; it* takes the place of *key.*]

Personal Pronouns

A *personal pronoun* is a pronoun that stands for the one speaking *(first person)*, the one spoken to *(second person)*, or the one spoken about *(third person)*.

FIRST PERSON I, me, my, mine, we, us, our, ours
SECOND PERSON you, your, yours
THIRD PERSON he, him, his, she, her, hers, it, its, they, them, their, theirs

EXAMPLE Did **she** borrow **my** algebra book and **your** calculator because **hers** are still at school? [*She* and *hers* are third-person pronouns; *my* is a first-person pronoun; and *your* is a second-person pronoun.]

EXERCISE A Underline the personal pronouns in the following sentences. Then, above each pronoun, write *1st* for *first person, 2nd* for *second person,* or *3rd* for *third person.* Hint: Some sentences contain more than one personal pronoun.

Examples 1. Will you be staying with us for the summer? [*You* is a second-person pronoun that refers to the one spoken to; *us* is a first-person pronoun that refers to the one speaking.]

  2. The bird has almost finished building its nest. [*Its* is a third-person pronoun that refers to the one spoken about.]

  1. In the 1840s and 1850s, many prospectors moved their families westward in search of gold.

  [Does the pronoun refer to the one speaking, the one spoken to, or the one spoken about?]

  2. Did she give you instructions for completing the assignment? [Which pronoun refers to the one spoken to? Which pronoun refers to the one spoken about?]

  3. Even the desert has its unique appeal, especially in the cool of its evenings.

  4. Did Angelique wear her new dress to the theater?

  5. They sometimes take me to school when I need a ride.

  GO ON ▶

3rd

6. Before Alexander Graham Bell invented the telephone, he worked in education of the

hearing impaired.

2nd

7. Your new haircut looks great!

3rd

8. She helped him write the editorial for the newspaper.

3rd

9. Many people claim that they have seen a large creature in Scotland's Loch Ness.

3rd

10. The sparrow picked up a tuft of lint and stuffed it into its nest.

Reflexive and Intensive Pronouns

A *reflexive pronoun* stands for the subject of the sentence and completes the meaning of the verb or acts as an object of a preposition. An *intensive pronoun* stresses its antecedent and is not required in order for the sentence to make sense. Reflexive and intensive pronouns end with the suffix *–self* or *–selves*.

> **REFLEXIVE** The cat taught **itself** how to open the screen door. [*Itself* refers to the subject *cat* and completes the meaning of the verb *taught*.]
>
> The children prepared breakfast for **themselves**. [*Themselves* refers to the subject *children* and is the object of the preposition *for*.]
>
> **INTENSIVE** Gail prepared dinner **herself**. [*Herself* emphasizes the antecedent *Gail*.]

TIP To determine whether a pronoun is reflexive or intensive, omit the pronoun from the sentence. If the sentence still makes sense, the pronoun is probably intensive. If the sentence does not make sense, the pronoun is reflexive.

> **EXAMPLES** Did you crochet this sweater **yourself**? [Without *yourself*, the sentence still makes sense, so the pronoun *yourself* must be intensive.]
>
> Did you crochet this sweater for **yourself**? [Without *yourself*, the sentence doesn't make sense, so the pronoun *yourself* must be reflexive.]

EXERCISE B Read each of the following sentences and decide whether the underlined pronoun is reflexive or intensive. Then, on the line provided, write *REF* for *reflexive* or *INT* for *intensive*.

Example __REF__ **1.** Did Emily forget to save a chair for herself? [*Herself* refers to the subject *Emily* and is the object of the preposition *for*.]

__INT__ **11.** Because no one else was available, the players kept score themselves. [Does the sentence make sense if you omit the pronoun?]

__REF__ **12.** Fred mailed a postcard to himself from Italy.

REF __REF__ **13.** Jill surprised even herself when she bowled a perfect game.

INT __REF__ **14.** Under the furniture's weight, the elevator itself began to groan.

__REF__ **15.** Do you plan to install the new sound system by yourself?

The Pronoun B: Demonstrative Pronouns, Interrogative Pronouns

1b. A *pronoun* is a word used in place of one or more nouns or pronouns.

Demonstrative Pronouns

A *demonstrative pronoun* points out a specific person, place, thing, or idea. The demonstrative pronouns are *this, that, these,* and *those. This* and *that* point out singular nouns. *These* and *those* point out plural nouns.

> **EXAMPLES** **This** is our favorite picnic spot. [*This* points out a singular place, *spot.*]
>
> Are **these** the plants from the nursery? [*These* points out the plural noun *plants.*]

NOTE *This, that, these,* and *those* can also be used to modify nouns or pronouns. When these words modify nouns or pronouns, they are called *demonstrative adjectives.* Demonstrative adjectives usually appear immediately before the nouns they modify.

> **PRONOUN** **That** is the last envelope in the box. [*That* stands for and points out the noun *envelope,* so it is a demonstrative pronoun.]
>
> **ADJECTIVE** **That** envelope is the last in the box. [*That* modifies and appears immediately before the noun *envelope,* so it is a demonstrative adjective.]

EXERCISE A Underline the demonstrative pronouns found in the following sentences.

Examples 1. <u>Those</u> are the only items that are on sale. [*Those* takes the place of *items,* which is a plural noun.]

2. Is <u>that</u> Gerald's locker at the end of the row? [*That* takes the place of *locker,* which is a singular noun.]

1. In spring, <u>these</u> grow faster than they do in summer. [Have you underlined a plural demonstrative pronoun?]

2. <u>That</u> is an unusual rock. [Have you underlined a singular demonstrative pronoun?]

3. Are <u>those</u> the same shoes that you saw in the catalog?

4. After they've been exposed to light, <u>these</u> glow in the dark.

5. <u>This</u> was the most challenging section of the exam.

6. Do <u>these</u> match the tablecloth and centerpiece?

7. <u>That</u> probably belongs to the neighbors.

8. Have <u>these</u> been tested for accuracy and durability?

GO ON

9. H. G. Wells wrote several interesting science fiction novels, but my favorite is this.

10. Those are among the finest impressionist paintings in the museum's collection.

Interrogative Pronouns

An *interrogative pronoun* introduces a question. The interrogative pronouns are *what, which, who, whom,* and *whose.*

> **EXAMPLES** **What** is the title of the last chapter in the book?
>
> **Who** called while I was away?

NOTE▶ Some interrogative pronouns can also function as adjectives. Remember that a pronoun takes the place of a noun or pronoun. An adjective makes the meaning of a noun or pronoun more specific.

> **PRONOUN** **Which** is the best Chinese restaurant? [*Which* takes the place of *restaurant.*]
>
> **ADJECTIVE** **Which** exit should we take when we enter the city? [*Which* modifies *exit.*]

EXERCISE B Underline the demonstrative and interrogative pronouns in each of the following sentences. Then, write *DEM* for *demonstrative* or *INT* for *interrogative* on the line provided.

Examples __INT__ **1.** What are the goals of the committee? [*What* introduces a question.]

__DEM__ **2.** Are these my grandmother's special recipes? [*These* points out specific

things, *recipes.*]

__INT__ **11.** Who is teaching calculus this semester? [Does the pronoun introduce a question or does it

point out a specific person?]

__DEM__ **12.** This is the only Steven Spielberg film I have ever seen. [Does the pronoun introduce a

question or does it point out a specific thing?]

__DEM__ **13.** Alvin took some photographs, but he didn't take these.

__INT__ **14.** Whose is the suitcase with the stickers all over it?

__DEM INT__ **15.** Are those the clothes we're donating to the shelter's rummage sale?

__INT__ **16.** When she calls, what should I tell Carolyn about our decision?

__INT__ **17.** Hey! Isn't that your dog running down the street?

__INT__ **18.** Which are the most popular attractions at the fair?

__INT__ **19.** Whom did you ask to make the announcements?

__DEM__ **20.** Of the fossils in this box, those are the only ones that have been cataloged.

The Pronoun C: Relative Pronouns, Indefinite Pronouns

1b.   A *pronoun* is a word used in place of one or more nouns or pronouns.

Relative Pronouns

A *relative pronoun* introduces a subordinate clause. The relative pronouns are *that, which, who, whom,* and *whose.*

> **EXAMPLES**   The UFO **that** we saw was only a weather balloon. [*That* introduces the subordinate clause *that we saw.*]
>
>   Broccoli, **which** is a dark green vegetable, may be served raw or cooked. [*Which* introduces the subordinate clause *which is a dark green vegetable.*]

> **REMINDER** A *clause* is a group of words that contains a subject and its verb. A *subordinate clause* has a subject and verb, but it does not express a complete thought and cannot stand alone as a sentence.

SUBORDINATE CLAUSE   which looks wilted

        SENTENCE   That plant, which looks wilted, is an ivy.

EXERCISE A Underline the relative pronoun in each of the following sentences.

Examples 1. The book that I bought at the auction is signed by the author. [*That* introduces the subordinate clause *that I bought at the auction.*]

        2. Mrs. Donaldson, who lives next door, knew my mother in high school. [*Who* introduces the subordinate clause *who lives next door.*]

1. Martina Navratilova, who is a well-known tennis player, won the Wimbledon women's championship nine times! [What word introduces a clause that cannot stand alone as a sentence?]

2. Jeff, whom we met last summer, recently moved to Canada. [Which word introduces a subordinate clause?]

3. Exploring the cave, the spelunkers discovered ancient petroglyphs, which are carvings and inscriptions on rock.

4. The store that we just passed is closed.

5. Derrick, whose project has been approved, has been working long hours.

6. I rode in the van with the scouts who were on their way to camp.

7. The Corrs, who are my favorite musicians, are from Ireland.

8. Glenette, whom we know well, prepares my parents' tax return every year.

9. The mirror that hangs in the estate's entry hall is two hundred years old.

10. Moles, which are small, burrowing animals, are often blind.

Indefinite Pronouns

An *indefinite pronoun* refers to a person, a place, a thing, or an idea that may or may not be specifically named.

NOTE Some indefinite pronouns can also function as adjectives. Remember that a pronoun takes the place of a noun or pronoun. An adjective makes the meaning of a noun or pronoun more specific.

> **PRONOUN** Can you fit **more** of the books into your backpack? [*More* is used as a pronoun that refers to a thing named in the sentence, *books,* but it does not name a specific book or modify *books.*]
>
> **ADJECTIVE** **More** people are going to volunteer to help. [*More* is used as an adjective modifying the noun *people* by telling *how many.*]

EXERCISE B Underline the indefinite pronouns in the following sentences. Hint: Some sentences may contain more than one indefinite pronoun.

Examples 1. Both of my brothers and many of their friends work at the mall. [*Both* refers to *brothers* and *many* refers to *friends.*]

      2. Can someone give me directions to the nearest gym? [*Someone* refers to a person who is not specifically named.]

11. Most of the players on the hockey team are from Sweden. [Which word takes the place of a noun or pronoun that is specifically named in the sentence?]

12. Did everyone find something to read during the trip? [Which words take the place of nouns or pronouns that are not specifically named in the sentence?]

13. Several of the students brought umbrellas, but few used them.

14. Marsha exclaimed, "I've never seen anything as spectacular as this fireworks display!"

15. I spend much of my time studying and playing sports.

16. None of these videocassettes have labels on them.

17. Many of Picasso's paintings were considered radical when he painted them, but some were not.

18. Since neither of these outfits appeals to you, we will look for another.

19. All of the baseball uniforms were donated by local businesses.

20. Either of these solutions to the problem will work.

The Adjective

| **1c.** | An *adjective* modifies a noun or a pronoun. |

Adjectives make the meanings of nouns and pronouns more specific by telling *what kind, which one, how many,* or *how much.*

WHAT KIND	**handmade** quilt	**red** sneakers	**state-of-the-art** equipment
WHICH ONE	**this** camera	**second** place	**last** word
HOW MANY	**seven** apples	**few** persons	**many** options
HOW MUCH	**more** bread	**much** thought	**enough** light

Adjectives usually come before the words they modify, but sometimes, for emphasis, they follow the words they modify.

EXAMPLES **Tall, green** cornstalks lined the highway. [The adjectives *Tall* and *green* come before the word they modify, *cornstalks.*]

The thundercloud, **large** and **dark,** loomed over the horizon. [The adjectives *large* and *dark* follow *thundercloud* for emphasis.]

Adjectives may be separated from the words they modify. A **predicate adjective,** for example, completes the meaning of a linking verb and modifies the subject of the verb.

EXAMPLE The dog seems **hungry.** [*Hungry* modifies the subject *dog* and completes the meaning of the linking verb *seems.*]

NOTE *A, an,* and *the* are special adjectives called *articles. A* and *an* are **indefinite articles** because they refer to any member of a group. *The* is the **definite article** because it refers to a specific member of a group.

EXERCISE A Underline the adjectives in each of the following sentences. Do not underline the articles *a, an,* and *the.* Hint: Sentences may contain more than one adjective.

Examples 1. Every year, loyal fans visit Graceland, the former home of the singer Elvis Presley.

[*Every* modifies *year* by telling "how much." *Loyal* modifies *fans* by telling "what kind."

Former modifies *home* by telling "which one."]

2. During this excavation, did archaeologists unearth more pieces of ancient pottery?

[*This* modifies *excavation* by telling "which one," *more* modifies *pieces* by telling "how

much," and *ancient* modifies *pottery* by telling "what kind."]

1. Four beautiful swans glided smoothly across the lake. [Which words make a noun more specific?]

2. With a soft cloth, Roger cleaned the dusty chandelier. [Which words come before nouns and

make their meanings more specific?]

3. After a long swim, did Kim relax on the sunny beach?

4. The first fifty customers received complimentary beverages.

GO ON

5. The mythological hero Hercules performed twelve difficult tasks.

6. I enjoy a fresh salad with crisp lettuce and juicy tomatoes.

7. Do the smooth dunes constantly shift in the barren desert?

8. The elephant, large and heavy, actually can be quite graceful.

9. My younger sister creates interesting sculptures out of unusual materials.

10. From the balcony, Zachary spotted several tiny blue eggs in a nest.

Adjectives and Other Parts of Speech

A word may be used as one part of speech in one situation and as a different part of speech in another situation. For example, the same word may be used as an adjective or noun or pronoun.

> **NOUN** The **telephone** is ringing. [The noun *telephone* is the subject of the sentence.]
>
> **ADJECTIVE** Did Rose receive a **telephone** call while she was away? [The adjective *telephone* modifies the noun *call*.]
>
> **PRONOUN** Are **those** empty? [The pronoun *those* takes the place of the noun *lockers*.]
>
> **ADJECTIVE** Are **those** lockers empty? [The adjective *those* modifies the noun *lockers*.]

Proper Adjectives

A *proper adjective* is an adjective that is formed from a proper noun.

> **EXAMPLES** **French** poodle [The proper adjective *French* is formed from the proper noun *France* and modifies *poodle*.]
>
> **Shakespearean** actor [The proper adjective *Shakespearean* is formed from the proper noun *Shakespeare* and modifies *actor*.]

EXERCISE B Underline the adjectives in each of the following sentences. Then, draw an arrow from each adjective to the word it modifies. Do not underline the articles *a, an,* and *the*. Hint: Sentences may contain more than one adjective.

Example 1. Jackie donated five dollars to the relief fund. [*Five* modifies *dollars* and *relief* modifies *fund*.]

11. Don't touch the hot burner on the new stove! [Which words make the meanings of the nouns more specific?]

12. Jennifer bought some clothes and a black purse at a popular store.

13. Every evening, Ms. Nordstrom strolls to a nearby Italian restaurant.

14. Is the new stereo still inside the cardboard box?

15. At the music festival, an Andean band will be performing Peruvian songs.

The Verb A

1d. A *verb* expresses action or state of being.

> **EXAMPLES** The cat **dashed** through the room. [*Dashed* expresses the cat's action.]
>
> The cat **seems** lively today. [*Seems* expresses the cat's state of being.]

Main Verbs and Helping Verbs

A *verb phrase* consists of at least one **main verb** and one or more **helping verbs.** (Helping verbs are also called *auxiliary verbs.*)

> **EXAMPLES** They **could** not **have found** the treasure without the map. [*Found* is the main verb. *Could* and *have* are helping verbs.]
>
> Dwight **will be spending** the holidays in Vermont. [*Spending* is the main verb. *Will* and *be* are helping verbs.]

Commonly used helping verbs include forms of *be,* forms of *have,* forms of *do,* and the modals *may, can, could, might, shall, should, must, will,* and *would.*

REMINDER A *modal* is a helping verb that is used with a main verb to express an attitude. Modals express necessity or possibility.

> **EXAMPLES** **Must** students take entrance exams before applying for admission? [Although it is separated from the main verb, *take, Must* is used to express necessity.]
>
> Chuck **may** bring his sister with him when he visits. [*May* is used with the main verb *bring* to express possibility.]

EXERCISE A Underline the verb phrase in each of the following sentences. Then, draw a second line under any helping verbs.

Examples 1. Kim is hosting a party. [*Is hosting* is the verb phrase; *is* is a helping verb.]

2. Will Vincent be guiding the tours of the facilities? [Although *Will* is separated from the main verb *guiding, Will* and *be* are part of the verb phrase *Will be guiding.*]

1. The problem could be resolved through a compromise. [Which word expresses action? Which two words help that main verb?]

2. Does the department store sell sporting goods? [Which word expresses action? Which word helps that main verb?]

3. Flamenco music may have originated in India.

4. Are you staying for the trophy's presentation?

5. In five minutes, I will have been jogging for half an hour.

6. The infant has been snoring softly.

7. Quincy has borrowed this book from the library five times.

8. As a student, Rachel must study anatomy and physiology.

9. That bank will finance loans to customers with poor credit ratings.

10. The gemstone sapphire can come in colors such as blue, yellow, and pale pink.

NOTE Words such as *not* (and the contraction *–n't*), *never, just,* and *always* are never part of a verb phrase. These words are adverbs.

EXAMPLES Tina and Valerie **have** never **met.** [The verb phrase *have met* does not include the adverb *never.*]

Wouldn't you **care** for some lemonade? [Although they are separated from each other, *Would* and *care* form the sentence's verb phrase, and the adverb *–n't*, a contraction of *not*, is not a part of the verb phrase.]

EXERCISE B Underline the verb phrases in each of the following sentences. Hint: Watch for helping verbs that are separated from main verbs, and remember that *not, –n't, never, just,* and *always* are adverbs.

Examples 1. Has Delores ever ridden a roller coaster? [*Ridden* is the main verb. *Has* is a helping verb.]

2. The bus driver must have been watching the road carefully! [*Watching* is the main verb. *Must, have,* and *been* are helping verbs.]

11. Because of an illness, Lance could not attend his own graduation party. [Have you underlined the verb phrase in this sentence? Are there any adverbs that should not be underlined?]

12. Does everyone understand the instructions? [Although the parts may be separated from each other, have you underlined all of the parts of the verb phrase in this sentence?]

13. According to some scholars, Shakespeare's plays may have been written by someone else.

14. Louis Braille, a French educator, had developed a system of printing for the blind.

15. Do your grandparents still live in Arkansas?

16. Might the impact of a large meteor have caused the extinction of the dinosaurs?

17. Will the election results be published in the newspaper?

18. Samantha has never before delivered a speech.

19. The soldiers were honored for their bravery and service.

20. Will you join us for a round of golf?

The Verb B: Action Verbs and Linking Verbs

Action Verbs

An *action verb* expresses either physical or mental activity.

> **EXAMPLES** Lana **moved** the furniture and **shampooed** the carpet. [*Moved* and *shampooed* are action verbs that express physical activities performed by the subject *Lana*.]
>
> In important decisions, Marcus always **considers** each alternative carefully. [*Considers* expresses a mental activity performed by the subject *Marcus*.]

EXERCISE A Underline the action verbs in the following sentences. Hint: A sentence may contain more than one action verb.

Examples 1. On the last morning of the campout, we <u>ate</u> breakfast at six and <u>left</u> at seven. [*Ate* and *left* express actions performed by the subject *we*.]

2. Does the puppy <u>know</u> its name yet? [*Does know* is a verb expressing the puppy's mental actions.]

1. After a trial, a jury sometimes deliberates for hours or even days. [What is the subject *jury* doing?]

2. Erica grabbed her sweater and dashed out the door. [Is the subject *Erica* performing more than one action in the sentence?]

3. Did the groundhog see his shadow this year?

4. English Puritans settled New England and established communities there.

5. We found some money in the park and took it to the police.

6. Several of our friends play soccer every weekend.

7. Ancient writings place the legendary island of Atlantis in the Atlantic Ocean, west of the Straits of Gibraltar.

8. They built a birdhouse and hung it from a branch of the oak tree.

9. Last spring, we planted hydrangeas in our flower garden.

10. Every Saturday, Stanley washes and vacuums his car.

Linking Verbs

A *linking verb* connects the subject to a word or word group in the predicate called a *subject complement*. A subject complement identifies or describes the subject and completes the meaning of the linking verb.

GO ON ➡

> **EXAMPLES** The woman in the navy blouse **is** my mother. [The linking verb *is* connects the subject complement *mother* to the subject *woman. Mother* identifies the subject *woman* and completes the meaning of the linking verb *is.*]
>
> Your zucchini casserole **smells** delicious. [The linking verb *smells* connects the subject complement *delicious* to the subject *casserole.* The subject complement *delicious* describes the subject *casserole.*]

NOTE Many linking verbs can be used as action verbs as well.

> **LINKING** The gardenias **smell** fragrant. [*Fragrant* describes the subject *gardenias.*]
>
> **ACTION** The horse **smelled** the fragrant gardenias. [*Smelled* describes an action performed by the subject *horse.*]

EXERCISE B Decide whether the underlined words in each of the following sentences are action verbs or linking verbs. Above each underlined verb, write *A* for *action verb* or *L* for *linking verb.*

Examples 1. Thomas Edison became a well-known inventor. [*Became* connects the subject *Thomas Edison* with the subject complement *inventor.*]

2. Everyone tried the vegetable stew, and it tasted delicious. [*Tried* expresses an action performed by the subject *Everyone. Tasted* connects the subject *it* to the subject complement *delicious.*]

11. The cat appears enthusiastic about her new collar. [Does the verb express an action or connect the subject to a subject complement?]

12. When I have a sore throat, my voice sounds scratchy. [Does either verb express an action? Does either verb connect the subject to a complement?]

13. The architect reviewed the plans once more before sending them to the client.

14. The rain smudged the ink on Clarence's report.

15. Does the room seem especially stuffy to you today?

16. The interior designer recommended neutral colors for our living room.

17. Mr. Shanks felt better after speaking with the doctor.

18. The family next door recently installed a satellite dish near their house.

19. Every time my grandfather visits, he looks at our family photo album.

20. Are you aware of the proposed safety regulations?

The Verb C: Transitive Verbs and Intransitive Verbs

Transitive Verbs

A *transitive verb* directs an action toward an *object*. An object is a word that tells *who* or *what* receives the action of the verb. The performer of the action is called a *subject*.

> **EXAMPLES**   We **placed** some napkins on the table. [*Napkins* is the object that receives the action of the verb *placed*.]
>
> Edgar Allan Poe **wrote** many stories and poems. [*Stories* and *poems* are the objects that receive the action of the verb *wrote*.]

EXERCISE A Underline the transitive verb in each of the following sentences. Then, draw two lines under the object of each transitive verb.

Examples 1. Professor Willa often reads books about the history of theater. [*Books* is the object of the transitive verb *reads*.]

   2. She also watches films adapted from stage plays. [*Films* is the object of the transitive verb *watches*.]

1. Aristotle's *Poetics* provides information about Greek tragedy. [What does the subject of the sentence do?]

2. In ancient Greek tragedies, actors wore buskins, which were thick-soled boots. [What is the verb of the sentence? What word completes the meaning of the verb?]

3. Writers of the Greek plays drew their subjects from myths.

4. The works of the poet Homer provided source material for some plays.

5. The Romans eventually adapted the Greeks' dramatic forms.

6. Later writers, such as Christopher Marlowe, introduced the overambitious tragic hero.

7. Some twentieth-century authors wrote tragedies about contemporary situations.

8. Many theatergoers prefer comedy to tragedy.

9. Comedy often provokes laughter from members of the audience.

10. Have you seen a play recently?

Intransitive Verbs

An *intransitive verb* does not express its action toward an object.

> **EXAMPLES**   Nelda **whispered** in Amelia's ear. [The intransitive verb *whispered* does not have an object.]
>
> The horse **whinnied** loudly. [The intransitive verb *whinnied* does not have an object.]

GO ON ▶

Some verbs can be transitive in one sentence and intransitive in another.

TRANSITIVE The climbers **ascended** the mountain carefully. [*Mountain* is the object of the transitive verb *ascended*.]

INTRANSITIVE The climbers **ascended** carefully. [The intransitive verb *ascended* does not have an object.]

TRANSITIVE The mockingbird **sang** a loud song. [*Song* is the object of the transitive verb *sang*.]

INTRANSITIVE The mockingbird **sang** loudly. [The intransitive verb *sang* does not have an object.]

TIP▶ If you're uncertain whether a verb can be used transitively, intransitively, or both, most dictionaries will help. Look carefully at any italicized or boldfaced letters appearing next to the listed verb or close to any of the verb's definitions. If the verb can be used transitively, the citation will probably include the letters *vt* (for *verb transitive*). If the verb can be used intransitively, the citation will probably include the letters *vi* (for *verb intransitive*).

EXERCISE B Decide whether the underlined verb is transitive or intransitive in each of the following sentences. Then, on the line provided, write *T* for *transitive verb* or *I* for *intransitive verb*. Hint: Look for an object of the verb. If the verb does not have an object, the verb is intransitive.

Examples ___T___ **1.** Timpanists <u>play</u> the kettledrums in an orchestra. [*Kettledrums* is the object of the transitive verb *play*.]

___I___ **2.** A bolt of lightning just <u>struck</u> nearby. [*Struck* does not take an object in this sentence.]

_____**11.** The German shepherd <u>barked</u> happily at passersby. [Does the verb have an object?]

_____**12.** All of the soloists <u>had memorized</u> their music. [What had the soloists memorized?]

_____**13.** The luggage finally <u>slid</u> onto the conveyor belt.

_____**14.** During the month of Ramadan, Muslims <u>fast</u> from dawn to sunset every day.

_____**15.** The van <u>swerved</u> suddenly after hitting a pothole.

_____**16.** Carl Jung and Sigmund Freud, both noted twentieth-century psychologists, often <u>disagreed</u>.

_____**17.** Did you know that hummingbirds <u>beat</u> their wings up to eighty times per second?

_____**18.** The mimes <u>entertained</u> the children at the birthday party.

_____**19.** Grandma Moses <u>began</u> her career as a painter late in her life.

_____**20.** Seated at large tables, several library patrons <u>were reading</u> silently.

The Adverb

1e. | An *adverb* modifies a verb, an adjective, or another adverb.

Adverbs make the meaning of a verb, adjective, or another adverb more specific by telling *how, when, where,* or *to what extent (how much or how long).*

Adverbs Modifying Verbs

An adverb makes the meaning of a verb more specific.

HOW	The rain **gently** fell. [*Gently* tells *how* the rain fell.]
WHEN	**Yesterday** I received your letter. [*Yesterday* tells *when* the letter was received.]
WHERE	Garland lives **here.** [*Here* tells *where* Garland lives.]
TO WHAT EXTENT	The coyote roamed **widely.** [*Widely* tells *to what extent* the coyote roamed.]

EXERCISE A Underline the adverbs in each of the following sentences. Then, draw an arrow from each adverb to the verb it modifies.

Example 1. Mark plays the guitar expertly. [*Expertly* modifies the verb *plays* by telling *how.*]

1. Although the car is old, it runs well. [*How* does the car run?]

2. Dustin carefully swept the pieces of the broken dish into a dustpan.

3. The veterinarian's office will open tomorrow at eight o'clock.

4. Casey always rides his scooter to track and field practice.

5. She sits there when she writes her letters.

Adverbs Modifying Adjectives

An adverb makes the meaning of an adjective more specific.

EXAMPLE That **particularly** slow computer needs to be repaired. [The adverb *particularly* makes the meaning of the adjective *slow* more specific by telling *to what extent.*]

EXERCISE B Underline the adverb in each of the following sentences. Then, draw an arrow from the adverb to the adjective it modifies.

Example 1. The book review was surprisingly favorable. [The adverb *surprisingly* modifies the predicate adjective *favorable.*]

GO ON ➡

Developmental Language Skills

6. Many of Franz Liszt's piano compositions are too difficult for me to play. [What word makes the meaning of an adjective in this sentence more specific?]

7. Always sociable, she makes friends wherever she goes.

8. The researchers are cautiously optimistic about the results of their experiments.

9. The volunteers were extremely helpful to the flood victims.

10. This process for identifying polluters has been reasonably successful in the past.

Adverbs Modifying Other Adverbs

An adverb makes the meaning of another adverb more specific.

> **EXAMPLE**   The game ended **very** quickly. [The adverb *very* makes the meaning of the adverb *quickly* more specific.]

EXERCISE C Underline the adverbs in each of the following sentences. Then, draw an arrow from each adverb to the word it modifies.

Examples 1. When I run too quickly, my stomach hurts. [The adverb *too* modifies the adverb *quickly*. The adverb *quickly* modifies the verb *run*.]

2. The caterpillar was moving slowly. [The adverb *slowly* modifies the verb *was moving*.]

11. Rudy speaks Russian quite fluently. [Which words modify verbs, adjectives, or adverbs?]

12. Jenny behaved rather squeamishly during biology class. [Which words modify verbs, adjectives, or adverbs?]

13. We talked only briefly before the show began.

14. The actors stood very rigidly, and onlookers thought that they were mannequins.

15. The train just barely missed the fallen tree.

16. The raccoon crept stealthily around the house.

17. Have you already bought your art supplies?

18. The ferret is somewhat clumsy when it wakes up in the evening.

19. Is she quite certain that this answer is correct?

20. Ed left rather hurriedly when he heard the news.

The Preposition

1f.   A *preposition* shows the relationship of a noun or pronoun, called the *object of the preposition,* to another word.

EXAMPLES   The car raced **across** the finish line. [*Across* shows the relationship of *line* to *raced*.]

The car **from** Canada roared loudly. [*From* shows the relationship of *Canada* to *car*.]

It sped **around** the track. [*Around* shows the relationship of *track* to *sped*.]

SOME COMMONLY USED PREPOSITIONS

about	before	during	near	to
above	behind	except	of	toward
after	beneath	for	on	up
against	beside	from	out	with
among	between	in	over	within
at	by	into	throughout	without

A preposition, its object, and any modifiers of the object form a *prepositional phrase.*

EXAMPLES   The ball rolled **under the truck.** [*Under* is a preposition. *Truck* is the object of the preposition *under*.]

I drank a glass **of fresh, cold water.** [*Of* is a preposition, and *water* is its object. *Fresh* and *cold* are modifiers of *water*.]

EXERCISE A Draw two lines under the preposition in each of the following sentences. Then, draw one line under the rest of the prepositional phrase.

Examples 1. The dish soap is stored under the kitchen sink. [The preposition *under* is part of a prepositional phrase that includes the article *the,* the modifier *kitchen,* and the object of the preposition, *sink.*]

2. Is my car parked in the garage? [The preposition *in* is part of a prepositional phrase that includes the article *the* and the object of the preposition, *garage.*]

1. The students formed a line along the wall. [What word shows the relationship between *wall* and *line*?]

2. Smoking is prohibited in the restaurant. [What word shows the relationship between *restaurant* and *is prohibited*?]

3. Did you leave the rake behind the shed?

4. Matt poured the orange juice into a glass.

5. Before the concert, the choir performed warm-up exercises.

6. Inside the bank vault, the money was securely locked.

7. I dropped my earring between the couch cushions.

8. The leopard walked slowly toward the deserted pond.

9. The new bus driver drove past my house.

10. Candidates posted campaign signs throughout the neighborhood.

Preposition or Adverb?

Some words that can be used as prepositions may also be used as adverbs. Remember that an adverb is a modifier. Adverbs do not take objects as do prepositions.

> **PREPOSITION** I had not heard that story **before** this morning. [The preposition *before* shows the relationship between the object *morning* and the verb *had heard*.]
>
> **ADVERB** I had not heard that story **before**. [*Before* is an adverb that modifies *had heard* by telling *when*.]

NOTE The word *to* can function as a preposition or as part of an *infinitive,* a verb form that often begins with *to*. Be careful not to confuse these distinct uses of the word *to*.

> **EXAMPLES** We need **to leave** at noon. [*To leave* is the infinitive form of the verb *leave*.]
>
> We are going **to the store**. [*To the store* is a prepositional phrase showing the relationship between the object *store* and the verb *are going*.]

Compound Prepositions

A preposition that consists of two or more words is a *compound preposition.*

COMMONLY USED COMPOUND PREPOSITIONS

according to	aside from	by means of	in place of	next to
along with	as of	in addition to	in spite of	on account of
apart from	because of	in front of	instead of	out of

> **EXAMPLE** **According to** the doctor, the patient should make a full recovery. [*According to* is a compound preposition. *Doctor* is the object of *According to*.]

EXERCISE B Underline the prepositional phrases in the following sentences. Then, draw a second line under any compound prepositions. Hint: A sentence may contain more than one prepositional phrase.

Example 1. Because of a food allergy, Antoine cannot eat strawberries. [*Because of* is a compound preposition that begins the prepositional phrase *Because of a food allergy*.]

11. Some early pioneers built homes out of logs and mud. [What is the prepositional phrase?]

12. There is a statue of Abraham Lincoln in front of the library.

13. In spite of protests, the board members implemented their original decision.

14. Along with exercise, nutritious foods are important for good health.

15. Aside from a few minor setbacks, the mission was a success.

The Conjunction and the Interjection

1g. A *conjunction* joins words or word groups.

Coordinating and Correlative Conjunctions

A *coordinating conjunction* joins words or word groups that are used in the same way. The seven coordinating conjunctions are *and, but, for, nor, or, so,* and *yet.*

> **EXAMPLES** We added oregano **and** parsley to the recipe. [*And* connects two words.]
>
> Check under the table **or** behind the chair. [*Or* connects two phrases.]
>
> The temperature was dropping rapidly, **so** I put on my heavy coat. [*So* joins two independent clauses.]

Correlative conjunctions are pairs of conjunctions that join words or word groups that are used in the same way. The correlative conjunctions are *both . . . and, not only . . . but also, either . . . or, neither . . . nor,* and *whether . . . or.*

> **EXAMPLE** **Neither** Neal **nor** Adam knew the time. [*Neither . . . nor* connect two words.]

EXERCISE A Identify the conjunctions in each of the following sentences. Then, draw one line under each coordinating conjunction and two lines under each correlative conjunction.

Example 1. Both Irene and Linda live in my apartment building. [*Both* and *and* are correlative conjunctions used to connect two nouns, *Irene* and *Linda*.]

1. The dog sleeps in the kitchen or in the hallway. [Which word connects two phrases?]

2. Neither Shane nor his brother has brown hair.

3. The defending champions lost the first game, but they won all of the others.

4. Franklin Roosevelt wanted to stimulate recovery from the Great Depression, so he proposed reforms known as the New Deal.

5. Both the playground and the swimming pool will open in May.

Subordinating Conjunctions

A *subordinating conjunction* begins a subordinate clause and connects the subordinate clause to an independent clause. Commonly used subordinating conjunctions include *after, although, because, before, how, if, in order that, so that, unless, until, whenever, whether, while,* and *why.*

> **EXAMPLES** **Because** we arrived late, we missed the opening ceremonies. [*Because* introduces the subordinate clause *Because we arrived late.*]
>
> Sheryl listened to classical music **while** she organized her room. [*While* introduces the subordinate clause *while she organized her room* and connects the subordinate clause to the independent clause *Sheryl listened to classical music.*]

GO ON

Developmental Language Skills

EXERCISE B Underline the subordinating conjunctions in the following sentences.

Example 1. Please hold these packages <u>while</u> I unlock the door. [*While* is a subordinating

conjunction that connects the subordinate clause *while I unlock the door* to the

independent clause *Please hold these packages.*]

6. Whenever I sing to the baby, she falls asleep. [Have you underlined a subordinating conjunction

connecting a subordinate clause to an independent clause?]

7. Though they have been to Chicago many times, the Wyatts are going there again in April.

8. We listened to the radio while we prepared lunch.

9. The Hawks will play the Eagles in the finals unless the Eagles lose to the Cardinals.

10. Because fluoride helps prevent cavities, dentists recommend its use to their patients.

Interjections

1h. An *interjection* expresses emotion and has no grammatical relation to the rest of the sentence.

Common interjections include *ah, aha, hey, oh, oops, ouch, uh-oh, well, whew,* and *wow.*

An interjection is often set off from the rest of the sentence by an exclamation point or a
comma. An exclamation point is used to indicate strong emotion. A comma is used to indicate
mild emotion.

> **EXAMPLES** **Uh-oh,** I think I left my notebook in the car. [*Uh-oh* is set off by a comma
> and expresses mild emotion.]
>
> **Wow!** That skyscraper is enormous! [*Wow* is set off by an exclamation
> point and is used to express strong emotion.]

EXERCISE C Underline the interjections in the following sentences.

Example 1. <u>Aha</u>! I see you have discovered the secret passageway! [The exclamation point

indicates strong emotion.]

11. Oh, did you hear about the new training program that starts next week? [Which word

expresses mild emotion?]

12. Ouch! I think I stepped on a piece of glass.

13. Well, at least we raised enough money to buy uniforms.

14. Whew! Those boxes are heavy!

15. Hey! Don't leave without us!

The Subject

The Simple Subject and the Complete Subject

2c. The *simple subject* is the main word or word group that tells *whom* or *what* the sentence is about. The *complete subject* consists of the simple subject and any words or word groups used to modify the simple subject.

SIMPLE SUBJECT   The **director** of the youth center planned many outdoor activities. [Who planned many outdoor activities? The director did. *Director* is the main word that tells *whom* the sentence is about.]

COMPLETE SUBJECT   **The director of the youth center** planned many outdoor activities. [Who planned many outdoor activities? The director of the youth center did. The complete subject, *The director of the youth center,* includes all the modifiers of the simple subject *director.*]

Sometimes the simple subject is also the complete subject.

EXAMPLE   **Baton Rouge** is the capital of Louisiana. [*Baton Rouge* is both the simple subject and the complete subject.]

TIP▶ The subject is never found in a prepositional phrase. Some common prepositions are *about, among, at, for, from, in, of, under,* and *with.* To help find the subject, cross out any preposition and the noun or pronoun that follows it.

EXAMPLES   The backpack ~~under the chair~~ is mine. [*Backpack,* not *chair,* is the subject of the sentence.]
Some ~~of the plants~~ need direct sunlight. [*Some,* not *plants,* is the subject of the sentence.]

EXERCISE A Underline the complete subject once in each of the following sentences. Then, underline the simple subject a second time. Hint: Remember that sometimes the simple subject is also the complete subject.

Examples 1. <u>All of these lawn mowers</u> are electric. [What are electric? All of these lawn mowers are. *All of these lawn mowers* is the complete subject. *All* is the simple subject.]

2. Can <u>an electric eel</u> really shock someone? [What can shock someone? An electric eel can. *An electric eel* is the complete subject. *Electric eel* is the simple subject.]

1. Ponce de León discovered Florida while searching for the fountain of youth. [Who discovered Florida?]

2. A school of fish swam beneath the glass-bottomed boat. [What swam beneath? Remember to cross out prepositional phrases.]

3. The combination to the safe is a secret.

4. Will the documents arrive by certified mail?

5. Maya Lin designed the Vietnam Veterans Memorial in Washington, D.C.

GO ON ▶

Developmental Language Skills

6. One of my favorite jazz composers is Duke Ellington.

7. Is hydrogen the most common element in the galaxy?

8. The state of Pennsylvania was named for Admiral Sir William Penn.

9. Boll weevils can cause extensive damage to cotton crops.

10. Have Mrs. Keene's first-grade class taken their pictures yet?

The Compound Subject

2e.   A *compound subject* consists of two or more subjects that are joined by a conjunction and that have the same verb.

Conjunctions commonly used to join the words of a compound subject are *and, or, neither . . . nor,* and *both . . . and.*

> **EXAMPLES**   Do **Minerva** and **Penny** attend the same school? [*Minerva* and *Penny* are parts of the compound subject joined by the conjunction *and*. They have the same verb, *attend*.]
>
> Neither the **judge** nor the **jury** believed the witness's testimony. [*Judge* and *jury* are parts of the compound subject joined by the conjunction *Neither . . . nor*. They have the same verb, *believed*.]

EXERCISE B Underline the simple subject in each of the following sentences. Remember to underline each word in a compound subject.

Examples 1. A box of paper clips and a package of paper are in the cabinet. [What are in the cabinet? A box and package are. *Box* and *package* are parts of the compound subject.]

2. Did Angela or her mother answer the phone? [Who answered the phone? Angela or her mother did. *Angela* and *mother* are parts of the compound subject joined by *or*.]

11. Will Beatrice or Yvonne sing the national anthem? [Who will sing the national anthem?]

12. A piece of tape and some glue held the kite together. [What held the kite together?]

13. For months, the team and their coach had been raising money for their trip.

14. Neither the library nor the bookstore has a copy of the book.

15. Lemons, limes, and oranges are classified as citrus fruits.

16. Did Cathy and John remodel the house themselves?

17. Both Juan and Caroline enjoyed reading the Romantic poetry of England.

18. Neither the pharmacist nor her assistant had heard of the new medicine.

19. Does Ned or his brother build model airplanes?

20. Cincinnati, Cleveland, and Dayton are all cities in Ohio.

The Predicate

The Simple Predicate and the Complete Predicate

2d. The **simple predicate,** or **verb,** is the main word or word group that tells something about the subject. The **complete predicate** consists of the verb and all the words used to modify the verb and complete its meaning.

SIMPLE PREDICATE (VERB)   The dog **barked** at the joggers. [*Barked* is the simple predicate and tells something about the subject, *dog.*]

Does Antonio **have** any brothers or sisters? [*Does have* is the simple predicate and asks something about the subject, *Antonio.*]

COMPLETE PREDICATE   The dog **barked at the joggers.** [*Barked at the joggers* is the complete predicate.]

Does Antonio **have any brothers or sisters?** [*Does have any brothers or sisters* is the complete predicate.]

REMINDER A simple predicate can be a one-word verb or verb phrase.

EXAMPLES   I **mowed** the lawn this morning. [The verb *mowed* tells something about the subject, *I.*]

I **will mow** the lawn. [The verb phrase *will mow* tells something about the subject, *I.*]

Sometimes the simple predicate is also the complete predicate.

EXAMPLE   **Was** the game **postponed?** [*Was postponed* is the simple predicate and the complete predicate.]

EXERCISE A Underline the complete predicate once in each of the following sentences. Then, underline the simple predicate, or verb, a second time. Be sure to underline all words in a verb phrase. Hint: Remember that sometimes the simple predicate is also the complete predicate.

Examples 1. The landscape designer chose drought-resistant plants. [The complete predicate tells something about the subject, *designer.* The simple predicate is *chose.*]

2. Did anyone notice the crack in the ceiling? [The complete predicate asks something about the subject, *anyone.* The simple predicate is *Did notice.*]

1. A jeweler measures the weight of diamonds in carats. [What does a jeweler do?]

2. The flight attendants always review safety procedures before takeoff. [What do the flight attendants do?]

3. Stephen Hawking has written several books about the universe.

4. Did Ellen ever answer your question?

5. The spider wasp had built a nest in the rotten pile of wood.

6. That company manufactures industrial machinery.

7. Have the customers received the advertisements in the mail?

8. A single raccoon stood on the trail.

9. The Suez Canal connects the Mediterranean Sea and the Red Sea.

10. Has the helicopter landed?

The Compound Verb

2f. A **compound verb** consists of two or more verbs that are joined by a conjunction and that have the same subject.

The parts of a compound verb are usually joined by the conjunction *and, but, or,* or *nor.*

> **EXAMPLE** The week before the exam, the teacher **answered** questions and **distributed** a study guide. [The verbs *answered* and *distributed* tell about the same subject, *teacher.* They are joined by the conjunction *and.*]

TIP▶ Be sure to include all parts of any verb phrases when you are identifying compound verbs.

> **EXAMPLE** **Should** we **sit** or **stand** when the officials enter? [*Should sit* and *stand* are parts of the compound verb.]

EXERCISE B Underline the simple predicate in each of the following sentences. Be sure to underline each part of a compound verb and all parts of a verb phrase.

Examples 1. Does this alarm clock ring or play music? [*Does ring* and *play* are parts of the compound verb and ask something about the subject, *alarm clock.*]

2. Becky picked some daisies and arranged them in a vase. [*Picked* and *arranged* are parts of the compound verb and tell something about the subject, *Becky.*]

11. Will you wash and vacuum the car? [What will you do?]

12. Mike's grandparents walk two miles a day and swim at the community pool. [What do Mike's grandparents do?]

13. Did they fly or drive to their destination?

14. Bill looked under the bed and found the other sock.

15. During the speech, the microphone malfunctioned and was replaced.

16. Everyone assembled the care packages or donated money for supplies.

17. Should I answer the phone or ignore it?

18. The bird caught a worm and then flew away.

19. Tina's little sister smiled and laughed at my jokes.

20. A newscaster reviews the headlines and reports the latest news.

The Direct Object and the Objective Complement

The Direct Object

2h.	A *direct object* is a noun, pronoun, or word group that tells who or what receives the action of the verb or that shows the result of the action.

Direct objects complete the meaning of action verbs. They answer the question *Whom?* or *What?* after the verb.

     S   **V**   **DO**

EXAMPLES The lawyers questioned numerous **witnesses** during the trial. [Questioned whom? Questioned witnesses. *Witnesses* is the direct object.]

    V S V DO
Did Ali see **them** at the store? [Did see whom? Did see them. *Them* is the direct object.]

An action verb may have more than one direct object. Two or more direct objects that complete the meaning of the same action verb are called a *compound direct object.*

    S   **V**   **DO**   **DO**

EXAMPLE They recommended the **soup** and the **salad.** [Recommended what? Recommended soup and salad. *Soup* and *salad* are parts of the compound direct object.]

NOTE▶ The direct object may come before the verb.

    DO   **S**   **V**

EXAMPLE What a delightful **performance** you gave! [Gave what? Gave a performance. *Performance* is the direct object.]

EXERCISE A Underline the direct object in each of the following sentences. Remember to underline all parts of a compound direct object.

Examples 1. Do you need a folder or a notebook? [Do need what? Do need a folder or a notebook. *Folder* and *notebook* are parts of the compound direct object.]

    2. The male sea horse carries the fertilized eggs in a pouch. [Carries what? Carries eggs. *Eggs* is the direct object.]

1. Has the research and development team tested the new circuit? [Which word answers the question *Has tested what?*]

2. Some bats eat rodents, birds, frogs, and lizards. [Which words answer the question *Eat what?*]

3. Do these boxes have lids?

4. Ancient South Americans built pyramids similar to those in Egypt.

5. A nurse recorded Julio's weight and his temperature.

6. All evening, the group discussed politics and current events.

7. Our cat sharpens its claws on the fence post.

GO ON ➡

8. General William Tecumseh Sherman commanded Union troops during the Civil War.

9. When will Grandmother visit us again?

10. I usually write poems and stories about my experiences.

The Objective Complement

2j. An *objective complement* is a word or word group that helps complete the meaning of a transitive verb by identifying or modifying the direct object.

Objective complements usually follow the direct object and give more information about the direct object. Objective complements can be nouns, pronouns, or adjectives.

                   S   **V**   **DO**   **OC**

EXAMPLES The coach appointed Rene **captain.** [The noun *captain* identifies the direct object, *Rene.*]

                   S   **V**   **DO** **OC**

The foreign exchange student made our home **his.** [The possessive pronoun *his* modifies the direct object, *home.*]

          S   **V**   **DO**   **OC**

Orin will paint the kitchen **white.** [The adjective *white* modifies the direct object, *kitchen.*]

EXERCISE B Underline the objective complement in each of the following sentences. Hint: Identify the direct object first, and then determine which word or word group identifies or modifies the direct object.

Examples 1. The mayor named Dr. Espinoza Citizen of the Year. [*Citizen of the Year* identifies the direct object, *Dr. Espinoza.*]

     2. Who will crown his successor king? [*King* identifies the direct object, *successor.*]

11. Did the commissioner appoint Colleen chairperson? [Which word identifies the direct object, *Colleen?*]

12. Some people call George Washington the father of our country. [Which word group identifies the direct object, *George Washington?*]

13. Most people consider Albert Einstein a genius.

14. Years of research had made him an expert.

15. The Swansons named their son William.

16. Did you paint the house blue?

17. The citizens elected Mrs. Brown senator.

18. Why did you call the cat Sparky?

19. The barber cut Gary's hair short.

20. Mr. Bailey always keeps his yard neat.

The Indirect Object

2i. An *indirect object* is a noun, pronoun, or word group that precedes a direct object and tells *to whom* or *to what* (or *for whom* or *for what*) the action of the verb is done.

           V   S   V   IO   DO

EXAMPLES   Did Vicky send her **friend** a get-well card? [Did send a card to whom? To her friend. *Friend* is the indirect object.]

           S   S   V   IO   DO

His grades and athletic ability earned **him** a scholarship. [Earned a scholarship for whom? For him. *Him* is the indirect object.]

           S   V   IO   DO

Aaron built his **cocker spaniel** a doghouse. [Built a doghouse for whom? For his cocker spaniel. *Cocker spaniel* is the indirect object.]

NOTE Don't confuse an indirect object with an object of a preposition. A noun or pronoun that follows the prepositions *to* or *for* is part of a prepositional phrase and is not an indirect object.

                            S   V   IO   DO

INDIRECT OBJECT   Felicia read her little **sister** a story. [Read a story to whom? To her sister. *Sister* is the indirect object.]

                             S   V   DO   OP

OBJECT OF A PREPOSITION   Felicia read a story **to** her little **sister.** [*Sister* is the object of the preposition *to*.]

EXERCISE A Underline the indirect object in each of the following sentences. Remember that the indirect object will not be part of a prepositional phrase.

Examples 1. The pitcher threw the batter a fastball. [Threw a fastball to whom? To the batter. *Batter* is the indirect object.]

     2. In a relay race, a runner passes a teammate a baton. [Passes a baton to whom? To a teammate. *Teammate* is the indirect object.]

1. The hotel gives guests free passes to local events. [Which word answers the question *Gives free passes to whom?*]

2. Would you sketch me a map of the campus? [Which word answers the question *Sketch a map for whom?*]

3. Tomorrow, Ms. Stanley will show our class some pictures from her trip to Argentina.

4. Every morning, my neighbor's dog brings him the paper.

5. Please give the gerbils some water.

6. The car dealer sold the family a roomy sedan.

7. The florist delivered Candice a beautiful flower arrangement.

8. At the drama competition, the judges awarded us first prize.

GO ON ➡

9. Will you sing me the song about candles?

10. The quarterback tossed the receiver the football.

The Compound Indirect Object

An action verb may have more than one indirect object. Two or more indirect objects of the same action verb are called *a compound indirect object.*

                                S   **V**   **IO**   **IO**   **DO**

EXAMPLE   Their mother bought **Thelma** and **Aileen** matching sweaters. [Bought sweaters for whom? For Thelma and Aileen. *Thelma* and *Aileen* are parts of the compound indirect object.]

EXERCISE B   Underline the compound indirect objects in the following sentences.

Examples 1. Aunt Judith mailed my <u>sister</u> and <u>me</u> a package from New Hampshire. [Mailed a package to whom? To my sister and me. *Sister* and *me* are parts of the compound indirect object.]

        2. Mr. Wilkins bought his <u>cat</u> and <u>dog</u> new collars. [Bought collars for what? For his cat and dog. *Cat* and *dog* are parts of the compound indirect object.]

11. The clerk handed me and another customer our receipts. [Which words answer the question *Handed receipts to whom?*]

12. Has Kent written Victor and Clara thank-you notes? [Which words answer the question *Has written notes to whom?*]

13. Mr. Benson taught Adam and Suzi Latin last year.

14. Did she send you or Sam a graduation invitation?

15. The computer virus caused individuals and companies problems.

16. I shipped my aunt and uncle a copy of my favorite CD.

17. The marathon organizers will present the volunteers and sponsors certificates of appreciation.

18. Has the veterinarian given Sapphire and Polly their shots?

19. My great-grandmother told my brother and me stories about the Great Depression.

20. For practice, Andrea read Clay and Ginger her speech.

The Predicate Nominative

2k. A *predicate nominative* is a word or word group that is in the predicate and that identifies the subject or refers to it.

A predicate nominative appears only in a sentence that has a linking verb. Common linking verbs include *is, was, will be, has been, could have been, become,* and *remain.*

S   V   PN

EXAMPLES In June, Mrs. Fleming became our new **principal.** [The noun *principal* refers to the subject, *Mrs. Fleming.*]

S   V   PN

Of all the comedians in the talent show, Ralph was the funniest **one.** [The pronoun *one* refers to the subject, *Ralph.*]

S   V   PN

The title of our newspaper will remain ***The Bulldog Beat.*** [The word group *The Bulldog Beat* refers to the subject, *title.*]

TIP To find the predicate nominative in a question, turn the question into a statement.

QUESTION Will Mrs. Bray be our substitute teacher?

S   V   PN

STATEMENT Mrs. Bray will be our substitute **teacher.** [The word order of the statement makes it easier to tell that *teacher* is the predicate nominative.]

EXERCISE A Underline the predicate nominative in each of the following sentences.

Examples 1. Snakes, lizards, and turtles are <u>reptiles</u>. [*Reptiles* refers to the subject, *Snakes, lizards, and turtles,* and completes the meaning of the linking verb, *are.*]

2. How long has Millicent been a <u>member</u> of the bowling league? [*Member* refers to the subject, *Millicent,* and completes the meaning of the linking verb, *has been.*]

1. Is that bright yellow bird a goldfinch? [Which word in the predicate identifies the subject, *bird,* and completes the meaning of the linking verb, *is*? Try turning the question into a statement.]

2. With more training, Evelyn could have been a concert violinist. [Which word in the predicate refers to the subject, *Evelyn,* and completes the meaning of the linking verb, *could have been*?]

3. Are the Barretts your next-door neighbors?

4. Dylan Thomas is my favorite poet.

5. The capital of Peru is Lima.

6. Those wooden shoes are souvenirs from a trip to Holland.

7. Despite the arthritis in his hands, my grandfather remains an avid gardener.

8. A gobbler is a male turkey.

GO ON

9. Was your mother a contestant on that trivia game show?

10. After graduation, Roberto became a mentor to younger students.

The Compound Predicate Nominative

A linking verb can have more than one predicate nominative. Two or more predicate nominatives of the same linking verb are called a *compound predicate nominative.*

                  V   S   PN   PN

EXAMPLE Are the school counselors **Ms. Childress** and **Mr. Jones?** [*Ms. Childress* and *Mr. Jones* identify the subject, *counselors.* Together, *Ms. Childress* and *Mr. Jones* make up the compound predicate nominative.]

NOTE Sometimes, a predicate nominative comes before the subject and the verb.

                           PN   S   V

EXAMPLE What a creative **artist** Anna is! [The noun *artist* refers to the subject, *Anna.*]

EXERCISE B Underline the predicate nominative in each of the following sentences. Remember to underline all parts of a compound predicate nominative.

Examples 1. Have you ever been a <u>cashier</u> or a <u>salesperson</u>? [*Cashier* and *salesperson* refer to the subject, *you,* and complete the meaning of the linking verb, *Have been.*]

      2. Good sources of vitamin C are <u>oranges</u>, <u>broccoli</u>, and <u>strawberries</u>. [*Oranges, broccoli,* and *strawberries* identify the subject, *sources,* and complete the meaning of the linking verb, *are.*]

11. What an extraordinary event the benefit concert was! [Which word in the predicate refers to the subject, *concert,* and completes the meaning of the linking verb, *was?*]

12. Is that a butterfly or a moth on the tree branch? [Which words in the predicate refer to the subject, *that,* and complete the meaning of the linking verb, *Is?*]

13. Lee's three favorite classes are science, math, and history.

14. The first two competitors were Ben and Lindsay.

15. Was the main character a liar or an honest man?

16. Are those paintings originals or reproductions?

17. He has been the president of the chess club for two years.

18. Stephanie's favorite types of music are jazz and rap.

19. Two basic seasonings are salt and pepper.

20. My next pet will be an iguana or a snake.

The Predicate Adjective

2l. A **predicate adjective** is an adjective that is in the predicate and that modifies the subject.

A predicate adjective completes the meaning of a linking verb and describes the subject. Common linking verbs include *is, was, will be, has been, could have been, appear, feel, grow, look, seem, smell, sound,* and *taste.*

                             S   V   PA

EXAMPLES The moon is **bright** this evening. [The adjective *bright* describes the subject, *moon,* and completes the meaning of the linking verb, *is.*]

           V   S   V   PA

Does that milk smell **sour**? [The adjective *sour* describes the subject, *milk,* and completes the meaning of the linking verb, *Does smell.*]

      S   V   PA

None of the lions seemed **afraid** of the film crew. [The adjective *afraid* describes the subject, *None,* and completes the meaning of the linking verb, *seemed.*]

EXERCISE A Underline the predicate adjective in each of the following sentences.

Examples 1. The passengers were becoming <u>restless</u>. [The adjective *restless* describes the subject, *passengers,* and completes the meaning of the linking verb, *were becoming.*]

        2. Does this picture look <u>straight</u> to you? [The adjective *straight* describes the subject, *picture,* and completes the meaning of the linking verb, *Does look.*]

1. All of the finalists seemed nervous before the last round. [Which word in the predicate describes the subject, *All,* and completes the meaning of the linking verb, *seemed*?]

2. Is your cousin's Great Dane friendly? [Which word in the predicate describes the subject, *Great Dane,* and completes the meaning of the linking verb, *Is*?]

3. The piano player's technique was flawless.

4. None of the avocados were ripe.

5. Was the service at the restaurant satisfactory?

6. My grandmother has always been patient with me.

7. This couch is really comfortable!

8. Standing in front of the fireplace, I finally felt warm.

9. Peter Carl Fabergé, a Russian jeweler, became famous for his magnificent jeweled Easter eggs.

10. Does the tomato soup taste salty?

GO ON

The Compound Predicate Adjective

A linking verb can have more than one predicate adjective. Two or more predicate adjectives of the same linking verb are called *a compound predicate adjective.*

                        S   V   PA   PA

EXAMPLES   Our leaders are **enthusiastic** and **supportive.** [The adjectives *enthusiastic* and *supportive* describe the subject, *leaders.*]

                   V   S   V   PA   PA

Do the demonstrators seem **angry** or **peaceful**? [The adjectives *angry* and *peaceful* describe the subject, *demonstrators.*]

NOTE Sometimes, a predicate adjective comes before the subject and the verb.

                  PA   S   V

EXAMPLE   How **lovely** these flowers are! [The adjective *lovely* describes the subject, *flowers.*]

EXERCISE B Underline the predicate adjective in each of the following sentences. Remember to underline all parts of a compound predicate adjective.

Examples 1. These jeans are <u>old</u> but <u>comfortable</u>. [The adjectives *old* and *comfortable* describe the subject, *jeans,* and complete the meaning of the linking verb, *are.*]

       2. Is the roof of the cabin <u>leaky</u> or <u>waterproof</u>? [The adjectives *leaky* and *waterproof* describe the subject, *roof,* and complete the meaning of the linking verb, *Is.*]

11. How beautiful the sunset looks this evening! [Which word in the predicate describes the subject, *sunset,* and completes the meaning of the linking verb, *looks?*]

12. The historical documents are incomplete yet useful to scholars. [Which words in the predicate describe the subject, *documents,* and complete the meaning of the linking verb, *are?*]

13. How bright those lights at the stadium are!

14. On a cold winter morning, warm oatmeal is delicious and soothing.

15. Does this skirt look navy or black to you?

16. The mother cat seemed loving and protective.

17. The basket of fruit was full this morning but empty by noon.

18. Snowboarding can be fun and exciting.

19. Do the strawberries taste sweet or sour?

20. After their rescue, the hikers appeared shaken but healthy.

Classifying Sentences by Purpose

2m. Sentences may be classified according to purpose.

(1) A **declarative sentence** makes a statement and ends with a period.

> **EXAMPLES** Raymond plays golf twice a week. [statement.]
> Someone left the window open. [statement]

(2) An **interrogative sentence** asks a question and ends with a question mark.

> **EXAMPLES** Will you be working late this evening? [question]
> What is the name of Louisa's younger sister? [question]

EXERCISE A Punctuate each sentence below with an appropriate end mark. Then, on the line provided, write *DEC* if the sentence is declarative or *INT* if the sentence is interrogative.

Example __INT__ **1.** Did you hear the alarm? [The sentence asks a question, so it's an interrogative

sentence and should end with a question mark.]

_____ **1.** Next year, my parents will celebrate their twenty-fifth wedding anniversary [Does the

sentence make a statement or ask a question?]

_____ **2.** How long did the Hundred Years' War between England and France actually last

_____ **3.** Dry ice, a solid form of carbon dioxide, is used as a refrigerant

_____ **4.** The American black bear and the grizzly bear are endangered species according to the

U.S. Fish and Wildlife Service

_____ **5.** Has anyone found a pair of glasses with wire frames

---

(3) An **imperative sentence** makes a request or gives a command. Most imperative sentences end with a period. A strong command ends with an exclamation point.

> **EXAMPLES** Please pass this book to her. [request]
> Remove your hats before you go inside. [command]
> Stand back! [strong command]

NOTE The subject of a command is always *you*. When *you* doesn't appear in imperative sentences, *you* is called the **understood subject.**

> **EXAMPLES** (You) Please pass this note to her. [request]
> (You) Remove your hats before you go inside. [command]
> (You) Stand back! [strong command]

The word *you* is the understood subject even when the person spoken to is addressed by name.

> **EXAMPLE** Chen, (you) read the poem by Gwendolyn Brooks. [In this request, *Chen* is
> used to get the listener's attention. *You,* not *Chen,* is the subject.]

GO ON ➡

for **CHAPTER 2: PARTS OF A SENTENCE**   pages 45–46   *continued*

(4) An *exclamatory sentence* shows excitement or expresses strong feeling and ends with an exclamation point.

> **EXAMPLES**   We're going to the playoffs! [The sentence expresses excitement.]
> What a good friend you are! [The sentence expresses strong feeling.]

EXERCISE B Punctuate each sentence below with an appropriate end mark: a period, a question mark, or an exclamation mark. Then, on the line provided, classify each sentence by writing *DEC* for declarative, *INT* for interrogative, *IMP* for imperative, and *EXC* for exclamatory.

Examples ___EXC___ **1.** What a great time I had! [The sentence expresses strong feeling, so it's an

exclamatory sentence and should end with an exclamation point.]

___IMP___ **2.** Take your umbrella with you. [The sentence expresses a command, so it's an

imperative sentence and should end with a period.]

_____ **6.** Please fasten your seatbelt [Does the sentence express excitement or express a command?]

_____ **7.** Will you bring an extra jacket for me [Does the sentence express a command or ask a

question?]

_____ **8.** Pewter, an alloy of tin, is used in many types of decorative objects

_____ **9.** Don't step on that broken glass

_____ **10.** Will your grandparents be arriving this week

_____ **11.** How beautiful you look tonight

_____ **12.** Watch out for that car

_____ **13.** Igloos are dome-shaped homes made from blocks of snow and ice

_____ **14.** Please send me your address and phone number after you move

_____ **15.** What an exceptional dancer she is

The Prepositional Phrase

3b. A *prepositional phrase* includes a preposition, the object of the preposition, and any modifiers of that object.

<table>
<tr><td></td><td>**P**</td><td></td><td>**OP**</td></tr>
</table>

EXAMPLES   **On that hot summer day,** the temperature reached one hundred degrees Fahrenheit. [*Day* is the object of the preposition *On. That, hot,* and *summer* modify *day.*]

             P   **OP**

The sunscreen **in the green bottle** smells like cinnamon. [*Bottle* is the object of the preposition *in. The* and *green* modify *bottle.*]

REMINDER A preposition shows the relationship of a noun or pronoun to another word.

EXERCISE A Underline each prepositional phrase in the following sentences. Then, draw a second line under each object of a preposition. Hint: Some sentences contain more than one prepositional phrase.

Example 1. The children ran happily in front of the breaking waves. [The compound preposition *in front of* begins the prepositional phrase *in front of the breaking waves. The* and *breaking* modify the object of the preposition, *waves.*]

1. When the sun beats down, we all rest under a beach umbrella. [Have you underlined the prepositional phrase and drawn two lines under the object of the preposition?]

2. Hey, don't pour water on my sand sculpture!

3. Because of the brisk coastal winds, even heavy kites fly well.

4. Cold water with a little lemon is a refreshing drink in this heat.

5. In addition to sunscreen, will you please wear this hat for the afternoon?

Adjective Phrases

3c. A prepositional phrase that modifies a noun or a pronoun is called an *adjective phrase.* An adjective phrase answers the question *what kind* or *which one.*

EXAMPLES   Tess enjoys novels **about animals.** [The adjective phrase *about animals* modifies the noun *novels* by telling what kind of novels.]

She read one book **from Florida about an aging raccoon.** [The adjective phrases *from Florida* and *about an aging raccoon* both modify the noun *book* by telling which one.]

Another book featured a cat **with thin stripes around its tail.** [The adjective phrase *with thin stripes* modifies *cat* by telling which one. The adjective phrase *around its tail* modifies the object of the first phrase, *stripes,* by telling what kind.]

GO ON

EXERCISE B Underline the adjective phrase in each of the following sentences. Then, draw two lines under the word or words the phrase modifies.

Example 1. Would you believe a <u>story</u> or <u>poem</u> <u>about a cat-loving canary</u>? [The preposition *about* begins an adjective phrase modifying *story* and *poem*.]

6. We may laugh, but performing dogs like Lassie show how smart dogs can be. [Have you underlined the adjective phrase in this sentence? Have you drawn two lines under the noun the phrase modifies?]

7. A dog's loyalty to its family often seems unshakable.

8. Does a cat really have a good sense of balance?

9. Movies and books about whales have been popular lately.

10. Have you seen that movie about a pig?

Adverb Phrases

3d. A prepositional phrase that modifies a verb, an adjective, or an adverb is called an **adverb phrase.** Adverb phrases describe verbs, adjectives, or other adverbs and tell *how, when, where, why,* or *to what extent.*

> **EXAMPLES** Ron put a CD **into the player** and started it. [The prepositional phrase *into the player* tells where Ron put the CD and modifies the verb *put.*]
> Amplified **by large speakers,** the music could be heard by the entire audience. [The prepositional phrase *by large speakers* tells how the music was amplified and modifies the adjective *Amplified.*]

EXERCISE C Underline each adverb phrase in the following sentences. Then, draw two lines under the word it modifies. Hint: Sentences may contain more than one adverb phrase.

Example 1. The DJ <u>played</u> jazz and blues <u>until late evening</u>. [The adverb phrase *until late evening* modifies the verb *played* by telling how long the DJ played jazz and blues.]

11. Collectors often find classic recordings at Tunes and Tones. [Have you underlined the adverb phrase in this sentence? Have you drawn two lines under the verb modified by the phrase?]

12. Famous for its diverse titles and many recordings, the shop stands between two restaurants.

13. During the annual summer sale, collectors swap CDs.

14. In the repair shop, technicians repair old turntables and speakers.

15. These old albums sound great despite the popping and crackling noises!

The Participle and the Participial Phrase

The Participle

3e. | A *participle* is a verb form that can be used as an adjective.

There are two kinds of participles: present participles and past participles. Present participles end in *–ing*. Most past participles end in *–d* or *–ed*, although some are formed in other ways. Participles can modify nouns and pronouns.

PRESENT PARTICIPLES	**shouting** boy	**yelping** coyote	**whining** tires
PAST PARTICIPLES	**praised** idea	**burst** bubble	**frozen** yogurt

REMINDER ▶ You will often see participles in verb phrases, such as *had been shouting* or *was praised*. If the participle appears with these helping verbs, it is not an adjective. It is part of the verb phrase.

> **ADJECTIVE**　The **sleeping** cat did not notice us enter the room.
> **VERB PHRASE**　The cat **was sleeping** on the back of the sofa.

EXERCISE A Underline the participles that are used as adjectives in the following sentences. Then, draw two lines under the word modified by the participle.

Example　1. They sat and talked as the flickering campfire warmed their hands. [The present

participle *flickering* modifies the noun *campfire*.]

1. Dangling, the bait lured the fish to the line. [Which word helps to modify a noun in this sentence?]

2. At the appointed time, stand up and shout!

3. Who smudged my freshly waxed car?

4. Each written word was easy to read.

5. We stopped and stared at the confusing sign.

The Participial Phrase

3f. | A *participial phrase* consists of a participle and any modifiers or complements the participle has. The entire phrase is used as an adjective. Participial phrases may use present or past participles to modify nouns and pronouns.

> **EXAMPLES**　**Sleeping peacefully,** the puppies snored lightly. [The adverb *peacefully* modifies the participle *Sleeping*. The entire participial phrase modifies the noun *puppies*.]
>
> The electrician, **shutting the cabinet door,** stepped back. [The noun *door* completes the participle *shutting*. The entire participial phrase modifies the noun *electrician*.]

GO ON ▶

> **TIP** Sometimes you will see other forms of a participle. In these forms, the helping verb *having* along with any other needed helping verbs is added to the past participle.
>
> **EXAMPLES** Her sister, **having formed** an opinion, was quick to speak up.
>
> **Having been assured** of the ride's safety, my parents rode the roller coaster.

EXERCISE B Underline the participial phrase in each of the following sentences. Then, draw two lines under the noun or pronoun the participial phrase modifies.

Example 1. Cracked by the heat, the pottery broke into two pieces. [The prepositional phrase *by the heat* modifies the participle *Cracked*. The entire participial phrase modifies the noun *pottery*.]

6. The new clay, formed into a lump, sat on a table. [Have you underlined the participle and prepositional phrase that form the participial phrase in this sentence? Have you drawn two lines under the noun the phrase modifies?]

7. Pressing his fingers into the clay, Karl smoothed out the wrinkles.

8. He placed the clay, moistened with water, onto the wheel.

9. Spinning the wheel with his feet, he began to form a new bowl.

10. Karl's new bowl, prepared more carefully, will last a long time.

EXERCISE C Using the verb suggested in the parentheses, add a meaningful participle to each participial phrase. Hint: If you're unsure of how to spell the past participle of an irregular verb, look the verb up in a dictionary.

Example 1. *(frost)* Glasses ___frosted___ in the freezer keep milk cold. [*Frost* is a regular verb, so adding *–ed* to it makes its past participle.]

11. *(Run)* _____ quickly, the hurdler prepared to jump. [Have you inserted a present participle that will help to make a participial phrase that modifies *hurdler*?]

12. *(paint)* The poster, _____ brightly, advertised the sale.

13. *(read)* Maddie lounged on the couch, _____ a magazine.

14. *(Draw)* _____ hastily on an envelope, the idea showed promise.

15. *(Cook)* _____ correctly, rice is neither sticky nor starchy.

The Gerund and the Gerund Phrase

The Gerund

3g. A *gerund* is a verb form ending in *–ing* that is used as a noun.

A gerund can be used as a subject, a predicate nominative, a direct object, an indirect object, or an object of a preposition.

SUBJECT	**Qualifying** should be your first priority.
PREDICATE NOMINATIVE	Isn't this computer program's primary purpose **calculating?**
DIRECT OBJECT	Clear and shallow surf invited **snorkeling.**
INDIRECT OBJECT	Ellis is going to give **jogging** a second attempt.
OBJECT OF A PREPOSITION	Before **marrying,** Trahn and Kala had been friends for almost seven years!

NOTE Both gerunds and present participles end in *–ing.* To tell them apart, decide how the word is used in the sentence. If the word is used as a noun, it is a gerund. If the word is used as an adjective, it is a present participle. If the word follows a helping verb, it is part of a verb phrase.

GERUND	Last year Hannah took two semesters of **typing.** [*Typing* is a gerund used as the object of the preposition *of.*]
PARTICIPLE	The **typing** clerk paused to answer the phone. [*Typing* is a participle used as an adjective that modifies *clerk.*]
PART OF A VERB PHRASE	Len is **typing** up his report now. [*Typing* is part of the verb phrase *is typing.*]

EXERCISE A Underline each gerund in the following sentences.

Example 1. Gardening is a healthy hobby. [*Gardening* is a gerund used as the subject of the sentence.]

1. Does Ms. Tyler enjoy welding? [Have you underlined a gerund used as a direct object?]

2. Today's speaker said, "Sharing has had more impact on this culture than most of us realize."

3. After the fourth thunderclap ended, the cat gave relaxing one final try.

4. Parking is a challenge at this mall!

5. He joked that the sparrows had better start to think about migrating.

3h. A *gerund phrase* consists of a gerund and any modifiers or complements the gerund has. The entire phrase is used as a noun.

SUBJECT	**Visiting Washington, D.C.,** was a memorable experience. [The gerund *Visiting* has a complement, *Washington, D.C.,* telling what was visited.]
PREDICATE NOMINATIVE	The cat's favorite game is **toying with crickets.** [The gerund *toying* is modified by a prepositional phrase, *with crickets.*]

GO ON ➡

DIRECT OBJECT	Our family vacations involve **meandering slowly toward historic sites.** [The gerund *meandering* is modified by the adverb *slowly* and by the prepositional phrase *toward historic sites.*]
INDIRECT OBJECT	Give **accurately organizing the data** your immediate attention. [The gerund *organizing* is modified by the adverb *accurately.* *Data* is the direct object of the gerund.]
OBJECT OF A PREPOSITION	The technicians have been trained for **responding quickly to emergencies.** [The gerund *responding* is the object of the preposition *for* and is modified by the adverb *quickly* and the prepositional phrase *to emergencies.*]

EXERCISE B Underline the gerund phrases in the following sentences.

Example 1. Carlos has hopes of <u>becoming a dental hygienist</u>. [*Becoming,* the gerund form of the

verb *become,* has a subject complement, *dental hygienist.*]

6. Does he enjoy working with people? [Have you underlined the gerund and its modifying

prepositional phrase?]

7. Helping people to relax is part of a dentist's job.

8. Carlos is good at putting people at ease.

9. His friends all speak of his humorous way of distracting people.

10. Studying to be a hygienist will take Carlos about two years.

EXERCISE C Use the verb in the parentheses to create a gerund to complete the gerund phrase. Hint: Make any necessary spelling changes when you add the –*ing* ending.

Example 1. (*Ask*) ___Asking___ for help is a sign of strength, not weakness. [Adding –*ing* to *Ask*

creates the gerund *Asking,* which is used as part of the gerund phrase *Asking for help.*]

11. (*Lift*) _____ weights strengthens your muscles and builds your stamina. [Have you

formed a gerund from *Lift*?]

12. (*add*) Lauren improved her training program by _____ more repetitions to each set.

13. (*feel*) She likes the _____ of muscles hard at work.

14. (*train*) How many hours a week does Lauren spend in _____ with weights?

15. (*Compete*) _____ in contests is her eventual goal.

The Infinitive and the Infinitive Phrase

The Infinitive

3i. An *infinitive* is a verb form that can be used as a noun, an adjective, or an adverb. Most infinitives begin with *to*.

NOUN	When he has a problem on his mind, Hal likes **to walk.** [The infinitive *to walk* is a noun, the direct object of the verb *likes*.]
ADVERB	An entire herd of deer was waiting **to eat.** [The infinitive *to eat* is an adverb modifying the verb phrase *was waiting*.]
ADJECTIVE	The machine's ability **to print** posters of multiple sizes is well known. [The infinitive *to print* is an adjective describing the noun *ability*.]

NOTE The word *to* is often used as a preposition. In general, when *to* is followed by a noun or pronoun, *to* is a preposition. When *to* is followed by a verb, *to* is part of an infinitive.

INFINITIVES	to allow	to number	to examine
PREPOSITIONAL PHRASES	to her	to the small box	to Kansas

EXERCISE A Underline the infinitive in each of the following sentences.

Example 1. To graduate is the goal of most juniors. [The sign of the infinitive, *To*, and the verb

graduate make up the infinitive. *To graduate* acts as a noun, the subject of the sentence.]

1. If I want hot tea, which is the button to push? [What infinitive modifies a noun?]

2. The colt tried to trot but tumbled down.

3. At any minute, we expected the bell to ring.

4. Have you heard the saying that to forgive is divine?

5. After the race, all the runners wanted was to rest.

The Infinitive Phrase

3j. An *infinitive phrase* consists of an infinitive and any modifiers or complements the infinitive has. The entire phrase can be used as a noun, an adjective, or an adverb.

NOUN	Roberto wants **to finish his homework before the game.** [The infinitive phrase acts as the sentence's direct object and includes the infinitive *to finish*, the infinitive's direct object *homework*, the direct object's modifier *his*, and the adverb phrase *before the game*.]
ADJECTIVE	Its capacity **to survive long periods of drought** makes this tree a good choice for a dry environment. [The infinitive phrase modifies the noun *capacity* and includes the infinitive *to survive*, the infinitive's direct object *periods*, and the direct object's modifiers *long* and *of drought*.]

GO ON ➡

> **ADVERB** **To make good bread at home,** use fresh, live yeast. [The infinitive phrase
> modifies the verb *use* and includes the infinitive *To make*, its direct object
> *bread*, the direct object's modifier *good*, and the adverb phrase *at home*.]

EXERCISE B Underline the infinitive phrase in each sentence. Then, draw a second line under the infinitive.

Example 1. Should we hurry to meet with Mark's sister? [The infinitive phrase acts as an adverb

explaining why we should hurry, and it includes both the infinitive and a prepositional

phrase.]

6. Did you remember to turn off the lights? [Have you underlined the infinitive phrase once and

drawn two lines under the infinitive?]

7. To restore a hundred-year-old steam locomotive is one of the historical society's goals.

8. Aren't horses able to sleep standing up?

9. The meteorologist expects rain to blow in early tomorrow.

10. Whose turn is it to wash the dishes?

In formal speech and writing, avoid using *split infinitives*. An infinitive is split when a modifying word or words come between the sign of the infinitive, *to*, and the verb form.

> **SPLIT INFINITIVE** What we want to most definitely increase is the size of our membership. [The modifiers *most* and *definitely* appear between the sign of the infinitive, *to*, and the verb form, *increase*.]
> **WHOLE INFINITIVE** What we most definitely want **to increase** is the size of our membership. [The parts of the infinitive are no longer separated from each other.]

EXERCISE C Use proofreading symbols to correct the split infinitives in each of the following sentences. Hint: Most sentences can be corrected in more than one way.

Example 1. Have your ant bites begun to (gradually) fade away? [The adverb *gradually* should not

split the infinitive *to fade*.]

11. To more easily achieve a goal, break it into small steps. [Where are the parts of the infinitive in

the sentence? What words should be moved in order to make the infinitive whole?]

12. The fox kits like to playfully and noisily pounce on each other.

13. The tree's broken stump began to miraculously grow again.

14. Do you have the strength to safely lift this box?

15. Don't forget to frequently and briskly stir the sauce, or it will scorch!

The Appositive and the Appositive Phrase

The Appositive

3k. An *appositive* is a noun or a pronoun placed beside another noun or pronoun to identify or describe it.

An appositive may be a single noun or pronoun, or it may be a compound noun or pronoun.

EXAMPLES Those trees, **oaks,** have been there for over fifty years. [The appositive *oaks* follows the more general noun *trees* and helps to identify it.]

As evening fell, the trees, **loblolly pines,** scented the air. [The compound noun *loblolly pines* follows the more general noun *trees* and helps to identify it.]

My uncle **David** raises trees on his tree farm. [The proper noun *David* follows the common noun *uncle* and helps to identify it.]

Evergreens, they look beautiful with winter snow on them. [The appositive *Evergreens* comes before the pronoun *they* and helps to describe it.]

EXERCISE A Underline the appositive in each of the following sentences. Then, draw two lines under the noun or pronoun that the appositive identifies or describes.

Example 1. Julian likes to shop at the grocery store Bag-It-Up. [The appositive *Bag-It-Up* identifies the noun *store*.]

1. The toughest obstacles, tree stumps, occasionally slowed the cross-country skiers. [Have you underlined a noun that helps to identify or describe another noun in this sentence?]

2. Unfortunately, it's time for my last chore, mopping.

3. The students, tenth graders, will receive corrected report cards.

4. Did you hear that my friend Matthew Clark is going to Germany this summer?

5. Some young people choose to become soldiers, marines.

The Appositive Phrase

3l. An *appositive phrase* consists of an appositive and any modifiers the appositive has.

EXAMPLE The percussion, **clashing cymbals and rattling snares,** kept the beat as the band marched. [The appositive phrase helps to describe the noun *percussion*.]

GO ON

TIP Appositives are often set off from the main sentence with commas. Appositive phrases are always set off from the main sentence with commas.

> **EXAMPLES** The nearest crossroad, **Sycamore,** is going to be resurfaced soon. [Commas set off the appositive from the rest of the sentence.]
>
> The flowers, **bright bluebonnets and delicate primroses,** decorated the highways. [Commas set off the appositive phrase from the rest of the sentence.]

EXERCISE B Underline the appositive phrase in each of the following sentences.

Examples 1. Can you help us find *Legacy of Pearl,* <u>a book on our summer reading list?</u> [The appositive phrase describes and follows the compound noun *Legacy of Pearl.*]

2. <u>My closest friend for years,</u> Anna has moved to another state. [The appositive phrase describes and precedes the noun *Anna.*]

6. He, the youngest child in the family, asked for an apple. [Have you underlined a phrase that helps to identify a pronoun in this sentence?]

7. Through the meadow, a field full of wildflowers, the cool river ran. [Have you underlined a phrase that helps to describe a noun in this sentence?]

8. A science fiction story set on Mars, the movie thrilled most viewers but frightened a few others.

9. Take down the window dressings, every single curtain and embroidered sash, and wash them.

10. Are you asking to drive this car, my restored 1967 sedan?

11. The room, a cozy study lined with shelves, was littered with books and newspapers.

12. Before we moved in, the house, an old-fashioned frame home, was in a sad state of disrepair.

13. Let's get those books, the mysteries and the romance novels, together and price them for the garage sale.

14. Avery's favorite kind of weather, windy, cool days, starts in October.

15. Join me in a round of applause, a token of gratitude, for our interesting speaker.

The Adjective Clause

4d. An *adjective clause* is a subordinate clause that modifies, or describes, a noun or a pronoun.

An adjective clause follows the noun or pronoun it describes and tells *what kind* or *which one*.

WHAT KIND Slate, **which is dense metamorphic rock,** can be used as patio flooring. [The adjective clause has a subject, *which*, and a verb, *is*. The clause follows the noun it modifies, *Slate*, and describes it, telling what kind of rock slate is.]

WHICH ONE The patio **that they recently installed** has a slate floor. [The adjective clause has a subject, *they*, and a verb, *installed*. The clause follows the noun it modifies, *patio*, and describes it, telling which patio has a slate floor.]

Most adjective clauses begin with a relative pronoun, such as *that, which, who, whom,* or *whose.* A *relative pronoun* shows the relationship of the clause to the word or words it modifies and usually functions as the subject of the clause or as an object of a preposition or verb.

EXAMPLES The painting, **which shows a girl reading a book,** is well known. [The relative pronoun *which* relates the subordinate clause to the noun it modifies, *painting*, and is the subject of the verb *shows*.]

The girl's mother, **for whom the painting was made,** was pleased with it. [The relative pronoun *whom* relates the subordinate clause to the noun it modifies, *mother*, and is the object of the preposition *for*.]

This is the second sketch **that Kim has finished.** [The relative pronoun *that* relates the subordinate clause to the noun it modifies, *sketch*, and is the direct object of the verb phrase *has finished*.]

NOTE Occasionally the words *when* and *where* can introduce adjective clauses. When they do, they are called *relative adverbs.* Relative adverbs also show the relationship of the subordinate clause to the word or words it modifies.

EXAMPLE I'll never forget the day **when my family moved.** [The relative adverb *when* relates the clause to the noun it modifies, *day*.]

EXERCISE A Underline each adjective clause in the sentences below. Then, draw two lines under the noun the adjective clause modifies.

Example 1. Who is the <u>man <u>whose music is playing right now?</u></u> [The adjective clause *whose music is playing right now* modifies the noun *man*.]

1. Machu Picchu, where visitors can see ancient Incan ruins, stands between two mountain

peaks. [What clause modifies a noun? Which noun does it modify?]

2. My grandfather, to whom I sent the letter, lives in Vermont.

3. Should we call the people whose names are on this list?

4. These are the students that began a lawn care business last summer.

5. Oh, yes—Wednesday is the day when we have to be at work an hour early.

Adjective clauses may be either *essential* or *nonessential* to a sentence's meaning. An *essential adjective clause* limits the possible meanings of a sentence. If you remove an essential adjective clause from a sentence, the sentence loses part of its basic message. A *nonessential adjective clause* adds information to the sentence but does not limit its meaning. If you remove a nonessential clause from a sentence, the sentence does not change in meaning. Nonessential adjective clauses are set off from the sentence with commas.

> **ESSENTIAL**   It's best not to eat fruit **that hasn't been washed.** [The adjective clause limits the sentence's meaning. Without the adjective clause, the meaning would change.]
>
> **NONESSENTIAL**   Apples, **which sometimes have a waxy coating,** should be gently scrubbed. [The adjective clause adds information to the sentence but does not limit its meaning. Without the adjective clause, the meaning stays the same.]

EXERCISE B Underline the adjective clause in each of the following sentences. Then, draw two lines under the noun the adjective clause modifies. If the clause is essential, write *E* on the line provided. If the clause is nonessential, write *NE* on the line provided.

Examples __NE__ **1.** Manhattan, which is a borough of New York City, is almost a city to itself. [The adjective clause adds information about *Manhattan* but does not change the meaning of the sentence.]

__E__ **2.** Is this the child who hit a home run? [The adjective clause modifies *child* and limits the meaning of the sentence.]

_____ **6.** Tanja is wearing the barrettes that she bought in Mexico. [Which clause modifies a noun in this sentence? Is the clause necessary to the sentence's basic meaning?]

_____ **7.** That's one movie that I'd really like to see! [Which clause modifies a noun in this sentence? Is the clause necessary to the sentence's basic meaning?]

_____ **8.** Grilled chicken, which is one of my favorite foods, is delicious.

_____ **9.** The boy, who came in third in the contest, was surprised about winning.

_____**10.** Todd recently spoke to a woman whose family lives in India.

_____**11.** The door, which was decorated with holly, stood wide open.

_____**12.** Would you hand me that hammer, which used to be my uncle's?

_____**13.** The audience listened closely to the musicians, who played their best.

_____**14.** The cartoon character that is such a smart aleck is known worldwide.

_____**15.** The velvet dress that the princess wore at her wedding is now on display at the museum.

The Noun Clause

4e. A *noun clause* is a subordinate clause that is used as a noun.

A noun clause may be used as a subject, a predicate nominative, a direct object, an indirect object, or an object of a preposition. Some words that commonly introduce noun clauses are *how, that, what, whatever, when, where, which, whichever, who, whoever,* and *whose.*

SUBJECT	**Whoever is last to yell "I'm it!"** is it. [The noun clause has a subject, *Whoever,* and a verb, *is.* The noun clause is the subject of the sentence.]
PREDICATE NOMINATIVE	A comic movie is **what John and Laura prefer to watch.** [The noun clause has a compound subject, *John and Laura,* and a verb, *prefer.* The clause is a predicate nominative and renames the sentence's subject, *movie.*]
DIRECT OBJECT	Will someone please tell me **what the correct answer is**? [The noun clause has a subject, *answer,* and a verb, *is.* The clause is the direct object of the verb *Will tell. Me* is the indirect object.]
INDIRECT OBJECT	Throw **whoever is open** the ball. [The noun clause has a subject, *whoever,* and a verb, *is.* The clause is the indirect object of the verb *Throw. Ball* is the direct object.]
OBJECT OF A PREPOSITION	Toni bought cards for **whoever had a birthday in July.** [The noun clause has a subject, *whoever,* and a verb, *had.* The clause is the object of the preposition *for.*]

EXERCISE A Underline the noun clause in each of the following sentences.

Examples 1. Has Thea decided <u>whether she will come with us</u>? [The noun clause *whether she will come with us* is the direct object of the verb phrase *Has decided.*]

    2. Brad's opinion is <u>that Ms. Andrews teaches Algebra II well</u>. [The noun clause *that Ms. Andrews teaches Algebra II well* is a predicate nominative that renames the sentence's subject, *opinion.*]

1. Carmen asked when the sun will rise and set tomorrow. [Which word group functions as a direct object in this sentence?]

2. The teacher gave whoever needed it extra time on the essay. [Which word group functions as an indirect object in this sentence?]

3. Whatever Aida writes is interesting.

GO ON

4. Why don't we offer a ride to whichever friends ask first?

5. The fact is that people and animals need clean air.

6. Does somebody know where I can buy free-range eggs?

7. Whoever can help clean up the park should be there at eight o'clock this Saturday morning.

8. Tell me this minute what we should do next!

9. That Jake wants to travel widely is well known to his family and friends.

10. The gymnasts will perform their routines at whatever time the judges find convenient.

NOTE You have learned to write phrases such as *for whom* and *with whomever* when the pronoun is the object of the preposition. When *who, whoever, whom,* or *whomever* is part of a noun clause, its function in that clause determines which form to use, not the preposition or verb that comes before the pronoun.

> **EXAMPLE** This cold water is for **whoever** is thirsty. [Although the entire noun clause functions as the object of the preposition *for, whoever* is the subject of the verb *is* within the clause itself. Therefore, the nominative case *whoever* is correct.]

EXERCISE B Underline the noun clause in each sentence. Then, on the line provided, write *S* if the noun clause is used as a subject, *PN* if it is used as a predicate nominative, *DO* if it is used as a direct object, *IO* if it is used as an indirect object, or *OP* if it is used as the object of a preposition.

Example ___*DO*___ **1.** Do you know how I can change this flat tire? [The noun clause *how I can change this flat tire* is the direct object of the verb phrase *Do know.*]

_____**11.** Whatever Amy plans to do will be fun. [Which word group functions as a noun in this

   sentence? How is the noun clause being used?]

_____**12.** Eric is a good friend to whoever needs him.

_____**13.** Good ideas are what we need now.

_____**14.** Yolanda asked me when the package would arrive.

_____**15.** Tell whoever comes through that door the good news.

The Adverb Clause

4f.   An *adverb clause* is a subordinate clause that modifies a verb, an adjective, or an adverb.

Adverb clauses begin with a subordinating conjunction and tell *how, when, where, why, to what extent,* or *under what condition.* Adverb clauses can appear at the beginning, in the middle, or at the end of sentences.

> **EXAMPLES**   **While you were out,** we ordered lunch. [The adverb clause has a subject, *you,* and a verb, *were.* The clause begins with the subordinating conjunction *While* and tells when the action of the sentence occurred.]
>
> Their dog, **even though it isn't hungry,** is eating all of the food in its bowl. [The adverb clause has a subject, *it,* and a verb, *is.* The clause begins with the subordinating conjunction *even though* and tells under what condition the dog is eating.]
>
> The lights went out abruptly **because a circuit breaker had tripped.** [The adverb clause has a subject, *circuit breaker,* and a verb, *had tripped.* The clause begins with the subordinating conjunction *because* and tells why the lights went out.]

EXERCISE A Underline the adverb clause in each sentence. Then, draw a second line under the subordinating conjunction that introduces the adverb clause.

Example 1. Unless it rains, we will do yardwork this afternoon. [The subordinating conjunction *Unless* begins the adverb clause *Unless it rains,* which modifies the verb phrase *will do* by telling under what conditions the action will occur.]

1. The deck must be refinished this year because the rain damaged it. [What clause modifies a verb phrase in this sentence by explaining why? What subordinating conjunction introduces the adverb clause?]

2. Anna didn't like basil until she tried the cinnamon variety.

3. Wherever we planted wildflowers, butterflies and hummingbirds gathered.

4. I will trim the hedges while you mow.

5. After we finish sweeping the sidewalk, we'll sit and watch the sunset.

EXERCISE B Underline the adverb clause in each of the following sentences. Then, draw two lines under the verb, adverb, or adjective that the clause modifies.

Example 1. Karen's family will move as soon as their new house is completed. [The adverb clause modifies the verb phrase *will move* by telling *when.*]

6. Will she attend the same school after they move? [What clause modifies a verb phrase in this sentence by telling when? Which verb phrase does it modify?]

GO ON

7. Happy because there are three bedrooms, Karen hopes that one will be all hers.

8. When the trees bud out in the spring, they will shade the backyard.

9. Put these boxes of books where they won't be in the way, please.

10. Karen and her brothers unpacked boxes while their parents arranged furniture.

4g. | Part of a clause may be left out when its meaning can be clearly understood from the context of the sentence. Such a clause is called an ***elliptical clause.***

> **COMPLETE CLAUSE** **While she was writing,** Nico kept humming to herself.
>
> **ELLIPTICAL CLAUSE** **While writing,** Nico kept humming to herself. [Both sentences and both adverb clauses mean the same thing. In the second sentence, the pronoun *she* and the verb *was* are understood, though not expressed.]

NOTE Be careful about choosing the case of a personal pronoun in elliptical clauses. Add the missing part of the clause back in to be sure that you've used a pronoun that is appropriate to your meaning.

> **EXAMPLES** Nico called Danielle more often than **me.** [Add the missing part of the clause back in to be sure that the sentence means what you intended: "Nico called Danielle more often than Nico called me."]
>
> Nico called Danielle more often than **I.** [Add the missing part of the clause back in to be sure that the sentence means what you intended: "Nico called Danielle more often than I called Danielle."]

EXERCISE C Underline the adverb clauses in the following sentences. Then, use proofreading symbols to make each adverb clause an elliptical clause. Make sure that the meaning of the revised sentence is the same as that of the original.

Example 1. Ellen wrote more poems than Gerald ~~wrote.~~ [The adverb clause *than Gerald wrote,*

which modifies the adjective *more,* becomes elliptical when the word *wrote* is removed.]

11. A starter on the track team, José ran faster than he had ever run before. [What clause modifies

an adverb? Which words in the adverb clause can be removed without changing its meaning?]

12. That large tank has more fish in it than this smaller tank has.

13. Does anyone play this game as well as we play it?

14. Try not to look at your hands while you are practicing the piano.

15. Ethan saved more money this year than he saved last year.

Sentence Structure A

Simple Sentences and Compound Sentences

4h. Depending on its structure, a sentence can be classified as simple, compound, complex, or compound-complex.

(1) A *simple sentence* has one and only one independent clause. It has no subordinate clauses. It may, however, have phrases and modifiers. It may also have a compound subject or verb.

EXAMPLES The candles shimmered on the elegantly set table. [The sentence contains an independent clause with a modifying prepositional phrase.]

These dishes are chipped and need repair. [The sentence contains an independent clause with a compound verb.]

Paint and plaster can make the damaged walls look like new. [The sentence contains an independent clause with a compound subject.]

(2) A *compound sentence* has two or more independent clauses. It has no subordinate clauses. Like a simple sentence, a compound sentence may have phrases and modifiers. It may also have a compound subject or verb.

EXAMPLES Many sales were underway, and the prices were low. [The sentence contains two independent clauses.]

We hiked from the car to the mall, we watched a good movie, and then we hiked back to the car. [The sentence contains three independent clauses.]

REMINDER An independent clause (or main clause) expresses a complete thought. It can stand by itself as a sentence. A subordinate clause (or dependent clause) has a verb and its subject but does not express a complete thought. It cannot stand by itself as a sentence.

EXERCISE A Underline each independent clause in the sentences below. Then, if the sentence is simple, write *S* for *simple* on the line provided. If the sentence is compound, write *C* for *compound*.

Example ___C___ **1.** The theater lights dimmed, and the play began. [Two independent clauses, joined by the conjunction *and,* form this compound sentence.]

_____ **1.** The audience sat spellbound and watched the play. [Are there two complete thoughts, each with its own subject and verb, or does a single subject have a compound verb?]

_____ **2.** The villain plotted an evil deed, but the heroine overheard his plans.

_____ **3.** The villain put his plan into action; however, the heroine saved the day.

_____ **4.** Then the final lines of the play were spoken by the defeated villain.

_____ **5.** The audience rose together and applauded the actors.

GO ON

Simple sentences can be joined to form compound sentences in one of three ways:

- Use a comma followed by a coordinating conjunction (*and, but, for, nor, or, so,* or *yet*).
- Use a semicolon.
- Use a semicolon, a conjunctive adverb or transitional expression, and a comma.

> **EXAMPLES** The sun rose**,** **but** the cloudy sky was still dark. [comma and coordinating conjunction]
>
> Rose says she is finished**;** are you finished, too? [semicolon]
>
> The game begins at 7:00**;** **however,** we should arrive early to get good seats. [semicolon, conjunctive adverb, and comma]

EXERCISE B Underline each independent clause in the sentences below. Then, if the sentence is simple, write *S* for *simple* on the line provided. If the sentence is compound, write *C* for *compound.*

Example __C__ **1.** Where are you going, and what are you going to do? [Two complete

thoughts, *where are you going* and *what are you going to do* are expressed in this

compound sentence.]

_____ **6.** Grilled vegetables are easy to prepare and taste wonderful. [Does the sentence have

more than one independent clause?]

_____ **7.** What color are your eyes, green or hazel?

_____ **8.** Josey wrapped the presents with colorful paper; meanwhile, Teresa set the table.

_____ **9.** First turn on the water, and then put in the soap.

_____ **10.** Smiling at the defendant, the judge dismissed the case.

EXERCISE C Use proofreading symbols to combine each of the following pairs of simple sentences to make compound sentences. Hint: There may be more than one way to combine the pairs of sentences.

Example 1. You will need paper for the quiz. You will need a pen or pencil. [The sentences can

be combined with a semicolon followed by a conjunctive adverb and a comma.]

11. Dwayne plays football. Rich prefers soccer. [Which one of the three ways listed above is the best

way to combine this pair of sentences?]

12. Exercise helps the body. Dancing strengthens the heart.

13. Terri rides horses. She knows how to care for them.

14. The music is great. This band is a favorite of mine.

15. I like broccoli. I like spinach.

Sentence Structure B

Complex Sentences and Compound-Complex Sentences

4h. Depending on its structure, a sentence can be classified as simple, compound, complex, or compound-complex.

(3) A *complex sentence* has one independent clause and at least one subordinate clause.

> **EXAMPLES** Kacy, who has just graduated, is planning to attend a nearby community college. [A subordinate clause, *who has just graduated,* modifies *Kacy,* the subject of the independent clause.]
>
> After she registers for classes, she will walk across the campus so that she knows her way around. [Two subordinate clauses, *After she registers for classes* and *so that she knows her way around,* modify the verb *will walk* in the independent clause.]

(4) A *compound-complex sentence* has two or more independent clauses, and like a complex sentence, it also contains at least one subordinate clause.

> **EXAMPLES** The photographer tickled the baby, who was sleeping through the appointment, and the baby woke up with a smile. [The sentence has two independent clauses and a subordinate clause, *who was sleeping through the appointment.*]
>
> Babies' moods change quickly, as the photographer knew, so he quickly snapped several good pictures while the baby giggled. [The sentence has two independent clauses and two subordinate clauses, *as the photographer knew* and *while the baby giggled.*]

REMINDER▶ An independent clause (or main clause) expresses a complete thought. It can stand by itself as a sentence. A subordinate clause (or dependent clause) has a verb and its subject but does not express a complete thought. It cannot stand by itself as a sentence.

EXERCISE A Underline each independent clause in the following sentences. Then, draw two lines under each subordinate clause. Hint: A complex or compound-complex sentence may have more than one subordinate clause.

Example 1. After they brought it home, the parents assembled the swing set so that the children could play on it. [The sentence has one independent clause and two subordinate clauses.]

1. Carly spoke the lines as if she had known them all her life. [Have you underlined the independent clause in this sentence? Have you drawn two lines under a subordinate clause?]

2. Because its skin is sensitive, take care while you brush the dog.

3. Open the windows that face east.

4. The ivy is growing faster than the fern.

5. Unless you have a better idea, we will hold a car wash.

EXERCISE B Underline the independent clauses in each of the following sentences. Then, draw two lines under each subordinate clause. If the sentence has only one independent clause in addition to any subordinate clauses, write *CX* for *complex* on the line provided. If the sentence has two or more independent clauses in addition to any subordinate clauses, write *CD-CX* for *compound-complex*.

Example _CD-CX_ **1.** If Shane has his way, he'll learn to play the saxophone; right now, he plays the drums. [The sentence has two independent clauses and a subordinate clause, so it is compound-complex.]

_____ **6.** Until the semester ends, I'll help you with math, and you help me with history. [How many independent clauses does the sentence have?]

_____ **7.** When night fell, the temperature dropped.

_____ **8.** The mechanics rebuilt the engine, which had a cracked block; then they rotated the car's tires.

_____ **9.** Because it's not the one you need, please put that book back.

_____ **10.** Ally chose a topic that she was interested in; then she gathered information.

EXERCISE C Identify each sentence as complex or compound-complex by writing *CX* for *complex* or *CD-CX* for *compound-complex* on the line provided. Hint: If you have trouble, underline and count the independent clauses as you did in Exercise B.

Example _CX_ **1.** How many people give up on a dream because it's hard to achieve? [The question has one independent clause and one subordinate clause, so the sentence is complex.]

_____ **11.** You should bring only one suitcase because we have limited space for luggage. [What section of the sentence can stand on its own, expressing a complete thought?]

_____ **12.** Carl wanted to make something for lunch that was quick and tasty, so he lightly toasted two slices of bread and added a few slices of avocado.

_____ **13.** Everyone should get enough sleep so that his or her body will stay healthy.

_____ **14.** The friends rode the Ferris wheel, and then, because they felt daring, they rode the roller coaster, too.

_____ **15.** Since we've made such good progress, do you think we'll be able to finish today?

for **CHAPTER 5: AGREEMENT** `pages 96–101`

Subject-Verb Agreement A

Singular and Plural Subjects

5b. | A verb should agree in number with its subject.

A subject and verb agree when they have the same number. When a word refers to one person, place, thing, or idea, it is *singular* in number. When a word refers to more than one person, place, thing, or idea, it is *plural* in number.

(1) Singular subjects take singular verbs.

                             S   V

EXAMPLE The **truck needs** a new windshield. [The singular verb *needs* agrees with the singular subject, *truck*.]

(2) Plural subjects take plural verbs.

                             S   V

EXAMPLE The **trucks need** new windshields. [The plural verb *need* agrees with the plural subject, *trucks*.]

NOTE Verb phrases also agree with their subjects. A verb phrase is made up of a main verb and one or more helping verbs. The first helping verb in the verb phrase agrees with the subject.

                      V   S   V

EXAMPLE **Does** your **grandmother play** the violin? [*Does play* is the verb phrase. The singular helping verb *Does* agrees with the singular subject, *grandmother*.]

EXERCISE A Circle the verb form in parentheses that agrees with the underlined subject in each of the following sentences.

Example 1. Many <u>students</u> (*juggles,* (*juggle*)) busy schedules. [The subject, *students*, is plural, so the verb must be plural, too.]

1. During swim practice, <u>Coach Owens</u> (*shows, show*) us how to improve our form. [Which verb agrees with the singular subject, *Coach Owens*?]

2. (*Does, Do*) the <u>apartments</u> have basketball courts?

3. My <u>grandparents</u> (*has, have*) been volunteering at the library for years.

4. The bicycle <u>tire</u> (*was, were*) flat.

5. <u>Bees</u> (*are, is*) attracted to these flowers.

Compound Subjects Joined by *And*

A *compound subject* is made up of two or more subjects that have the same verb.

GO ON

5e. Subjects joined by *and* usually take a plural verb.

> EXAMPLE   **Tony and Roland tutor** younger students who need help with math
> homework. [The subjects *Tony* and *Roland* are joined by *and*, so the
> plural verb *tutor* agrees with the compound subject.]

EXERCISE B Circle the verb form in parentheses that agrees with the underlined compound subject in
each of the following sentences.

Example 1. Ana and her friends (*were*, *was*) watching the baseball game. [The subjects *Ana* and

friends are joined by *and*, so the plural helping verb *were* agrees with the subject.]

6. (*Is, Are*) the phones and fax machines working now? [Which verb agrees with the compound

subject joined by *and*?]

7. Alligators and snakes (*live, lives*) in the swamps near my house.

8. Ruben, Chris, and he (*has, have*) been practicing for the track tournament.

9. At the park, joggers, walkers, and riders (*share, shares*) the trail.

10. A writer and a photographer from the newspaper (*were, was*) at the charity auction.

Compound Subjects Joined by *Or* or *Nor*

For compound subjects joined by *or* or *nor*, the verb should agree with the subject nearer to it.

> EXAMPLES   The **twins or Dena visits** Uncle Alfred every weekend. [The singular
> subject, *Dena*, is nearer to the verb *visits*. The singular verb *visits* agrees
> with the singular subject, *Dena*.]
> **Dena or** the **twins visit** Uncle Alfred every weekend. [The plural subject,
> *twins*, is nearer to the verb *visit*. The plural verb *visit* agrees with the
> plural subject, *twins*.]

EXERCISE C Circle the verb form in parentheses that agrees with the underlined compound subject in
each of the following sentences.

Example 1. A flashlight or candles (*is*, *are*) useful during an electricity outage. [The plural subject,

candles, is nearer to the verb, so the plural verb *are* agrees with the plural subject, *candles*.]

11. (*Are, Is*) your father or your brothers going fishing with you? [Which verb agrees with *father*,

the subject nearer to the verb?]

12. Neither the table nor the chairs (*needs, need*) a fresh coat of paint.

13. In the afternoons, Frank or Angie (*takes, take*) the dog for a walk.

14. Overhead, a swallow or a lark (*is, are*) singing cheerfully.

15. Snails or slugs (*has, have*) been eating the leaves of my potted plants.

Subject-Verb Agreement B

Intervening Phrases and Clauses

5c. The number of a subject usually is not determined by a word in a phrase or a clause following the subject.

Sometimes a phrase or a clause comes between the subject and its verb. Usually, the words in the phrase or clause do not affect agreement between the subject and the verb.

> **EXAMPLE** **Kangaroos,** which most people associate with Australia, **are** also **found** in Tasmania and New Guinea. [The plural subject *Kangaroos* takes the plural helping verb *are*. The subordinate clause does not affect agreement, even though the clause comes between the subject and the verb.]

EXERCISE A Circle the verb form in parentheses that agrees with the underlined subject in each of the following sentences.

Example 1. The painting of the flowers (*was*, were) a gift from my aunt. [The subject, *painting*, is singular, so the verb must be singular, too.]

1. My uncle, who collects antiques, (*owns, own*) a bed-and-breakfast in Vermont. [Which verb agrees with the singular subject *uncle*?]

2. Frequently, the lights in the hallway (*flickers, flicker*).

3. The box of books (*is, are*) quite heavy.

4. Earthworms, which feed on decaying organisms, (*helps, help*) to improve soil conditions.

5. Your pictures from the camping trip (*has, have*) been developed.

Indefinite Pronouns

A pronoun that does not refer to a specific person, place, thing, or idea is called an *indefinite pronoun.* When an indefinite pronoun is used as a subject, the verb agrees with the pronoun.

5d. Some indefinite pronouns are singular, some are plural, and some can be singular or plural, depending on how they are used.

(1) The following indefinite pronouns are singular: *anybody, anyone, anything, each, either, everybody, everyone, everything, neither, nobody, no one, nothing, one, somebody, someone,* and *something.*

> **EXAMPLE** **Each** of my friends **has signed** my yearbook. [The singular helping verb, *has*, agrees with the singular subject, *Each*.]

(2) The following indefinite pronouns are plural: *both, few, many,* and *several.*

> **EXAMPLE** **Many** of my friends **have signed** my yearbook already. [The plural helping verb, *have*, agrees with the plural subject, *Many*.]

GO ON

EXERCISE B Circle the verb form in parentheses that agrees with the underlined subject in each of the following sentences.

Example 1. <u>Neither</u> of those movies *(interest,* (interests)*)* me. [*Neither* is a singular indefinite pronoun. It takes the singular verb *interests*.]

6. After I jog several miles, <u>nothing</u> *(is, are)* as refreshing as a cold glass of water. [Which verb agrees with the singular indefinite pronoun *nothing*?]

7. <u>Several</u> of the map pencils *(need, needs)* to be sharpened.

8. *(Have, Has)* <u>either</u> of your dogs learned to sit yet?

9. <u>One</u> of my cats *(paws, paw)* the television screen when it sees a bird or lizard.

10. In the afternoon, <u>both</u> of my sisters *(plays, play)* tennis.

---

(3) The indefinite pronouns *all, any, more, most, none,* and *some* may be singular or plural, depending on their meaning in a sentence.

Often, the phrase that follows these indefinite pronouns determines the number. If the noun in that phrase is singular, then the pronoun is also singular. If the noun in that phrase is plural, then the pronoun is also plural.

EXAMPLES **Most** of the **tape has been used.** [The subject *Most* is singular because it refers to the singular noun *tape*. The singular helping verb *has* agrees with the singular subject *Most*.]

Most of the **supplies were** in stock. [The subject *Most* is plural because it refers to the plural noun *supplies*. The plural verb *were* agrees with the plural subject *Most*.]

EXERCISE C Circle the verb form in parentheses that agrees with the underlined subject in each of the following sentences.

Example 1. Each week, <u>all</u> of the newspaper articles *(is,* (are)*)* written by students. [*All* refers to the plural noun *articles* and takes the plural helping verb *are*.]

11. *(Do, Does)* <u>any</u> of the parrots know how to say "hello"? [Is the noun in the phrase that follows *any* singular or plural? Which verb agrees with the subject?]

12. <u>Some</u> of the children *(is, are)* playing basketball in the gym.

13. *(Have, Has)* <u>more</u> of the shipment been delivered?

14. Because of the static, <u>most</u> of the message *(was, were)* hard to understand.

15. Next week, <u>none</u> of the computer labs *(is, are)* reserved.

Subject-Verb Agreement C

Collective Nouns

| **5i.** | A collective noun may be either singular or plural, depending on its meaning in a sentence. |

If a collective noun refers to a group as one unit, then it is singular. If a collective noun refers to individual members or parts of a group, then it is plural. Some common collective nouns are *army, assembly, audience, band, club, flock, family, group, herd, staff,* and *team.*

> **SINGULAR** The **staff decides** where to hold the awards ceremony. [The members of the staff make a decision together, so they are acting as a unit. *Staff* is singular and takes the singular verb *decides.*]
>
> **PLURAL** The **staff are eating** soups, salads, or sandwiches. [The individual members of the staff are eating. Not everyone is eating the same thing at the same time. *Staff* is plural and takes the plural helping verb *are.*]

EXERCISE A Decide whether the underlined subject refers to a group or to individual members of a group. Then, circle the verb form in parentheses that agrees with the underlined subject in each of the following sentences.

Example 1. The <u>band</u> *(is, (are))* changing into their uniforms. [The individual members of the band are changing, so *band* is plural and takes the plural helping verb *are.*]

1. Each morning, the <u>flock</u> of geese *(finds, find)* their favorite spots on the pond. [Are the geese acting as a unit (singular) or as individuals (plural)?]

2. Jasmine's <u>family</u> usually *(has, have)* its reunion at Lake Sam Rayburn in Texas.

3. On Mondays, the <u>club</u> *(submits, submit)* its suggestions for the week's activities.

4. The <u>audience</u> *(is, are)* arriving in fancy dresses and tuxedos.

5. After the game, the <u>team</u> *(shake, shakes)* hands with their opponents.

Expressions of Amount

| **5j.** | An expression of an amount (a measurement, a percentage, or a fraction, for example) may be singular or plural, depending on how it is used. |

If the expression of an amount refers to a unit, then it is singular. If the expression of an amount refers to separate units, then it is plural.

> **SINGULAR** **Six apples is** enough for a pie. [*Six apples* refers to one unit or group of apples, so the singular verb *is* agrees.]
>
> **PLURAL** **Six apples are** rolling across the table. [*Six apples* refers to individual pieces of fruit, so the plural helping verb *are* agrees.]

GO ON

EXERCISE B Circle the verb form in parentheses that agrees with the underlined subject in each of the following sentences.

Example 1. Eight tomatoes (*are*, *is*) in each package. [*Eight tomatoes* refers to individual tomatoes, so the plural verb *are* agrees.]

6. Two hundred acres (*provides, provide*) enough grassland for a small herd of cattle. [Does *Two hundred acres* refer to a unit of land or individual pieces of land?]

7. I'll wait for a sale; sixty-five dollars (*are, is*) too much to pay for these shoes.

8. One thousand pennies (*were, was*) in the jar.

9. In the auditorium, three speakers (*distribute, distributes*) the sound.

10. We decided to fly to Phoenix because nine hundred miles (*are, is*) too far to drive.

To determine whether a fraction or percentage is singular or plural, look at the phrase that follows the fraction or percentage. If the noun in that phrase is singular, then the fraction or percentage is also singular. If the noun in that phrase is plural, then the fraction or percentage is also plural.

> **SINGULAR** **Three quarters** of the yard **has** rocky soil. [The fraction *Three quarters* refers to the singular word *yard*. The singular verb *has* agrees.]

> **PLURAL** **Three quarters** of the flowers **have wilted.** [The fraction *Three quarters* refers to the plural word *flowers*. The plural helping verb *have* agrees.]

An expression of measurement is usually singular. Some expressions of measurement are length, weight, capacity, and area.

> **EXAMPLE** **Twelve fluid ounces fills** my sports bottle. [*Twelve fluid ounces* is an expression of measurement and capacity, so it is singular. The singular verb *fills* agrees.]

EXERCISE C Circle the verb form in parentheses that agrees with the underlined subject in each of the following sentences.

Example 1. Ten percent of my allowance (*goes*, *go*) into a bank account. [*Ten percent* refers to the singular noun *allowance*, so it is singular. The singular verb *goes* agrees.]

11. Sixty-four square feet (*is, are*) the area of the room. [Is an expression of measurement usually singular or plural?]

12. Three fifths of the new bridge (*have, has*) been completed.

13. At birth, seven pounds (*was, were*) the weight of the baby.

14. In this day-care group, two thirds of the children (*does, do*) not eat sweets.

15. (*Was, Were*) fifteen percent of these dollar bills printed this year?

Subject-Verb Agreement D
When the Subject Follows the Verb

5h.　When the subject follows the verb, find the subject and make sure that the verb agrees with it.

The subject usually follows the verb in two kinds of sentences: (1) questions and (2) sentences beginning with *here* or *there*.

> **EXAMPLES**　**Was** the **invitation** in the mail? [*Invitation* is the subject of the sentence. The singular verb *Was* agrees with the singular subject *invitation*.]
>
> There **were** two **invitations** in the mail. [*There* is not the subject. *Invitations* is the subject of the sentence. The plural verb *were* agrees with the plural subject *invitations*.]

NOTE The contractions *here's*, *there's*, and *where's* each contain the word *is* (*here is, there is, where is*). Because *is* is a singular verb, make sure you use these contractions only with singular subjects.

> **STANDARD**　Here's your invitation. [*Here **is** your **invitation**. The singular verb *is* agrees with the singular subject, *invitation*.]
>
> **NONSTANDARD**　Here's your invitations. [*Here **is** your **invitations**. The singular verb *is* does not agree with the plural subject *invitations*, so the sentence should be revised to Here **are** your **invitations**.]

EXERCISE A Circle the word or word group in parentheses that agrees with the underlined subject in each of the following sentences.

Example 1. (*Here's*, Here are) a birthday <u>card</u> for Willis. [The singular subject *card* takes the

singular verb *is* in *Here's*.]

1. Here (*comes*, *come*) the top five <u>runners</u> in the marathon. [Which verb agrees with the plural

   subject *runners*?]

2. (*Where's*, *Where are*) the <u>food</u> for the fish?

3. (*Has*, *Have*) there been many telephone <u>calls</u> today?

4. There (*was*, *were*) enough <u>blankets</u> donated for 250 families.

5. When (*is*, *are*) a good <u>time</u> for a debate team meeting?

Don't and *Doesn't*

5o.　The contractions *don't* and *doesn't* should agree with their subjects.

The contraction *don't* stands for the words *do not*. Because *do* is a plural verb, you should use *don't* with plural subjects and with the pronouns *I* and *you*.

GO ON

> **EXAMPLES** Those **plants don't look** healthy. [*Don't* agrees with the plural subject, *plants*.]
>
> **I don't drink** soft drinks. [*Don't* agrees with the pronoun *I*.]
>
> **Don't you play** the saxophone? [*Don't* agrees with the pronoun *you*.]
>
> The contraction *doesn't* stands for the words *does not*. Because *does* is a singular verb, you should use *doesn't* with singular subjects, except with the pronouns *I* and *you*.
>
> **EXAMPLE** **Fredric doesn't** have his library card with him. [*Doesn't* agrees with the singular subject, *Fredric*.]

EXERCISE B Circle the contraction in parentheses that agrees with the underlined subject in each of the following sentences.

Example 1. The light in the basement (*doesn't*, *don't*) work. [*Doesn't* agrees with the singular subject, *light*.]

6. (*Don't*, *Doesn't*) I have a doctor's appointment today? [Which contraction agrees with the pronoun *I*?]

7. Our car (*doesn't*, *don't*) have a CD player.

8. You (*doesn't*, *don't*) want to miss the band's final performance!

9. Why (*don't*, *doesn't*) we go camping this weekend?

10. The dog food (*don't*, *doesn't*) come in a bigger package.

EXERCISE C Underline the subject in each of the following sentences. Then, circle the word in parentheses that agrees with the underlined subject.

Example 1. Many people (*doesn't*, *don't*) feel safe during a lightning storm. [*People* is the subject of the sentence. *Don't* agrees with the plural subject, *people*.]

11. Lightning (*don't*, *doesn't*) have to be a source of fear. [Which word is the subject of the sentence? Which contraction agrees with the subject?]

12. There (*is*, *are*) many safety tips listed on the National Lightning Safety Institute's Web site. [Which word is the subject of the sentence? Which verb agrees with the subject?]

13. Where (*is*, *are*) people safe during a lightning storm?

14. There (*is*, *are*) danger from lightning in open spaces and near trees.

15. Small shelters (*doesn't*, *don't*) provide total safety.

Pronoun-Antecedent Agreement A

A pronoun is a word that takes the place of a noun or another pronoun. The word a pronoun replaces is called the pronoun's *antecedent.*

5q. A pronoun should agree in number, gender, and person with its antecedent.

(1) Singular pronouns refer to singular antecedents. Plural pronouns refer to plural antecedents.

> **SINGULAR** **Tina** said that **she** was excited about the field trip. [The singular pronoun *she* refers to the singular noun *Tina.*]
>
> **PLURAL** **They** met after school to complete **their** project. [*Their* refers to the plural pronoun *They.*]

(2) Some singular pronouns indicate gender.

Sometimes singular pronouns also show gender. The *masculine pronouns*—he, him, his, himself—refer to males. The *feminine pronouns*—she, her, hers, herself—refer to females. The *neuter pronouns*—it, its, itself—refer to places, things, ideas, and sometimes to animals. Plural pronouns do not show gender.

> **EXAMPLES** **Roberto** practiced **his** speech before class. [The masculine pronoun *his* agrees with its masculine antecedent, *Roberto.*]
>
> The **stapler** is jammed, and I can't get **it** to work. [The neuter pronoun *it* agrees with its neuter antecedent, *stapler.*]

EXERCISE A In each of the following sentences, an antecedent has been underlined for you. On the line provided, write an appropriate pronoun that agrees with the underlined antecedent.

Example 1. When we go on road trips, my <u>brother</u> always brings ____*his*____ CD player and

headphones. [*His* agrees with the singular, masculine antecedent *brother.*]

1. How quickly do these <u>batteries</u> lose _____ charge? [Which pronoun would agree with the

plural antecedent, *batteries*?]

2. <u>Katie</u> usually spends Sunday afternoon with _____ grandparents.

3. The kitchen <u>sink</u> was leaking, so we called a plumber to fix _____.

4. At my aunt's wedding, <u>Michael</u> looked so handsome in _____ tuxedo.

5. If your <u>parents</u> can volunteer for the Fall Festival, _____ should contact Ms. Reynolds.

---

(3) *Person* indicates whether a pronoun refers to the one speaking *(first person)*, the one spoken to *(second person)*, or the one spoken about *(third person).*

First-person pronouns include *I, me, my, mine, we, us, our,* and *ours.* Second-person pronouns include *you, your,* and *yours.* Third-person pronouns include *he, him, his, she, her, hers, it, its, they, them, their,* and *theirs.*

GO ON ➡

> **EXAMPLES** My mother and **I** took **our** seats. [first person]
>
> Mark, **you** should bring **your** bicycle. [second person]
>
> The puppies wagged **their** tails. [third person]

EXERCISE B In each of the following sentences, an antecedent has been underlined for you. On the line provided, write an appropriate pronoun that agrees with the underlined antecedent.

Example 1. I take ____my____ dog for a walk every afternoon. [*My* agrees with the first-person antecedent *I*.]

6. Yesterday afternoon, we washed _____ cars. [Which first-person pronoun would agree with the plural antecedent *we*?]

7. The ducks build _____ nests under the bridge in the park.

8. You shouldn't leave _____ dirty clothes on the bathroom floor.

9. Did I forget _____ jacket at the restaurant?

10. Roland colored the picture and gave _____ to his brother.

5s. | Use a plural pronoun to refer to two or more antecedents joined by *and*.

> **EXAMPLE** **Tina, Julia, and he** carried umbrellas with **them.** [Because *Tina, Julia,* and *he* are joined by the conjunction *and*, they act as a plural antecedent.]

5t. | Use a singular pronoun to refer to two or more singular antecedents joined by *or* or *nor*.

> **EXAMPLE** **Anthony or Jeff** parked **his** car in the shade. [Because *Anthony* and *Jeff* are singular, masculine antecedents joined by the conjunction *or*, they require the singular, masculine pronoun *his*.]

EXERCISE C In each of the following sentences, the compound antecedent has been underlined for you. On the line provided, write an appropriate pronoun that agrees with the underlined antecedent.

Example 1. Theodore, Misty, and Charlotte will give ____their____ presentation next. [Because the antecedents are joined by *and*, they require the plural pronoun *their*.]

11. Does the den or the kitchen need _____ walls repainted? [Do antecedents joined by *or* require a singular or plural pronoun?]

12. Ms. Moon, Melissa, or Mom will let you ride with _____.

13. If the weather is pleasant, my brothers and sisters spend most of _____ time outside.

14. Neither the fruit salad nor the green salad has nuts in _____.

15. When Carl saw Lyle, Karen, and Jerry, did he wave to _____?

Pronoun-Antecedent Agreement B

Indefinite Pronouns

5r. Some indefinite pronouns are singular, and some are plural. Other indefinite pronouns can be either singular or plural, depending on their meaning.

(1) Use singular pronouns to refer to the indefinite pronouns *anybody, anyone, anything, each, either, everybody, everyone, everything, neither, nobody, no one, nothing, one, somebody, someone,* and *something.*

> **EXAMPLES** **Everyone** tried **his or her** best. [*His or her* agrees in number with the antecedent *Everyone* because both are singular. *His or her* agrees in gender because *Everyone* may include both males and females.]
>
> Did **one** of the girls bring **her** math book? [*Her* agrees with the antecedent *one* in number because both are singular. *Her* agrees in gender because the phrase *of the girls* indicates *one* is feminine.]

(2) Use plural pronouns to refer to the indefinite pronouns *both, few, many,* and *several.*

> **EXAMPLE** **Many** of the trees lose **their** leaves during the winter months. [The pronoun *their* agrees with the antecedent *Many* because both are plural.]

EXERCISE A Circle the pronoun or pronoun group in parentheses that agrees with the underlined antecedent in each of the following sentences.

Example 1. Neither of the contestants felt well before (*his or her*, *their*) recital. [*Neither* is always singular and may refer to both males and females, so *his or her* agrees in number and gender.]

1. Because the library's roof leaked, many of the books were ruined, and (*it, they*) had to be replaced. [Which pronoun agrees with *many* in number?]

2. Either of the girls could have done the yardwork (*herself, themselves*).

3. Did everything in the biology lab have a proper label on (*it, them*)?

4. Several of the tomato plants have come loose from (*their, its*) stakes.

5. A few of the students said that (*he or she, they*) would distribute fliers.

---

(3) Use a singular or plural pronoun to refer to the indefinite pronoun *all, any, more, most, none,* or *some,* depending on how it is used in the sentence.

Look at the phrase that follows these indefinite pronouns. If the noun in the phrase is singular, then the pronoun is also singular. If the noun in the phrase is plural, then the pronoun is also plural.

GO ON

> **EXAMPLES**   **Most** of the track had **its** surface smoothed. [*Most* refers to the singular noun *track*. Therefore, the singular pronoun *its* is correct.]
>
> **Most** of the runners said **they** like the new track surface. [*Most* refers to the plural noun *runners*. Therefore, the plural pronoun *they* is correct.]

EXERCISE B Circle the pronoun in parentheses that agrees with the underlined antecedent in each of the following sentences.

Example 1. <u>Most</u> of the tablecloth had coffee stains on (*it*, them). [*Most* refers to the singular noun *tablecloth*. Therefore, the singular pronoun *it* is correct.]

6. Do <u>some</u> of the nearby restaurants have (*its, their*) menus online? [Is the noun in the phrase following *some* singular or plural?]

7. <u>Most</u> of the leaf had bugs crawling on (*them, it*).

8. How many <u>more</u> of the envelopes need to have the return address written on (*them, it*)?

9. Did <u>all</u> of the boys agree (*he, they*) would go to the museum?

10. In the morning, <u>all</u> of the wall should be dry enough for (*its, their*) second coat of paint.

Relative Pronouns

5x. The gender and number of a relative pronoun (such as *who, which,* or *that*) are determined by its antecedent.

> **EXAMPLE**   **Kate, who** composed **her** own musical score, won first prize at the talent show. [The singular, feminine noun *Kate* is the antecedent of *who.* Therefore, the singular, feminine pronoun *her* agrees with *who.*]

EXERCISE C Circle the pronoun in parentheses that agrees with the underlined antecedent in each of the following sentences.

Example 1. The horse <u>that</u> has a white stripe on (*its*, their) nose is named Dudley. [The singular, neuter noun *horse* is the antecedent of *that.* Therefore, the singular, neuter pronoun *its* agrees with *that.*]

11. The man <u>who</u> is waving (*its, his*) hand is my uncle. [Is the antecedent of *who* singular or plural? Is the antecedent of *who* masculine, feminine, or neuter?]

12. Is the table <u>that</u> has the large flower arrangement on (*it, them*) reserved?

13. At noon, the spectators <u>who</u> purchased (*her, their*) tickets in advance will be admitted.

14. These weeds, <u>which</u> have thorns on (*it, them*), grow quickly.

15. The bird <u>that</u> is carrying straw in (*its, their*) beak must be making a nest.

Personal Pronouns A

The Nominative Case

6a.   The subject of a verb should be in the nominative case.

The *subject of a verb* tells *whom* or *what* the sentence is about. Nominative case personal pronouns include *I, you, he, she, it, we,* and *they.*

> **EXAMPLES**   **They** bought concert tickets. [*They* is the subject of the verb *bought.*]
>
> Will **he** and **she** attend the concert? [*He* and *she* make up the compound subject of the verb phrase *Will attend.* Both pronouns in the compound subject are in the nominative case.]

6b.   A predicate nominative should be in the nominative case.

A *predicate nominative* is a word or word group in the predicate and completes the meaning of a linking verb. A predicate nominative identifies or refers to the subject of the verb.

Often a predicate nominative follows a form of the verb *be.* Common forms of the verb *be* are *am, is, are, was, were, be, been,* and *being.*

> **EXAMPLES**   The two winners were **they.** [The predicate nominative *they* completes the meaning of the verb *were* and identifies the subject *winners.*]
>
> The new technicians are **she** and **I.** [*She* and *I* form the compound predicate nominative that identifies *technicians.*]

EXERCISE A Underline the correct form of the pronoun in parentheses in each of the following sentences.

Examples 1. Did (*them, they*) announce who would be speaking first? [The pronoun is the subject of the verb phrase *Did announce,* so it should be in the nominative case.]

  2. The guest speakers will be (*she, her*) and (*I, me*). [The pronouns form a compound predicate nominative identifying the subject *speakers.* Both pronouns should be in the nominative case.]

1. For English class, (*her, she*) and (*me, I*) wrote reports about Ernest Hemingway. [Pronouns in a compound subject should be in what case?]

2. The candidates that the board has selected are (*him, he*) and (*her, she*). [Pronouns in a compound predicate nominative should be in what case?]

3. After work, (*they, them*) relaxed by the pool.

4. (*I, Me*) knocked on her door and called out, "It is (*me, I*)!"

5. Did (*him, he*) say that the dance teachers are Reggie and (*them, they*)?

6. (*She, Her*) found an old bicycle near the creek.

7. When the tournament is over, the winners shall be (*us, we*)!

8. Few people knew it, but the president's speechwriter was (*she, her*).

9. (*They, Them*) and (*we, us*) played basketball against each other.

10. The person to clean up the spilled orange juice should have been (*me, I*).

The Possessive Case

Possessive pronouns show ownership. Some possessive pronouns, such as *mine, yours, his, hers, its, ours,* and *theirs,* may be used as subjects or predicate nominatives.

> **EXAMPLES** **His** is the last house on the left. [*His* is the subject of the verb *is.*]
>
> The last bicycle on the right is **mine.** [*Mine* is a predicate nominative identifying the subject *bicycle.*]

The possessive pronouns *my, your, his, her, its, our,* and *their* are used to describe nouns.

> **EXAMPLES** **His** toolbox is in the truck. [*His* describes *toolbox.*]
>
> Todd is **our** neighbor. [*Our* describes *neighbor.*]

NOTE▶ When a pronoun comes before a gerund and is used to describe the gerund, the pronoun should be in the possessive case. A *gerund* is a verb form that ends in *–ing* and is used as a noun.

> **EXAMPLES** **His** joking with the audience made them all laugh. [*His* comes before and describes the gerund *joking.* The gerund *joking* is the subject of the sentence.]
>
> Did Todd supervise **your** loading of the truck? [*Your* comes before and describes the gerund *loading.* The gerund *loading* is the direct object of the verb phrase *Did supervise.*]

EXERCISE B Underline the correct form of the pronoun in parentheses in each of the following sentences.

Example 1. The coach didn't approve of (*him, <u>his</u>*) yelling at the umpire. [The pronoun comes before and describes the gerund *yelling,* so the pronoun should be in the possessive case.]

11. Last summer (*our, us*) assisting the basketball coach was fun. [Which case should the pronoun that comes before and describes the gerund be in?]

12. The pickup truck in front of the music store is (*her, hers*).

13. Did the kids laugh at (*mine, my*) funny skit?

14. Detective Rivera's favorite stories are of (*his, him*) outsmarting clever criminals.

15. In the fall, (*them, theirs*) is the cabin we plan to stay in for a weekend.

Personal Pronouns B

The Objective Case

6c. A direct object should be in the objective case.

A **direct object** tells *who* or *what* receives the action of the verb. Objective case personal pronouns include *me, you, him, her, it, us,* and *them.*

> **EXAMPLE** The invitation surprised **me.** [*Me* receives the action of the verb *surprised.*]

6d. An indirect object should be in the objective case.

An **indirect object** tells *to whom* or *to what* (or *for whom* or *for what*) the action of a verb is done.

> **IO   DO**
> **EXAMPLE** Josh gave **us** invitations. [The indirect object *us* tells to whom invitations have been given. The direct object *invitations* receives the action of the verb *gave.*]

EXERCISE A Underline the correct form of the pronoun in parentheses in each of the following sentences.

Examples 1. If you have room in your car, you can bring *(he, him)* with you. [The pronoun is a direct object of the verb *bring,* so the pronoun should be in the objective case.]

2. The librarian handed Kim and *(I, me)* some new novels. [The pronoun is an indirect object that tells to whom the librarian handed the novels, so it should be in the objective case.]

1. Of all the after-school activities, sports interests *(them, they)* the most. [Should a pronoun used as a direct object be in the nominative or in the objective case?]

2. Elena should give *(her, she)* a call this afternoon. [Should a pronoun used as an indirect object be in the nominative or in the objective case?]

3. Ms. Williams gave *(we, us)* a list of books about sports.

4. When her puppy began to squirm, the veterinarian gently calmed *(he, him).*

5. Jamal lent *(I, me)* a copy of *Many Stones* by Carolyn Coman.

6. This book about a sixteen-year-old in South Africa interested Jamal and *(I, me).*

7. I lent a cousin and *(him, he)* a copy of *Foul Ball.*

8. As it closed, the door bumped *(her, she)* on the arm.

9. Clarice's uncle baked *(us, we)* some biscuits.

10. Please, help *(us, we)* find a book about soccer.

GO ON

6e. An object of a preposition should be in the objective case.

An *object of a preposition* is the noun or pronoun that a preposition relates to another word. A prepositional phrase consists of a preposition, an object of the preposition, and any modifiers of that object. Some commonly used prepositions are *in, to, about, next to, around, under, besides,* and *because of.*

> **EXAMPLE** A fly keeps buzzing around **me**. [*Me* is the object of the preposition *around*.]

EXERCISE B Underline the correct form of the pronoun in parentheses in each of the following sentences.

Example 1. He has been keeping the phone near *(him, he).* [The pronoun is the object of the preposition *near,* so it should be in the objective case.]

11. In PE, Ms. Williams selected several books for Jason and *(she, her).* [Should a pronoun used as an object of a preposition be in the nominative or in the objective case?]

12. Some books were so popular that she kept a sign-up sheet next to *(they, them).*

13. Will you send a copy of *Hoops* by Walter Dean Myers to Lisa and *(me, I)*?

14. I love baseball and soccer, and I read everything I can about *(they, them).*

15. Above *(he, him),* a cicada began to buzz noisily.

The Possessive Case

Possessive pronouns show ownership. Some possessive pronouns, such as *mine, yours, his, hers, its, ours,* and *theirs,* are used as objects.

> **DIRECT OBJECT** She brought **hers** to the beach. [*Hers* receives the action of the verb *brought.*]
>
> **INDIRECT OBJECT** Jill gave **hers** a coat of paint. [*Hers* answers the question *What did Jill give a coat of paint to?*]

EXERCISE C Underline the correct form of the pronoun in parentheses in each of the following sentences.

Example 1. While looking for his own umbrella, Michael found *(hers, she)* under a desk. [A possessive pronoun should be used to indicate possession.]

16. Once Ms. Cooper sees these essays, she'll give *(he, his)* an A. [Should the pronoun be in the possessive or in the nominative case?]

17. After she asked to use our hammer, did Velma use *(their, theirs)* instead?

18. When she'd finished studying her own leaf, Jewel studied *(his, he)* as well.

19. My lawn mower is broken, but you can borrow *(she, hers).*

20. Dave lost his catcher's mitt, so Adam offered *(his, him).*

Special Problems in Pronoun Usage

The Relative Pronouns Who and Whom

The pronouns *who* and *whoever* are in the nominative case. The pronouns *whom* and *whomever* are in the objective case. To decide which form to use, find the clause in which the pronoun appears and determine how the pronoun is used in that clause.

If the pronoun is used as a subject or predicate nominative in the clause, the pronoun should be in the nominative case.

> **EXAMPLE** The award winner will be **who** collects the most litter. [Because *who* is the subject of the subordinate clause *who collects the most litter*, it is in the nominative case.]

If the pronoun is used as a direct object, an indirect object, or an object of a preposition in the clause, then the pronoun should be in the objective case.

> **EXAMPLES** Lian, **whom** we all miss, moved away in November. [*Whom* is the direct object of the verb *miss* in the subordinate clause *whom we all miss*.]
>
> She was a scientist about **whom** we know very little. [*Whom* is the object of the preposition *about*.]

EXERCISE A Underline the correct form of the pronoun in parentheses in each of the following sentences.

Example 1. *(Who, Whom)* did Li ask to the prom? [The pronoun is the direct object of the verb *did ask*, so the pronoun should be in the objective case.]

1. The eldest senator is *(who, whom)*? [What case is appropriate for a predicate nominative?]

2. The children flocked to the person *(who, whom)* they knew best.

3. Felicia, in *(who, whom)* the group placed its trust, became its next treasurer.

4. Richard, *(who, whom)* the dog gave the ball, threw the ball out into the yard again.

5. The sportscaster finally announced *(who, whom)* won the game.

Appositives

6i. A pronoun used as an appositive is in the same case as the word to which it refers.

An *appositive* is placed next to another noun or pronoun. The appositive identifies or refers to that noun or pronoun.

> **EXAMPLE** The owners, **Marta** and **he,** will remodel the store. [The appositives *Marta* and *he* identify the noun *owners*.]

An appositive should be in the same case as the noun or pronoun the appositive identifies. If the appositive identifies a word in the nominative case, then the appositive should be nominative. If the appositive identifies a word in the objective case, then the appositive should be objective.

GO ON

EXAMPLES   The new owners, Marta and **he,** plan to rearrange the store's aisles. [The appositive phrase *Marta and he* refers to the subject *owners,* so the pronoun is in the nominative case.]

We met the new owners, Marta and **him.** [The appositive phrase *Marta and him* refers to the direct object *owners,* so the pronoun is in the objective case.]

NOTE Sometimes the pronoun *we* or *us* is followed by an appositive. To determine which pronoun, *we* or *us,* to use, remove the appositive from the sentence. Whichever form of the pronoun is correct without the appositive will be the correct pronoun to use.

EXAMPLE   *(We, Us)* juniors want the college brochures.

ASK   *We want the college brochures or Us want the college brochures?*

ANSWER   The pronoun functions as the subject of the sentence, so the pronoun should be in the nominative case. *We* is the correct choice: **We** *juniors want the college brochures.*

EXERCISE B Underline the correct form of the pronoun in parentheses in each of the following sentences.

Examples 1. All players should see their team captain, Shawn, Sue, or *(I, me).* [The pronoun is an appositive identifying *captain. Captain* is the direct object of the verb phrase *should see,* so the pronoun should be in the objective case.]

2. The winners of the state finals are *(us, we)* Eagles! [The pronoun is followed by the appositive *Eagles* and functions as the sentence's predicate nominative. The pronoun should be in the nominative case.]

6. Once a week my best friends, Trina and *(her, she),* take a yoga class with me. [Which pronoun is in the same case as the subject *friends*?]

7. As a kind gesture, *(us, we)* grandkids do all of the repairs on Grandma's house. [Is the pronoun a subject or an object in this sentence?]

8. I baked a loaf of raisin bread for our neighbors, Ms. Thomas and *(them, they).*

9. At the assembly there will be speeches from the two finalists, Troy and *(I, me).*

10. Are the team leaders the Wilson brothers, Ray and *(he, him)?*

11. The baby sitters, Cindy, Sara, and *(I, me),* will bring games and snacks.

12. Did you finally meet the authors, Doug and *(her, she)?*

13. When will someone give *(us, we)* volunteers a lunch break?

14. This year, the hosts of the block party are your neighbors, Neil and *(they, them).*

15. While in Germany, Shari sent her cousins, Phil and *(me, I),* several postcards.

Clear Reference A

Ambiguous Reference

You may remember that a pronoun stands for a word or word group called its antecedent. In clear writing, readers can find the antecedent of each pronoun and are able to understand each pronoun's meaning. A pronoun should refer clearly to its antecedent.

> **EXAMPLE**   Mark worked hard on his report, and **he** got an *A* on **it.** [The antecedent of *he* is *Mark,* and the antecedent of *it* is *report.*]

One problem with pronoun reference is ***ambiguous reference.*** This problem occurs when a pronoun can refer to more than one word or word group in the sentence. Sentences with an ambiguous reference should be revised so that the pronoun refers clearly to its antecedent. There is usually more than one way to revise a sentence with an ambiguous reference.

7b.	Avoid an ***ambiguous reference,*** which occurs when any one of two or more words could be a pronoun's antecedent.

> **AMBIGUOUS**   When Don saw Carlos in the gym, he was doing a set of push-ups. [The antecedent of *he* is unclear. Is Don or Carlos doing the push-ups?]
>
> **CLEAR**   When Don was doing a set of push-ups in the gym, **he** saw Carlos. [In this revision, *he* refers clearly to *Don.*]
>
> **CLEAR**   When Don saw Carlos in the gym, **Don** was doing a set of push-ups. [Sometimes, you can correct an ambiguous reference by replacing the pronoun with a noun.]

EXERCISE A Read each of the following sentences. Then, decide whether the underlined pronoun refers clearly to one antecedent or refers ambiguously to more than one antecedent. If the pronoun reference is clear, write *C* on the line provided. If the pronoun reference is ambiguous, write *A* on the line provided. Hint: Draw an arrow from the pronoun to the antecedent. If you can draw only one arrow, the pronoun reference is clear. If you can draw more than one arrow, the pronoun reference is ambiguous.

Example _____A_____ **1.** When I hit the metal post with the car fender, it bent. [*It* could refer to *post* or

fender. Did the post bend, or did the fender bend? The pronoun reference is

ambiguous.]

_____ **1.** Although she didn't know it, Isabel and Joan had grown up in the same town. [Could

she refer to more than one word or word group, or is the reference clear?]

_____ **2.** When Alex spoke to Ruben, he said that tomorrow's game has been rescheduled.

_____ **3.** Did Mr. Thompson meet with Tara because he wanted to discuss scholarships?

_____ **4.** While Claudia was painting a portrait of Luisa, she smiled.

_____ **5.** After the camper saw bear cubs, he talked with the forest ranger.

GO ON ➡

General Reference

Another problem with pronoun reference is *general reference.* This problem occurs when a pronoun refers to a general idea rather than to a specific antecedent. Writers are most likely to slip into general reference when they use words like *it, that, this, such,* and *which.* These words may be easy to understand in speech, but they can be misinterpreted in unclear writing. A pronoun should always refer to a specific antecedent, not to a general idea.

7c. Avoid a *general reference,* which is the use of a pronoun that refers to a general idea rather than to a specific antecedent.

> **GENERAL** Hank is kind to his little brother. That is what I like about him. [*That* does not have a specific antecedent. Instead, it refers to the general idea of Hank's kindness.]
>
> **CLEAR** Hank is kind to his little brother. **His kindness** is what I like about him. [In this sentence, the word group *His kindness* is more exact than *That.*]
>
> **CLEAR** Because Hank is kind to his little brother, I like him. [In this sentence, the writer uses exact language and avoids general reference.]

EXERCISE B Correct the general pronoun reference error in each of the following sentences. Write the revised sentence on the line provided. Hint: There is more than one way to revise each sentence. The unclear pronoun has been underlined.

Example 1. During our trip to Montana, we visited our cousins, and it was the best part of the trip. [*It* does not have a specific antecedent, so *it* is replaced by a specific reference.]

During our trip to Montana, we visited our cousins, and seeing them was the best

part of the trip.

6. The class elected Claire the new class treasurer, which was a surprise to me. [What exactly was a surprise?] _____

7. My neighbor speaks French beautifully and enjoys helping me study. This allows me to practice my French outside of class. _____

_____

8. One of the judges knew a contestant. That wasn't fair. _____

_____

9. The coloration of some animals helps them blend into their surroundings, which gives them extra protection from predators. _____

_____

10. Do you love music and dance? Is that why you enjoy ballets so much? _____

_____

Clear Reference B
Weak Reference

One problem with pronoun reference is *weak reference.* This problem occurs when a pronoun's antecedent has been suggested but is missing from the sentence. A sentence with a weak reference should be revised so that the pronoun refers to a specific antecedent, not to a suggested one.

7d. Avoid a *weak reference,* which occurs when a pronoun refers to an antecedent that has been suggested but not expressed.

> **WEAK**   My aunt's dedication to teaching has inspired me, and I want to be one, too. [What is the antecedent of *one*? It is not stated.]
>
> **CLEAR**   My aunt's dedication to teaching has inspired me, and I want to be a **teacher,** too. [The pronoun *one* is replaced with a specific noun, *teacher.*]

EXERCISE A Correct the weak pronoun reference error in each of the following sentences. Write the revised sentence on the line provided. Hint: There is more than one way to revise each sentence. The unclear pronoun has been underlined.

Example 1. Jerry's brother is on the police force. As one of them, he has sworn to uphold the

law. [The antecedent of *them* is not stated, so the phrase *one of them* is replaced with

the specific phrase, *a police officer.*]

Jerry's brother is on the police force. As a police officer, he has sworn to uphold the law.

1. Although Danny admires marathon runners, he has never participated in one. [Which word

could you use to replace the pronoun *one*?]

_____

2. The flash on the camera isn't getting a charge, but I just replaced them last week.

_____

3. We put some more birdseed in the feeder, but we haven't seen any yet.

_____

4. Carlton believes in conserving energy, so he switches them off whenever he leaves the room.

_____

5. The letter needed extra postage, so I put another one on it.

_____

GO ON

Indefinite Reference

Another problem with pronoun reference is *indefinite reference.* This problem occurs when a pronoun—usually *it, they,* and *you*—does not refer to any particular person or thing and is not necessary for the sentence to make sense. A sentence with an indefinite reference should be revised to eliminate the unnecessary pronoun.

7e.   Avoid an *indefinite reference*—the use of a pronoun that refers to no particular person or thing and that is unnecessary to the meaning and structure of a sentence.

> **INDEFINITE**   In that magazine article, **it** says yoga is becoming quite popular in America. [*It* does not refer to a particular person or thing. *It* is not necessary to the meaning of the sentence.]
>
> **CLEAR**   That magazine article says yoga is becoming quite popular in America.
>
> **INDEFINITE**   During the Great Depression, **you** had financial difficulties. [*You* does not refer to the reader or to any other particular antecedent.]
>
> **CLEAR**   During the Great Depression, many people had financial difficulties.

EXERCISE B Correct the weak and indefinite references in each of the following sentences. Write the revised sentence on the line provided. The unclear pronoun is underlined.

Example 1. Kyle is excited about playing at the piano recital; he has been practicing <u>it</u> for weeks. [The antecedent of *it* is not stated, so the pronoun *it* is replaced with the phrase *his composition.*]

Kyle is excited about playing at the piano recital; he has been practicing his composition

for weeks.

6. On the news program, <u>it</u> said the mayor is running for reelection. [Is the pronoun *it* necessary to the meaning of the sentence?]

_____

7. Luke planned the guest list for his party and called <u>them</u> with the details.

_____

8. Were the roads icy in your town? Did <u>it</u> make the roads dangerous?

_____

9. At the library, <u>they</u> have CDs and videotapes available for checkout.

_____

10. In the recipe, does <u>it</u> say that the eggs are added before the flour?

_____

Principal Parts of Verbs A

The Principal Parts of Verbs

Every verb has four principal parts, and each principal part is a different form of the same verb.

8a. The principal parts of a verb are the **base form,** the **present participle,** the **past,** and the **past participle.** All other verb forms are derived from these principal parts.

BASE FORM	carry	edit	fly
PRESENT PARTICIPLE	[is] carrying	[is] editing	[is] flying
PAST	carried	edited	flew
PAST PARTICIPLE	[have] carried	[have] edited	[have] flown

NOTE Some teachers prefer to call the base form of a verb the *infinitive.* Follow your teacher's instructions when you label this verb form.

When present participle and past participle forms are used as verbs in sentences, they need **helping verbs.** Commonly used helping verbs are forms of *be* (such as *was* and *is*) and forms of *have* (such as *has* and *had*).

NOTE When you join a helping verb and a present or past participle, you have made a *verb phrase.* In the chart above, for example, *is carrying, is editing, is flying, have carried, have edited,* and *have flown* are verb phrases.

EXERCISE A Label the form of each of the following verbs. On the line provided, write *base, present participle, past,* or *past participle.*

Examples _present participle_ **1.** [is] laughing [Forms of *be* are used with present participles.]

past participle **2.** [has] forgotten [Forms of *have* are used with past participles.]

_____ **1.** wrote [How is the past form of a verb formed?]

_____ **2.** [has] fallen [How is the past participle of a verb formed?]

_____ **3.** repair

_____ **4.** [is] cheering

_____ **5.** [has] bought

_____ **6.** surrounded

_____ **7.** [is] bouncing

_____ **8.** understand

_____ **9.** [has] bitten

_____ **10.** [is] gossiping

GO ON

Regular Verbs

All verbs form the present participle by adding *–ing* to the base form.

BASE FORM	watch	memorize
PRESENT PARTICIPLE	[is] watch**ing**	[is] memoriz**ing**

8b. A *regular verb* forms its past and past participle by adding *–d* or *–ed* to the base form.

BASE FORM	celebrate	trust
PAST	celebrate**d**	trust**ed**
PAST PARTICIPLE	[have] celebrate**d**	[have] trust**ed**

EXERCISE B Complete the following chart by writing in the base form, the present participle, the past, and the past participle of each verb that is provided.

	Base Form	Present Participle	Past	Past Participle
Examples 1.	graduate	[is] graduating	graduated	[have] graduated

[The base form of the present participle *[is] graduating* is *graduate,* the past form is

graduated, and the past participle is *[have] graduated.*]

2.	gain	[is] gaining	gained	[have] gained

[The present participle of the regular verb *gain* is *[is] gaining,* the past form is *gained,* and

the past participle is *[have] gained.*]

	Base Form	Present Participle	Past	Past Participle
11.	chew	[is] _____	_____	[have] _____
12.	_____	[is] surprising	_____	[have] _____
13.	_____	[is] _____	_____	[have] swallowed
14.	_____	[is] _____	answered	[have] _____
15.	_____	[is] grating	_____	[have] _____
16.	prepare	[is] _____	_____	[have] _____
17.	_____	[is] _____	_____	[have] mowed
18.	_____	[is] _____	dropped	[have] _____
19.	_____	[is] laughing	_____	[have] _____
20.	dream	[is] _____	_____	[have] _____

Principal Parts of Verbs B

Irregular Verbs

8c. | An *irregular verb* forms its past and past participle in some other way than by adding –*d* or –*ed* to the base form.

Generally, the past and past participle forms of irregular verbs are formed in one of four ways:

- by changing vowels
- by changing consonants
- by changing vowels and consonants
- by making no change

	BASE FORM	PRESENT PARTICIPLE	PAST	PAST PARTICIPLE
VOWELS	ring	[is] ringing	rang	[have] rung
CONSONANTS	make	[is] making	made	[have] made
VOWELS + CONSONANTS	think	[is] thinking	thought	[have] thought
NO CHANGE	put	[is] putting	put	[have] put

EXERCISE A Complete the following chart. Fill in the missing verb forms for each verb. Hint: If you are unsure of a verb form, check a dictionary for its spelling.

	Base Form	Present Participle	Past	Past Participle
Examples 1.	grow	[is] growing	grew	[have] grown

[The present participle of the irregular verb *grow* is *[is] growing,* the past form is *grew,*

and the past participle is *[have] grown.*]

2.	read	[is] reading	read	[have] read

[The present participle of the irregular verb *read* is *[is] reading,* the past form is *read,* and

the past participle is *[have] read.*]

	Base Form	Present Participle	Past	Past Participle
1.	deal	[is] _____	_____	[have] _____
2.	forget	[is] _____	_____	[have] _____
3.	ride	[is] _____	_____	[have] _____
4.	cut	[is] _____	_____	[have] _____
5.	give	[is] _____	_____	[have] _____
6.	know	[is] _____	_____	[have] _____
7.	do	[is] _____	_____	[have] _____
8.	set	[is] _____	_____	[have] _____

GO ON ➡

9. burst   [is] _____   _____   [have] _____

10. take   [is] _____   _____   [have] _____

Avoid these common errors when you form the past and past participle forms of irregular verbs:

(1) using the past form with a helping verb

    NONSTANDARD Maria has forgave you.

    STANDARD Maria **forgave** you.

(2) using the past participle form without a helping verb

    NONSTANDARD Corey rung the school bell.

    STANDARD Corey **has rung** the school bell.

(3) adding *–d, –ed,* or *–t* to the base form

    NONSTANDARD Kim throwed a ball to Hector.

    STANDARD Kim **threw** a ball to Hector.

EXERCISE B Underline the correct verb form in parentheses in each of the following sentences.

Examples 1. Since before 3000 B.C., people *(have rode, have ridden)* donkeys. [Because the past

      form *rode* is not used with a helping verb, *have ridden* is the correct form of the past

      participle of *ride.*]

    2. Have you *(built, builded)* a new pen for the donkey, Mitch? [Because *build* forms its

      past participle by changing the *d* to a *t,* the correct form is *Have built.*]

11. Mitch and I *(have gave, gave)* the donkey fresh water and sweet hay. [How is the past form of the

irregular verb *give* formed?]

12. Mitch, who is a farmer, *(has keeped, has kept)* a donkey for years. [How is the past participle of the

irregular verb *keep* formed?]

13. Yesterday evening I *(heared, heard)* the donkey bray.

14. Mr. Hugo, my science teacher, *(taught, teached)* us about donkeys.

15. I *(have did, did)* my homework on this subject.

16. An adult donkey *(has grown, has growed)* a large head in proportion to its body.

17. In my report, I *(wrote, writed)* about the long ears and large heads of donkeys.

18. Have you ever *(saw, seen)* a mule?

19. A mule *(has come, has came)* from a cross between a donkey and a horse.

20. Mitch's donkey *(has burst, has bursted)* through the fence between our farms.

Sit and *Set*, *Rise* and *Raise*, *Lie* and *Lay*

Sit and *Set*

The verb *sit* means "to be in a seated, upright position" or "to be in a place." *Sit* seldom takes an object. The forms of *sit* are *sit*, *[is] sitting*, *sat*, and *[have] sat*. The verb *set* means "to put [something] in a place." *Set* usually takes an object. The forms of *set* are *set*, *is setting*, *set*, and *[have] set*.

> **EXAMPLES** The plasterboard **is sitting** inside the garage, so we **are setting** the boxes of tile in the kitchen. [*Is sitting* does not have an object. *Are setting* has an object, *boxes*.]
>
> The dog **sat** next to the sprinkler and **set** the stick next to it. [*Sat* does not have an object. *Set* has an object, *stick*.]
>
> **Had** Lily **sat** down after Anthony **had set** a chair there? [*Had sat* does not have an object. *Had set* has an object, *chair*.]

EXERCISE A Underline the correct form of *sit* or *set* in the parentheses in each of the following sentences. Hint: Forms of *sit* do not take objects. Forms of *set* usually take objects.

Example 1. Has Ricky (<u>sat</u>, set) in the doctor's office long? Did he (sat, <u>set</u>) his feet on a stool?

> [*Sat* does not have an object. *Set* has an object, *feet*.]

1. The bench is (*sitting, setting*) on the porch, and Beth is (*sitting, setting*) plates on it.

2. May I (*sit, set*) in this chair or (*sit, set*) my books in it?

3. You may (*sit, set*) your bags on this table, and you may (*sit, set*) over there.

4. My cat (*sat, set*) nearby as I (*sat, set*) the new turtle in the aquarium.

5. Flora has (*sat, set*) the groceries in the car, and Frank has (*sat, set*) in the front seat.

Rise and *Raise*

The verb *rise* means "to go up" or "to get up." *Rise* does not take an object. The forms of *rise* are *rise*, *[is] rising*, *rose*, and *have risen*. The verb *raise* means "to lift up" or "to cause [something] to rise." *Raise* usually takes an object. The forms of *raise* are *raise*, *[is] raising*, *raised*, and *[have] raised*.

> **EXAMPLES** The sun **is rising,** and Gary **is raising** the window. [*Is rising* does not have an object. *Is raising* has an object, *window*.]
>
> The ballerina **rose** gracefully and **raised** her foot. [*Rose* does not have an object. *Raised* has an object, *foot*.]
>
> The hot air balloon **has** finally **risen** into the sky, so the reporters **have raised** their cameras to take photographs. [*Has risen* does not have an object. *Have raised* has an object, *cameras*.]

GO ON ➡

EXERCISE B Underline the correct form of the verb in parentheses in each of the following items. Hint: Forms of *rise* do not take objects. Forms of *raise* usually take objects.

Example 1. At his entrance, the veterans *(had risen, had raised)* and *(had risen, had raised)* their

hands in salute. [*Had risen* does not have an object. *Had raised* has an object, *hands.*]

6. We *(rise, raise)* early because the cheery sunlight *(rises, raises)* our spirits.

7. During the discussion, several issues *(rose, raised)*. Someone *(rose, raised)* the question of money.

8. Dust *(had risen, had raised)* in the wind before we *(had risen, had raised)* the car's windows.

9. Will you *(be rising, be raising)* my allowance? Prices *(are rising, are raising)*.

10. The dolphin *(rose, raised)* from the water and *(rose, raised)* its mouth for a fish.

Lie and *Lay*

The verb *lie* means "to rest," "to recline," or "to be in a place." *Lie* does not take an object. The forms of *lie* are *lie*, [*is*] *lying*, *lay*, and [*have*] *lain*. The verb **lay** means "to put [something] in a place." *Lay* generally takes an object. The forms of *lay* are *lay*, [*is*] *laying*, *laid*, and [*have*] *laid*.

> **EXAMPLES** We **are laying** the files on the counter next to where the cat **is lying.** [*Are laying* has an object, *files. Is lying* does not have an object.]
>
> May I **lay** my coat on this chair and then **lie** on your sofa? [*Lay* has an object, *coat. Lie* has no object.]
>
> The cat **has laid** its toy under the table where the cat **has** often **lain.** [*Has laid* has an object, *toy. Has lain* does not have an object.]

EXERCISE C Underline the correct form of *lie* or *lay* in parentheses in each of the following sentences. Hint: Forms of *lay* usually take an object. Forms of *lie* do not take an object.

Example 1. Walt has *(lain, laid)* the papers on the desk, where the others have *(lain, laid)* for a

few days. [*Laid* has an object, *papers. Lain* does not have an object.]

11. Please *(lie, lay)* the mail on the table before you *(lie, lay)* down for a nap.

12. I was *(lying, laying)* on the beach when Jan *(lay, laid)* her towel beside me.

13. The hamster *(lay, laid)* asleep in its nest, so I quietly *(lay, laid)* its food nearby.

14. Burt has *(lain, laid)* the gardening tools out, for the leaves have *(lain, laid)* on the lawn too long.

15. For the picnic, I'll *(lie, lay)* out the food and drinks, and then I'll *(lie, lay)* in the hammock.

Tense

Verb Tense

8d.   The *tense* of a verb indicates the time of the action or of the state of being expressed by the verb.

Every verb in English has six tenses.

PAST	We **were** singers. We **sang.** [existing or happening in the past]
PRESENT	We **are** singers. We **sing.** [existing or happening now]
FUTURE	We **will be** singers. We **will sing.** [existing or happening in the future]
PAST PERFECT	We **had been** singers. We **had sung.** [existing or happening before a specific time in the past]
PRESENT PERFECT	We **have been** singers. We **have sung.** [existing or happening sometime before now; may be continuing now]
FUTURE PERFECT	We **will have been** singers. We **will have sung.** [existing or happening before a specific time in the future]

EXERCISE A   Write the missing forms of the verbs on the lines provided.

Present	Past	Future
Example 1. repair	repaired	will repair [To form the past tense of *repair*,

—ed is added. The helping verb *will* is added to form the future tense.]

Present	Past	Future
1. hike	_____	_____
2. _____	_____	will serve
3. _____	revised	_____
4. practice	_____	_____
5. _____	studied	_____

TIP Helping verbs are used with the *future, present perfect, past perfect,* and *future perfect* tenses.

FUTURE	The birds **will** migrate. [The birds are going to migrate at some future time.]
PRESENT PERFECT	The birds **have** migrated. [The birds have already migrated.]
PAST PERFECT	The birds **had** migrated. [The birds migrated before a specific time in the past.]
FUTURE PERFECT	The birds **will have** migrated. [The birds will have migrated before a specific time in the future.]

GO ON

EXERCISE B Write the missing forms of the verbs on the lines provided.

	Present Perfect	**Past Perfect**	**Future Perfect**
Example 1.	have spoken	had spoken	will have spoken

[The helping verb *have* is used with the past participle form of *speak* to form the present perfect tense. The helping verbs *will* and *have* are used to form the future perfect tense.]

Present Perfect	**Past Perfect**	**Future Perfect**
6. have recorded	_____	_____
7. _____	had baked	_____
8. _____	_____	will have swept
9. have assigned	_____	_____
10. _____	had locked	_____

EXERCISE C Identify the tense of the underlined verb in each of the following sentences. On the line provided, write *past, present, future, past perfect, present perfect,* or *future perfect.*

Examples _past perfect_ **1.** <u>Had</u> they <u>heard</u> about the hard lives of circus elephants? [This action happened before a specific time in the past.]

present perfect **2.** Since 1995, people <u>have brought</u> several former circus elephants to a special place in Tennessee. [This action happened sometime before now.]

_____**11.** On the Internet, I <u>found</u> a Web site for The Elephant Sanctuary. [Did this action happen in the past or before a specific time in the past?]

_____**12.** Jenny and Bunny <u>are</u> elephants. [Is this state of being occurring now?]

_____**13.** The two elephants <u>live</u> in The Elephant Sanctuary in Tennessee.

_____**14.** Had Bunny <u>lived</u> in an animal park before?

_____**15.** All of the elephants in this sanctuary <u>have worked</u> in circuses or parks.

_____**16.** Now, however, they <u>will roam</u> the two hundred acres of their new home.

_____**17.** Bunny and the other elephants <u>have enjoyed</u> their healthy habitat.

_____**18.** During the cold winters, they <u>sleep</u> in a warm barn.

_____**19.** Will they <u>play</u> in the mud holes in the rainy springtime?

_____**20.** The sanctuary <u>will have improved</u> the lives of many elephants.

HOLT HANDBOOK | Fifth Course

Progressive Forms of Verbs

Each verb tense has a form called the *progressive form.* The progressive form is not a separate tense. It is another form of each of the six tenses and expresses continuing action or state of being.

The progressive form of a verb consists of two parts: **(1)** a form of the verb *be* in the appropriate tense—present, past, future, present perfect, past perfect, or future perfect—and **(2)** the present participle (*–ing* form) of the verb.

The Present and Present Perfect Progressive Forms

The *present progressive form* indicates that an action is or has been occurring in the present.

> **EXAMPLES**   The attendant **is cleaning** the windshield. [The present progressive form consists of the present tense of *be* and the present participle *cleaning.*]
>
> The attendant **has been cleaning** the windshield. [The present perfect progressive form consists of the present perfect tense of *be* and the present participle *cleaning.*]

EXERCISE A Using the directions in parentheses, write the correct form of the verb on the line provided.

Example 1. The store ___has been closing___ at six o'clock. (present perfect progressive form of *close.*) [The present perfect progressive form of *close* is *has been closing.*]

1. The neighbor's dog _____ at a squirrel on our roof. (present progressive form of *bark*) [How is the present progressive form of a verb formed?]

2. We _____ the recycling bins almost once a week. (present perfect progressive form of *fill*)

3. Three horses _____ along the ravine. (present progressive form of *gallop*)

4. Now that the storm's winds have died down, many trees _____ to one side. (present progressive form of *lean*)

5. Their class _____ the development of early stone tools. (present perfect progressive form of *study*)

The Future and Future Perfect Progressive Forms

The *future progressive form* of a verb indicates that an action will be occurring or will have been occurring at some time in the future.

> **FUTURE PROGRESSIVE**   will be singing
>
> **FUTURE PERFECT PROGRESSIVE**   will have been singing

GO ON

EXERCISE B Using the directions in parentheses, write the correct form of the verb on the line provided.

Example 1. The band ____will have been playing____ for most of the evening. (future perfect

progressive form of *play*) [The future perfect progressive form of *play* is *will have been*

playing.]

6. Once the car is packed, they _____ for the airport. (future progressive form

of *leave*) [How is the future progressive formed?]

7. New employees _____ a seminar on sales techniques before they begin.

(future perfect progressive form of *attend*)

8. Vanya _____ the overseas managers. (future progressive form of *contact*)

9. At six o'clock, that lizard _____ on that limb for four hours. (future perfect

progressive form of *bask*)

10. Once volleyball practice has ended, Leo _____ to the orthodontist. (future

progressive form of *go*)

The Past and Past Perfect Progressive Forms

The *past progressive form* of a verb indicates that an action was occurring or had been occurring
at some time in the past.

> **PAST PROGRESSIVE**   was, were singing
> **PAST PERFECT PROGRESSIVE**   had been singing

EXERCISE C Using the directions in parentheses, write the correct form of the verb on the line provided.

Example 1. The shuttle bus ____had been running____ earlier today. (past perfect progressive form of

run.) [The past perfect progressive form of the verb *run* is *had been running*.]

11. Nicky and Sarah _____ uncertain about the homework assignment. (past

perfect progressive form of *feel*) [How is the past perfect progressive formed?]

12. Until today, snow _____ the ground. (past progressive form of *cover*)

13. Last June, the ice skater already _____ regularly for ten years. (past perfect

progressive form of *perform*)

14. When they questioned him, the officers _____ the witness for some time.

(past perfect progressive form of *watch*)

15. Mike and Claudia _____ to meet us there. (past progressive form of *plan*)

The Uses of Tenses

The Present, Past, and Future Tenses

8e. Each of the six tenses has its own uses.

The *present tense* expresses an action or a state of being that is occurring now, is customary, states a general truth, or is meant to convey a literary or historical present.

> **EXAMPLES** Anica **listens** to songs on her CD player. [The present tense shows that Anica is currently listening to songs, or it shows that her listening is customary.]
>
> Carmen **finds** certain television shows entertaining. [The present tense shows that Carmen generally finds certain shows entertaining.]
>
> The hero **discovers** a doorway into the underworld. [The present tense is used to summarize a plot event within a literary work.]
>
> The peasants then **leave** their rural homes. [The present tense is used to make a historical event seem current.]

The *past tense* expresses an action or a state of being that occurred in the past.

> **EXAMPLES** Roy **danced** to a song. [The past tense shows that Roy has ceased to dance.]
>
> Roy **was dancing** to songs on the radio. [The past progressive form shows that Roy was dancing at some time in the past.]

The *future tense* expresses an action or a state of being that will occur. The future tense is formed with the helping verb *will*.

> **EXAMPLES** The wheel **will** not **spin**. [The future tense is formed with the helping verb *will*.]
>
> Soon the mechanic **will be balancing** our tires. [The future progressive tense is formed with the helping verb *will*, the verb *be*, and the present participle of the verb *balance*.]

EXERCISE A Identify the tense of the underlined verb in each of the following sentences. Write *present*, *present progressive*, *past*, *past progressive*, *future* or *future progressive* on the line provided. Hint: Progressive forms of verbs are formed with helping verbs.

Example ___past progressive___ **1.** Were the mice nibbling at the cheese in the trap? [The verb phrase *were nibbling* indicates that the action occurred at some time in the past.]

_____ **1.** Thelma is pouring a glass of ice water for you. [Did this action occur in the present or the past?]

_____ **2.** Will you be staying for the cast party after the play?

_____ **3.** They were looking for the lost calf until late in the afternoon.

_____ **4.** The detective seems suspicious of the suspect's actions.

_____ **5.** Next summer, we will go on many picnics.   **GO ON** ➡

The Present Perfect, Past Perfect, and Future Perfect Tenses

The *present perfect tense* expresses an action or a state of being that occurred at an indefinite time in the past. It is also used to express an action or a state of being that began in the past and continues into the present. The present perfect tense is formed with the helping verbs *have* or *has*.

> **EXAMPLES** Roy **has danced** to songs on the radio. [The use of the present perfect tense shows that Roy danced at some time in the past.]
>
> Mary **has been leading** the youth choir since April. [The use of the present perfect progressive tense shows that Mary began leading the choir in the past and continues to do so in the present.]

The *past perfect tense* expresses an action or a state of being that ended before some other past action or state of being. The past perfect tense is formed with the helping verb *had*.

> **EXAMPLES** Roy **had danced** to songs on the radio. [The use of the past perfect tense shows that Roy ceased to dance before some other past event.]
>
> Mary **had been leading** the youth choir when the power went out. [The use of the past perfect progressive tense shows that Mary had been leading the choir before a specific event occurred in the past.]

The *future perfect tense* expresses an action or a state of being that will end before some other future occurrence. The future perfect tense is formed with the helping verbs *will have*.

> **EXAMPLES** By three o'clock, Roy **will have danced** to twenty songs. [The use of the future perfect tense shows that Roy will have danced at some time in the future.]
>
> By August, Mary **will have been leading** the choir for five months. [The use of the future perfect progressive tense shows that Mary will have been leading the choir at some specific time in the future.]

EXERCISE B Identify the tense of the underlined verb in each of the following sentences. Write *present perfect, present perfect progressive, past perfect, past perfect progressive, future perfect,* or *future perfect progressive* on the line provided. Hint: The progressive tenses of these verbs are formed with the helping verbs *have, has,* or *had.*

Example __future perfect progressive__ **1.** By Friday, <u>will</u> the band <u>have practiced</u> its set? [The action will end before a certain time in the future, so it is in the future perfect progressive tense.]

_____ **6.** The team <u>had practiced</u> its plays. [Did this action happen in the past, or does it happen in the present?]

_____ **7.** By the fall, the prairie grasses <u>will have been growing</u> for months!

_____ **8.** An armadillo <u>has dug</u> in the front flower bed.

_____ **9.** <u>Had</u> the engine <u>been idling</u> roughly?

_____ **10.** The drought <u>has affected</u> lake levels.

Consistency of Tense

When you write about events that take place at the same time, use verbs that are in the same tense. When you write about events that occur at different times, use verbs that are in different tenses.

Events That Occur at the Same Time

8f.   Use tense forms correctly to show relationships between verbs in a sentence. Do not change needlessly from one tense to another.

When describing events that occur at the same time, use verbs in the same tense.

> **INCONSISTENT**   Scott **whistled** as he **walks** home. [*Whistled* is past tense, and *walks* is present tense.]
>
> **CONSISTENT**   Scott **whistled** as he **walked** home. [Both actions happened in the past.]
>
> **CONSISTENT**   Scott **whistles** as he **walks** home. [Both actions happen in the present.]

EXERCISE A   Use proofreading symbols to correct the error in consistency of verb tense in each of the following sentences. Hint: There may be more than one way to correct each sentence. Choose the way that makes the most sense.

Examples 1. Across the lake ~~was~~ a cabin, and near it is a barn. [Since the cabin and the barn exist
  is

at the same time, both verbs should be in the present tense.]

2. While Dad was raking the leaves, Jina ~~trims~~ the hedge. [Since Dad and Jina were
  was trimming

working at the same time, the verbs should be in the same tense.]

1. When I walked into the pizza parlor, I see an old friend of mine. [Do both verbs in this sentence

show that the actions happened in the past?]

2. The raccoon is near the lake when it saw a water moccasin. [Are both verbs in this sentence in

the same tense?]

3. Did you pay your money at the door when you are walking in?

4. That afternoon, Gabriella was slicing apples for a pie and makes a delicious pie crust.

5. Under the bridge flowed the dark river, and the bright moon will reflect on the water.

6. Polly jumps into the air and slammed the volleyball across the net.

7. After school we will study together, or we begin our art project.

8. As I spray water from the garden hose, the dog jumped into the stream.

GO ON

9. He finds the textbook that you lost.

10. A group of us is going to a movie on Friday, and we take our dates.

Events That Occur at Different Times

When describing events that occur at different times, use verbs in different tenses to show the order of events.

> **EXAMPLES**   Jerome **works** at the hospital now, but he **worked** as a lifeguard last summer. [Jerome works at the hospital in the present, so *works* is in the present tense. At a specific time before his current work at the hospital, Jerome worked as a lifeguard, so *worked* is in the past tense.]
>
> Ever since Jerome **got** this job, he **has dreamt** of a career in medicine. [Jerome got his job at a specific time in the past, so *got* is in the past tense. His dreams of a career in medicine began at a specific time in the past and continue into the present, so *has dreamt* is in the present perfect tense.]

The tenses you use depend on the meaning you intend to express.

> **EXAMPLES**   Marty **says** that he **has** the money for the trip. [Both verbs are in the present tense. Both actions are occurring now.]
>
> Marty **says** that he **will have** the money for the trip. [*Says* is in the present tense, showing that this action is happening now. *Will have* is in the future tense, showing that this action will happen in the future.]

EXERCISE B In each of the following sentences describing events that happen at different times, underline the correct form of the verb in parentheses to show the order of events.

Example 1. Did you cover your ears when the siren *(sounds, was sounding)*? [The past progressive verb *was sounding* shows that the action was ongoing at a specified time in the past.]

11. I set the alarm for seven o'clock so that I *(will wake, wake)* in time to get ready. [Which verb expresses an action that happens at a future time?]

12. Tanya promised that she *(calls, will call)* me this weekend.

13. Was the class taking a test when the principal *(stopped, is stopping)* by the room?

14. Cedric likes spinach now, but he *(dislikes, disliked)* it as a child.

15. Unfortunately, the tire had gone flat just before I *(needed, need)* the car.

Active Voice and Passive Voice

Identifying Active Voice and Passive Voice

Voice is the form a verb takes to show whether the subject performs or receives the action. When the subject performs the action of the verb, the verb is in the *active voice.* When the subject receives the action of the verb, the verb is in the *passive voice.*

ACTIVE VOICE Ms. Hart **graded** our papers. [The subject, *Ms. Hart,* performs the action of the verb *graded.*]

PASSIVE VOICE Our papers **were graded** by Ms. Hart. [The subject, *papers,* receives the action of the verb phrase *were graded.*]

ACTIVE VOICE A falling limb **rang** the bell. [The subject, *limb,* performs the action of the verb *rang.*]

PASSIVE VOICE The bell **was rung** by a falling limb. [The subject, *bell,* receives the action of the verb phrase *was rung.*]

In passive voice, the verb phrase always includes a form of *be* and the past participle of the main verb. Other helping verbs may also be included.

EXAMPLES The mirror **was broken.** [*Was* is a form of *be. Broken* is the past participle of the verb *break.*]

The mirror **has been broken.** [*Been* is a form of *be.* The helping verb *has* is included in the verb phrase *has been broken.*]

EXERCISE A Decide whether the underlined verb or verb phrase in each of the following sentences is in the active or in the passive voice. Then, write *A* for *active voice* or *P* for *passive voice* on the line provided.

Examples __P__ **1.** Was the homeless cat adopted by a nice family? [The subject, *cat,* receives the action of the verb phrase *Was adopted.*]

__A__ **2.** Your sister has promised to bring my books. [The subject, *sister,* performs the action of the verb phrase *has promised.*]

_____ **1.** During the earthquake, city hall was damaged by fire. [Does *city hall* perform the action of the verb, or does *city hall* receive the action?]

_____ **2.** Outside the door, I scraped the mud from my boots. [Does *I* perform the action of the verb, or does *I* receive the action?]

_____ **3.** The entire wedding will be planned by a professional wedding planner.

_____ **4.** I am surprised by your creativity.

_____ **5.** Michelle's enthusiasm greatly inspired the team.

_____ **6.** Please dust the furniture in the family room.

_____ **7.** Had the winners been announced by the next day?

_____ **8.** Was this Web site created by your brother, Cliff?

GO ON ➡

_____ **9.** At their favorite theater Dawn and Alison <u>watched</u> a movie.

_____ **10.** The pasta salad <u>has been shared</u> by Rick and Lucia.

The Uses of the Passive Voice

The active voice generally produces clearer and stronger sentences than the passive voice. However, when you don't know or don't want to reveal the performer of the action, or when you want to emphasize the receiver of the action, the passive voice is useful.

> **EXAMPLES** A window **was broken.** [Who or what broke the window is unknown.]
> Several insults **were hurled.** [The performer of the action is not revealed.]
> The museum **has received** many donations. [The receiver of the donations, the museum, is emphasized.]

EXERCISE B Revise each of the following sentences so that the verb is in the active voice. Then, write your new sentence on the line provided. Hint: You will need to add or change words in order to revise some sentences.

Example 1. Was the family car washed by Hannah and Harley? [Because the subject of the sentence, *car*, receives the action of the verb phrase *was washed*, the sentence is in the passive voice. The sentence can be revised so that a new subject, *Hannah and Harley*, now performs the action of the verb.]

Did Hannah and Harley wash the family car?

11. A delicious dinner was cooked by Mabel. [Does the subject of this sentence perform the action, or does the subject receive the action?]

_____

12. All roads in town were briefly flooded after the storm.

_____

13. These old coins were lost during the seventeenth century.

_____

14. Coral reefs were chosen as the subject of my report.

_____

15. Has the firewood been chopped by anyone yet?

_____

Troublesome Modifiers A

A modifier is a word or word group that makes the meaning of another word or word group more specific.

> **EXAMPLES** What a **colorful** shirt! [*Colorful* is an adjective describing the noun *shirt*.]
>
> We finished **quickly.** [*Quickly* is an adverb describing the verb *finished*.]

Certain pairs of modifiers such as *bad* and *badly* or *good* and *well* can be confusing. The following information will help you use these modifiers correctly when you write.

Bad and *Badly*

Bad is an adjective. Adjectives describe nouns and pronouns. *Badly* is an adverb. Adverbs describe verbs, adjectives, and other adverbs.

> **ADJECTIVE** That was a **bad** movie. [*Bad* is an adjective describing the noun *movie*.]
>
> **ADVERB** Clara burned the toast **badly.** [*Badly* is an adverb describing the verb *burned*.]

NOTE▶ When used as a predicate adjective, only *bad,* which is an adjective, should follow a linking verb such as *feel, look, taste, sound,* or *smell*.

> **NONSTANDARD** The cook feels badly for having overcooked the rice. [*Badly* is an adverb. *Badly* should not follow the linking verb *feels* or be used to describe a noun.]
>
> **STANDARD** The cook feels **bad** for having overcooked the rice. [The adjective *bad* describes the noun *cook* and follows the linking verb *feels*.]
>
> It looks **bad.** [The adjective *bad* describes the pronoun *It* and follows the linking verb *looks*.]

EXERCISE A Underline the correct choice of modifier in parentheses in each of the following sentences. Hint: Remember that only *bad* should follow a linking verb.

Examples 1. Did it look (*bad, badly*) after the paint faded? [The adjective *bad* describes the pronoun *it* and follows the linking verb *look*.]

2. Because I didn't use a ruler, I drew the lines (*bad, badly*). [The adverb *badly* describes the verb *drew*.]

1. This stale bread tastes (*bad, badly*). [Which modifier should follow a linking verb?]

2. I never treat animals (*bad, badly*). [Which modifier should be used to describe a verb?]

3. Does the damage from the rust seem (*bad, badly*)?

4. John, those bright blue curtains look (*bad, badly*) in that window.

5. Lee says that he (*bad, badly*) wants to learn how to speak French.

6. There is a *(bad, badly)* scratch on one lens of this pair of binoculars.

7. Dented *(bad, badly)* in the accident, the car's fender will have to be replaced.

8. That pattern may have been a *(bad, badly)* choice for a set of formal dishes.

9. That apple didn't taste *(bad, badly)* with the oatmeal.

10. This wobbly bench must have been assembled *(bad, badly)*.

Good and *Well*

Good is an adjective. An adjective describes nouns or pronouns. When describing a verb, use the adverb *well*, meaning "capably" or "satisfactorily," instead of the adjective *good*. *Well* may be used as either an adjective or an adverb.

> **NONSTANDARD** Mario sings good. [Because the adjective *good* describes nouns or pronouns, it should not be used to describe the verb *sings*.]
>
> **STANDARD** Mario sings **well.** [The adverb *well* describes the verb *sings*.]
>
> Mario sings **good** songs. [The adjective *good* describes the noun *songs*.]

EXERCISE B Underline the correct choice of modifier in parentheses in each of the following sentences. Hint: Remember that *good* is an adjective. *Good* should only be used to describe nouns or pronouns.

Examples 1. As an actor, Jenna always performs *(good, well)*. [The adverb *well* describes the verb *performs*.]

        2. Was Stan's casserole *(good, well)*? [The adjective *good* describes the noun *casserole*.]

11. The entire team played *(good, well)*. [Should a verb be described by *good* or by *well*?]

12. Dan drew a really *(good, well)* picture of the pond. [Should a noun be described by *good* or by *well*?]

13. Before the meeting I'll clean the house so that it looks *(good, well)*.

14. The senator feels *(good, well)* about keeping his campaign promises.

15. For his age, Shawn reads quite *(good, well)*.

16. Is the new employee working *(good, well)* with the others?

17. *(Good, Well)* mornings often lead to pleasant afternoons.

18. You look *(good, well)* in your tuxedo.

19. Did you swim *(good, well)* at last week's competition?

20. Scooter, our dog, runs really *(good, well)* when the grass is short.

Troublesome Modifiers B

A modifier is a word or word group that makes the meaning of another word or word group more specific.

> **EXAMPLES** **Fresh** fruit was sitting on the counter. [*Fresh* is an adjective describing the noun *fruit*.]
>
> We spoke **quietly.** [*Quietly* is an adverb used to describe the verb *spoke*.]

Certain pairs of modifiers such as *slow* and *slowly* or *real* and *really* can be confusing. The following information will help you use these modifiers correctly when you write.

Slow and *Slowly*

Slow can be used as either an adjective or an adverb. *Slowly* is used only as an adverb. In formal writing it is better to use *slowly* instead of *slow* as an adverb.

> **ADJECTIVE** That pitch was a **slow** curveball. [*Slow* describes the noun *curveball*.]
>
> That one was **slow.** [*Slow* describes the pronoun *one*.]
>
> **ADVERB** The aquarium filled **slowly.** [*Slowly* describes the verb *filled*.]
>
> The detective gazed at the **slowly** fading signature. [*Slowly* describes the adjective *fading*. *Fading* describes the noun *signature*.]

EXERCISE A Underline the modifier in parentheses that is correct according to standard, formal English in each of the following sentences. Hint: Use *slowly* as an adverb to describe verbs or adjectives.

Examples 1. Is this Internet connection (*slow, slowly*)? [The adjective *slow* describes the noun *connection*.]

    2. The Web page loaded (*slow, slowly*) in my browser. [The adverb *slowly* describes the verb *loaded*.]

1. He (*slow, slowly*) sang the song. [Should a verb be described by *slow* or by *slowly*?]

2. (*Slow, Slowly*) and carefully crafted, this serving bowl has lasted for hundreds of years. [Should the adjective *crafted*, which describes *bowl*, be described by *slow* or by *slowly*?]

3. Should this song's tempo be quite this (*slow, slowly*)?

4. At the beach a gull (*slow, slowly*) walked along the water's edge.

5. Lift that heavy box (*slow, slowly*).

6. (*Slow, Slowly*), calm, and smooth actions quieted the excited horse.

7. Because the geometry problems were complex, Jaime worked (*slow, slowly*).

8. The bus was (*slow, slowly*), but we arrived on time.

9. The herd of deer moved *(slow, slowly)* into the underbrush.

10. As a beginner, the ice skater was *(slow, slowly)* and careful on the ice.

Real and *Really*

Real is an adjective meaning "actual" or "true." Adjectives describe nouns and pronouns. *Really* is an adverb meaning "truly" or "actually." Adverbs describe verbs, adjectives, and other adverbs.

> **ADJECTIVE** Does the recipe use **real** cream? [*Real* describes the noun *cream*.]
>
> That looks **real.** [*Real* follows the linking verb *looks* and describes the demonstrative pronoun *That*.]
>
> **ADVERB** In thirty seconds Lloyd **really** named fifty capital cities. [*Really* describes the verb *named*.]
>
> With field glasses she could see the butterfly **really** clearly. [*Really* describes the adverb *clearly*. *Clearly* describes the verb phrase *could see*.]

EXERCISE B Underline the modifier in parentheses that is correct according to standard, formal English in each of the following sentences.

Examples 1. Katie, our cat, walks *(real, really)* quietly. [The adverb *really* should be used to describe the adverb *quietly*.]

2. In the play at school, the "snow" wasn't *(real, really)*. [The adjective *real* should be used to describe the noun *snow*.]

11. On career day the students met a *(real, really)* Hollywood actor. [Should the adjective *real* or the adverb *really* describe the noun *actor*?]

12. That spaghetti is *(real, really)* hot! [Should the adjective *real* or the adverb *really* describe the adjective *hot*?]

13. Her fear of the dark is *(real, really)*.

14. Is this autograph *(real, really)*?

15. In the story doesn't Pinocchio become a *(real, really)* boy?

16. I'm glad that Will is my partner because he is *(real, really)* creative.

17. That company has a bright future, for it is *(real, really)* productive.

18. Does one of these ideas seem *(real, really)* good to you?

19. I was *(real, really)* glad to hear about your promotion.

20. Give the dog a *(real, really)* good bath, please.

98

Degrees of Comparison

Regular Comparison

Modifiers can be used to compare one thing to another or to compare more than two things.

9c. Modifiers change form to show comparison.

The three degrees of comparison are the *positive,* the *comparative,* and the *superlative.* To show a decrease in the qualities modifiers express, all modifiers form the comparative degree by using *less* and the superlative degree by using *least.*

	POSITIVE	COMPARATIVE	SUPERLATIVE
ONE SYLLABLE	small	small**er**	small**est**
TWO SYLLABLES	happy	happi**er**	happi**est**
	random	**more** random	**most** random
THREE OR MORE	specific	**more** specific	**most** specific
SYLLABLES	unfortunate	**more** unfortunate	**most** unfortunate
DECREASING	full	**less** full	**least** full
	likely	**less** likely	**least** likely
	hesitant	**less** hesitant	**least** hesitant

EXERCISE A According to the instructions in each of the following items, write the comparative and superlative degrees of the modifiers on the lines provided. Hint: Change spellings if needed.

		Comparative	Superlative
Examples	1. decreasing degrees of *crisp*	less crisp	least crisp

[The decreasing degrees of *crisp* are formed by using *less* and *least.*]

	2. increasing degrees of *beautifully*	more beautifully	most beautifully

[Because *beautifully* has more than two syllables, the comparative and superlative

degrees of *beautifully* are formed by adding *more* and *most.*]

	Comparative	Superlative
1. increasing degrees of *sneaky*	_____	_____

[How can the increasing degrees of comparison for a two-syllable modifier be formed?]

2. increasing degrees of *comforting* _____ _____

[How are the increasing degrees of comparison for a three-syllable modifier formed?]

3. decreasing degrees of *round* _____ _____

4. increasing degrees of *flat* _____ _____

5. decreasing degrees of *colorful* _____ _____

GO ON

Developmental Language Skills

6. increasing degrees of *quickly* _____ _____

7. increasing degrees of *habitual* _____ _____

8. decreasing degrees of *ready* _____ _____

9. increasing degrees of *coldly* _____ _____

10. decreasing degrees of *blue* _____ _____

Irregular Comparison

Some modifiers are formed in different ways.

POSITIVE	COMPARATIVE	SUPERLATIVE
bad	worse	worst
ill	worse	worst
good	better	best
well	better	best
little	less	least
many	more	most
much	more	most
far	farther *or* further	farthest *or* furthest

EXERCISE B Underline the correct modifier in parentheses in each of the following sentences.

Examples 1. Thompson's Market has (*gooder, better*) prices than Mick's Market. [*Better* is the comparative degree of the adjective *good*.]

2. Was that the (*more worse, worst*) cold virus of the year? [*Worst* is the superlative degree of the adjective *bad*.]

11. The (*baddest, worst*) mosquitoes are in those marshes. [How is the superlative degree of *bad* formed?]

12. This phone has a (*better, gooder*) sounding ring. [How is the comparative degree of *good* formed?]

13. Last night's meteor shower may have been the (*most, maniest*) impressive in decades.

14. The drink on the left has (*littler, less*) taste than the drink on the right.

15. Now that she's started sneezing, Mariana feels even (*badder, worse*) than she did yesterday.

16. Who drove (*more far, farther*) in order to get here, Len or Nathan?

17. The Clay Pot is one of the (*best, goodest*) restaurants in town.

18. They cleaned up one of the (*baddest, worst*) piles of trash along that highway.

19. (*Manier, More*) monarch butterflies have visited our flower box than have ever visited before.

20. The museum downtown has the (*best, most good*) collection of gemstones I've ever seen.

Use of Comparisons

9d. Use the comparative degree when comparing two things. Use the superlative degree when comparing more than two things.

TWO THINGS	The light in the kitchen is bright**er** than the light in the den. [Two things are compared, so the comparative degree is used.]
MORE THAN TWO	Of all the lights in the house, the light in the study is bright**est.** [More than two things are compared, so the superlative degree is used.]

EXERCISE A Underline the correct modifier in parentheses in each of the following sentences.

Example 1. Between the two, isn't Frank's cat *(heaviest, heavier)*? [Only two things are being compared, so the comparative degree is used.]

1. Who was *(least, less)* curious about your secret, DeShawn, Angelo, or Nancy? [Which degree of comparison should be used when more than two things are compared?]

2. In the litter of six puppies, the black and gray puppy looked *(cuter, cutest)*.

3. Which of the two runners can sprint *(farthest, farther)* in sixty seconds?

4. The *(newest, newer)* mouse pad is on the table with the others.

5. Of the four sets of golf clubs available, the first set is *(lighter, lightest)*.

9e. Avoid using double comparisons.

A ***double comparison*** is the use of two modifiers in the comparative degree or two modifiers in the superlative degree to describe the same word.

DOUBLE	Peggy is more older than Janet. [*Older* already describes *Peggy*. The use of *more* creates a needless double comparison.]
	Of the three packages, this one is most smallest. [*Smallest* already describes *packages*. The use of *most* creates a needless double comparison.]
STANDARD	Peggy is **older** than Janet. [The adjective *older* describes Peggy.]
	Of the three packages, this one is **smallest.** [The adjective *smallest* describes *packages*.]

9f. Include the word *other* or *else* when comparing one member of a group with the rest of the group.

ILLOGICAL	Janet is younger than everyone in her class. [Janet is a member of her own class, so she cannot be younger than everyone: She cannot be younger than herself.]
LOGICAL	Janet is younger than everyone **else** in her class. [Janet can be younger than everyone *else* in her class.]

GO ON

| **9g.** | Be sure comparisons are clear. |

Make certain that the items being compared are clearly indicated and that the comparison is complete, especially if the comparison could be misunderstood.

> **UNCLEAR** Virgil's comments were nicer than Paula. [*Comments* cannot logically be compared to a person, *Paula*. The items being compared are unclear.]
>
> **CLEAR** Virgil's comments were nicer than Paula**'s comments.** [Virgil's *comments* can be compared to Paula's *comments*.]
>
> **UNCLEAR** Angela takes breakfast to her grandparents more frequently than anyone else. [*Anyone else* can refer to other persons to whom Angela takes breakfast, or it can refer to other persons who, like Angela, take breakfast to her grandparents. The comparison is incomplete.]
>
> **CLEAR** Angela takes breakfast to her grandparents more frequently than **she takes breakfast to** anyone else. [It is clear that *anyone else* refers to other persons to whom Angela takes breakfast.]

EXERCISE B Decide whether each of the following sentences uses a comparison correctly or incorrectly. On the line provided, write *C* for *correct* or *I* for *incorrect*.

Examples ___I___ **1.** This pepper is hotter than all the peppers. [To avoid an illogical comparison, the word *other* should be used before *peppers*.]

___I___ **2.** We have known Tim longer than Diane. [To avoid an incomplete comparison, the sentence might read *We have known Tim longer than we have known Diane.*]

_____ **6.** Is this highway busier than any other highway in the city? [Is this comparison complete?]

_____ **7.** The head cheerleader's voice is more louder than everyone else's voice. [Should two modifiers in the comparative degree describe the same noun?]

_____ **8.** Mateo finished his assignment faster than anyone in his study group.

_____ **9.** This book's title is more interesting than that book.

_____ **10.** Sandra visits them more often than Jodi.

_____ **11.** With the use of a computer, the calculations can be completed faster than they can be completed without one.

_____ **12.** The average temperature in Phoenix is higher than Denver.

_____ **13.** Dr. Endo said, "These birds hide more cleverly than any animals."

_____ **14.** A visit to that gallery will be shorter than another gallery.

_____ **15.** The grass along the sidewalk is more greener than the grass near the house.

Placement of Modifiers A

Misplaced Modifiers

10a. Avoid using misplaced modifiers.

A *misplaced modifier* is a word or word group that describes the wrong word or word group in a sentence. To avoid writing a misplaced modifier, place the modifier as close as possible to the word or word group the modifier describes.

Misplaced Words, Phrases, and Clauses

MISPLACED	Excited, the ride was full of children. [Placed immediately before the noun *ride*, the modifier *Excited* describes *ride*. Can the *ride* be *excited*?]
CLEAR	The ride was full of **excited** children. [Placed immediately before the noun *children*, the modifier *excited* describes *children*. The children are excited.]
MISPLACED	The cat watched the ball twitching its whiskers. [The modifying phrase *twitching its whiskers* describes *ball*. Can the *ball* be *twitching its whiskers*?]
CLEAR	**Twitching its whiskers,** the cat watched the ball. [The modifying phrase *twitching its whiskers* modifies *cat.*]
MISPLACED	The gazelle leapt the fence, which had been growing impatient. [The modifying clause *which had been growing impatient* describes *fence*. Can the *fence* have *been growing impatient*?]
CLEAR	The gazelle, **which had been growing impatient,** leapt the fence. [The modifying clause is placed near the noun it modifies, *gazelle*.]

EXERCISE A Underline the misplaced modifier in each of the following sentences. Then, use proofreading symbols to show where the modifier should go in the sentence.

Examples 1. <u>Worried</u>, the message did not reach the family. [*Worried* should modify *family* rather than *message.*]

    2. Lava from the volcano poured down the hillside, <u>which had belched smoke for years.</u> [The adjective phrase *which had belched smoke for years* should modify *volcano* rather than *hillside.*]

1. Tired, the noise of the passing train didn't wake the little boy. [What adjective in the sentence is misplaced?]

2. I found the book in my locker that I thought I had lost. [What adjective clause in the sentence is misplaced?]

3. Waiting, the clock was the focus of the assembly line workers.

4. Nervous, the awards were presented to the contestants.

GO ON

5. The girl apologized for the broken window with the baseball glove.

6. Disappointed, a fourth-place ribbon was awarded to the runner.

7. The sweater is hanging in the hall closet with a moth hole in it.

8. She knew, prepared, that the interview would go well.

9. The ropes course is popular with students, thrilling and challenging.

10. The snow covered the countryside, which had been falling all night long.

Squinting Modifiers

10b. Avoid misplacing a modifying word, phrase, or clause so that it seems to modify either of two words. Such a misplaced modifier is often called a *squinting,* or a *two-way, modifier.*

> **SQUINTING** The teacher said when the bell rang she would let her class study. [It is unclear whether the class will be allowed to study when the bell rings or whether the teacher spoke when the bell rang.]
>
> **CLEAR** **When the bell rang,** the teacher said she would let her class study. [The teacher spoke when the bell rang.]
>
> **CLEAR** The teacher said she would let her class study **when the bell rang.** [The class will be allowed to study when the bell rings.]

EXERCISE B Underline the squinting modifier in each of the following sentences. Then, use proofreading symbols to show where the modifier could be placed to make the sentence clear. Hint: There is more than one way to correct each sentence; show only one correction.

Example 1. The announcer said <u>before the game</u> two players were replaced. [The sentence now clearly says that the announcer said that two players were replaced prior to the game.]

11. The newscaster said yesterday no one was hurt in the accident. [Did the newscaster speak yesterday, or did the accident occur yesterday?]

12. Michael said when he woke up this morning he was really hungry.

13. She told me during class I could use her computer.

14. The child's mother said after lunch she would take him to the playground.

15. The director said once the play was over the cast would have a party.

Placement of Modifiers B

Dangling Modifiers

| **10c.** | Avoid using dangling modifiers. |

A *dangling modifier* is a modifier that does not clearly and sensibly modify any word or word group in the sentence.

To correct a dangling modifier, add or replace words to make the meaning of the sentence sensible and clear.

> **DANGLING** Happy, a new phone was purchased. [Was the phone happy?]
>
> **CLEAR** **Happy, Kim** purchased a new phone. [The independent clause that follows the modifier *Happy* has been rewritten with a new subject, *Kim.*]
>
> **DANGLING** Having adjusted the carburetor, the engine still idled roughly. [Who adjusted the carburetor?]
>
> **CLEAR** **After Mike adjusted the carburetor,** the engine still idled roughly. [A subject, *Mike,* has been added to the word group that begins the sentence, and the word *Having* has been replaced.]

EXERCISE A Underline the dangling modifier in each of the following sentences.

Examples 1. <u>After completing the bibliography,</u> the research paper was finished. [The adverb phrase *After completing the bibliography* does not clearly and sensibly modify a word or word group. *Who* or *what* completed the bibliography?]

2. The jacket was returned to the store, <u>having decided it was too short.</u> [The participial phrase *having decided it was too short* does not clearly and sensibly modify a word or word group. *Who* or *what* decided that the jacket was too short?]

1. Having left the house too late for the movie, a Chinese restaurant was the destination. [Is it clear *who* left the house?]

2. Meowing loudly, the noise came from the garage. [Is it clear *what* was meowing loudly?]

3. Not wanting to miss the program, the VCR was programmed.

4. Thrilled by the unexpected goal, the excitement grew.

5. While visiting my aunt's house, storm clouds gathered.

6. Lost, the map's faulty directions were misleading.

7. Researching in the library, the online catalog was very helpful.

8. Following the strong scent, the trail led to a clump of trees.

9. Listening with rapt attention, the disc jockey gave the contest's final clue.

10. After working on the farm all summer, his muscles had grown strong.

> **NOTE** Dangling modifiers often happen when a writer combines sentences that have different subjects. Sometimes a writer revises one part of a sentence without looking at the rest of the sentence.
>
> | ORIGINAL | Craig was sitting in the dark movie theater. His weary eyelids drooped shut. [The two sentences have different subjects, *Craig* and *eyelids*.] |
> |---|---|
> | DANGLING | Sitting in the dark movie theater, Craig's weary eyelids drooped shut. [The writer has combined the sentences by inserting a participial phrase from one sentence into the other, but the combination doesn't make sense. Craig's *eyelids* are not *sitting in the dark movie theater*. Instead, *Craig* is.] |
> | CLEAR | **While Craig was sitting in the dark movie theater,** his weary eyelids drooped shut. [The writer has combined the sentences by making the first sentence into a subordinate clause with *Craig* as its subject. The subject of the independent clause is *eyelids*.] |

EXERCISE B Underline the dangling modifier in each of the following sentences. Then, on the line provided, rewrite each sentence to eliminate the dangling modifier. Hint: There is more than one way to correctly revise each dangling modifier.

Example 1. Enjoying her walk in the garden, the roses were just beginning to bloom. [The subject *She* has been added to the sentence. The present participle *Enjoying* has been changed to a main verb, *enjoyed,* and the independent clause *the roses were just beginning to bloom* has been changed into a subordinate clause explaining why she enjoyed her walk.]

She enjoyed her walk in the garden because the roses were just beginning to bloom.

11. Frustrated by the traffic on the highway, a different way home was decided. [Who was frustrated by the traffic?]

_____

12. Pulling with all their might, the wagon was still stuck in the mud.

_____

13. Barking to be let inside, the newspaper was brought in.

_____

14. Having covered the lawn, Ray raked the fallen leaves into a pile.

_____

15. After watching the weather report, the windows were closed.

_____

Glossary of Usage A

accept, except *Accept* is a verb meaning "to receive favorably." The word *except* can be a preposition or a verb. When *except* is a preposition, it means "excluding." When *except* is a verb, it means "to leave out."

> **EXAMPLES** Will you **accept** the gift? [The verb *accept* means "to receive favorably."]
>
> She liked all colors **except** blue. [The preposition *except* means "excluding."]
>
> They should not **except** him from jury duty. [The verb *except* means "to leave out."]

a lot *A lot* is always two words and is always informal. *A lot* can be used as a noun or as an adverb. When *a lot* is used as a noun, it means "a large amount" or "a large number." When *a lot* is used as an adverb, it means "a great deal" or "very much."

> **EXAMPLES** Mrs. Chester donated **a lot** of old clothes. [*A lot* is used as a noun and is two words.]
>
> Ray finished the test **a lot** sooner than he thought he would. [*A lot* is used as an adverb describing *sooner* and is two words.]

EXERCISE A Underline the word in parentheses that correctly completes the meaning of each of the following sentences.

Example 1. There sure is (<u>a lot</u>, alot) of noise in here! [*A lot* is a noun meaning "a large amount," and it should be two words.]

1. Were you (*excepted, accepted*) from taking the exam? [Which word is a verb meaning "left out"?]

2. During the study (*alot, a lot*) of gorillas sat down next to her.

3. Everyone (*except, accept*) Mr. Pania is able to come to the party.

4. Tina (*excepted, accepted*) the invitation to join the honor society.

5. Let's go early so that we avoid (*a lot, alot*) of the traffic.

at *At* should not end questions or clauses that begin with *where*.

> **NONSTANDARD** Where is the auditorium at?   I don't know where I left my shoes at.
>
> **STANDARD** Where is the auditorium?   I don't know where I left my shoes.

beside, besides *Beside* is a preposition meaning "next to." *Besides* can be a preposition or an adverb. When *besides* is a preposition, it means "in addition to." When *besides* is an adverb, it means "moreover."

> **EXAMPLES** Sit **beside** me. [*Beside* means "next to."]
>
> No one finished the homework **besides** me. [*Besides* means "in addition to."]
>
> The homework wasn't hard; **besides,** I had some extra time to work on it. [The adverb *besides* means "moreover."]

GO ON ➡

between, among   Use *between* when referring to only two items or to more than two items when each item is being compared to each of the other items. Use *among* when you refer to more than two items and are not comparing each item to each of the other items.

> **EXAMPLES**   My brother sat **between** my mother and my father. [*Between* is used because only two items, *mother* and *father* are referred to.]
>
> Those are the differences **between** raspberries, blackberries, and gooseberries. [*Between* is used because each item is compared to each of the other items.]
>
> The seven clerks divided the work **among** themselves. [*Among* is used because more than two items are referred to.]

done   *Done* is the past participle of the verb *do*. *Did* is the past form of the verb *do*. Always use a helping verb before the past participle *done*. Do not use *done* instead of *did*.

> **NONSTANDARD**   She already done the assignment.
>
> **STANDARD**   She **had** already **done** the assignment. [The verb *had done* is the past perfect form of the verb *do*. It includes *had*—the past form of the helping verb *has*—and the past participle *done*.]
>
> **STANDARD**   She already **did** the assignment. [The verb *did* is the past form of the verb *do*.]

EXERCISE B Underline the word in parentheses that correctly completes each of the following sentences.

Example 1. Would anyone (*beside*, <u>*besides*</u>) Justin like more free time? [The preposition *besides* means "in addition to," so the correct choice is *besides*.]

6. Where in the house did the dog find that box of (*treats at, treats*)? [Should *at* end a question that begins with *Where*?]

7. Please put your backpacks (*beside, besides*) your chairs. [Which word means "next to"?]

8. The drill bits are lying wherever the drill (*is, is at*).

9. (*Beside, Besides*) Max and Santos, has anyone else been told about the meeting?

10. Nothing (*beside, besides*) a few crumbs of bread remained.

11. Describe some similarities (*between, among*) Spanish, French, and Italian.

12. Divide the four sandwiches (*between, among*) the three of us.

13. The gymnast (*did, done*) a flip and landed perfectly upright.

14. I folded the clothes after I (*done, did*) the laundry.

15. Are there any differences (*between, among*) these two jackets?

Glossary of Usage B

don't, doesn't   *Don't* is the contraction of *do not*. *Doesn't* is the contraction of *does not*. Use *doesn't* with singular subjects except *I* and *you*. Use *don't* with plural subjects and *I* and *you*.

> **EXAMPLES**   My mother **doesn't** like garlic. [The subject is singular, so the contraction is *doesn't*.]
>
> Our cats **don't** eat garlic. [The subject is plural, so the contraction is *don't*.]
>
> I **don't** like garlic, either. [The subject of the verb is *I*, so the contraction is *don't*.]

fewer, less   Use *fewer* to describe a noun that can be counted. *Fewer* tells "how many" about the noun. Use *less* to describe an uncountable noun. *Less* tells "how much" about the noun.

> **EXAMPLES**   Tanya says that we should eat **fewer** servings of sugary snacks than we do. [*Servings* is a countable noun, so the correct adjective is *fewer*, which tells "how many" servings.]
>
> Mr. Ortiz says that many students drink **less** water than they should. [*Water* is uncountable, so the correct adjective is *less*, which tells "how much" water.]

EXERCISE A Underline the word in parentheses in each of the following sentences that correctly completes the sentence.

Examples 1. He (*don't*, *doesn't*) want to go swimming. [The subject of the verb is the singular pronoun *He*, so *doesn't* is the correct contraction to use.]

2. Kim thought the coach should schedule (*fewer*, *less*) practices. [The noun *practices* can be counted, so the correct word is *fewer*.]

1. Why (*don't*, *doesn't*) you bring your guitar when you come over? [Does the subject *you* take the contraction *don't* or does it take *doesn't*?]

2. If the engine is properly tuned, will it use (*fewer*, *less*) gasoline? [Is the noun *gasoline* countable?]

3. In winter, those trees (*don't*, *doesn't*) have any leaves.

4. (*Fewer*, *Less*) children are at tonight's game than were here last week.

5. Mary (*don't*, *doesn't*) have a driver's license yet.

6. Our dog (*don't*, *doesn't*) dislike cats at all.

7. This set of shelves holds (*fewer*, *less*) gallons of milk than the old set held.

8. I (*don't*, *doesn't*) remember the words to that song.

9. When she shops carefully, she spends (*fewer*, *less*) money.

10. My mother has (*fewer*, *less*) days of vacation this year.

GO ON

hisself, theirself,* and *theirselves Use *himself* instead of *hisself*. Use *themselves* instead of *theirself* or *theirselves*. *Hisself, theirself,* and *theirselves* are nonstandard forms.

NONSTANDARD	The children made lunch theirselves.
STANDARD	The children made lunch **themselves.**
NONSTANDARD	He is teaching hisself Russian.
STANDARD	He is teaching **himself** Russian.

kind of* and *sort of In formal speech or writing, avoid using *kind of* or *sort of* instead of the adverbs *rather* or *somewhat*.

NONSTANDARD	The governor's speech was kind of long.
STANDARD	The governor's speech was **somewhat** long.
	The governor's speech was **rather** long.

EXERCISE B Underline the word in parentheses that is correct according to formal, standard English in each of the following sentences.

Examples 1. The students built the greenhouses (*theirself, themselves, theirselves*). [*Themselves* is the correct, standard form. *Theirself* and *theirselves* are nonstandard.]

2. The teacher explained that the exam would be (*rather, sort of*) long. [*Sort of* is informal usage, so *rather* is the better choice.]

11. Has your little brother learned to tie his shoes by (*hisself, himself*)? [Which of the two pronouns is correct standard English?]

12. Would it be possible for us to move along (*somewhat, kind of*) faster? [Which word is in standard, formal English?]

13. He bought (*himself, hisself*) a new bicycle helmet.

14. Although the truck runs (*kind of, rather*) noisily, the cab's interior is quiet.

15. Brian drove (*hisself, himself*) to his dentist appointment.

16. All children have to learn to do certain tasks for (*theirselves, themselves, theirself*).

17. The oven's temperature was (*sort of, rather*) high.

18. My understanding of electronics is (*somewhat, kind of*) weak.

19. Many young animals can't take care of (*themselves, theirself, theirselves*).

20. The chemical reaction turned the solution (*sort of, somewhat*) blue.

Glossary of Usage C

supposed to, used to,* and *try to   Avoid omitting the *–d* ending of the past forms of *suppose* and *use,* especially before *to.* Use *try to* rather than *try and.*

> **NONSTANDARD**   He use to say he would try and call us once a week.
>
> **STANDARD**   He **used to** say he would **try to** call us once a week. [The past form of *use* has a *–d* ending, and *try to* is correct.]

than, then   *Than* is a subordinating conjunction used in comparisons. *Then* is an adverb telling *when* and usually means "after that" or "at that time."

> **NONSTANDARD**   I woke up earlier then I usually do.
>
> **STANDARD**   I woke up earlier **than** I usually do.
>
> **NONSTANDARD**   I got dressed and than went for a walk.
>
> **STANDARD**   I got dressed and **then** went for a walk.

EXERCISE A Underline the word in parentheses that is correct according to formal, standard English in each of the following sentences.

Examples 1. Karen was *(suppose, supposed)* to meet us at five o'clock. [The past form of *suppose* should have a *–d* ending.]

    2. Are these socks cleaner *(than, then)* those are? [One pair of socks is being compared to others, so *than* is the correct word to use.]

1. Are we *(suppose, supposed)* to turn in these projects next week? [How is the past form of *suppose* formed?]

2. First, we'll cook breakfast, and *(than, then)* we can decide what to do. [Which word, *then* or *than,* is used as an adverb telling *when*?]

3. The pelican is going to try *(and, to)* catch another fish.

4. These eggs are larger *(than, then)* the ones we usually buy.

5. A raccoon *(use, used)* to live in a park around the corner from our house.

6. I don't think I can eat more *(than, then)* two oranges.

7. We should try *(to, and)* write to each other more often.

8. Before he began his new hobby, my uncle *(used, use)* to watch television every night.

9. Remove the wrapper and *(than, then)* open the package.

10. What shall we do *(than, then)*?

GO ON

them*, *this here*, and *that there   This, that, these, and those are the standard forms of demonstrative adjectives. Do not use *them* instead of *those*. Do not add *here* or *there* after *this* or *that*.

NONSTANDARD	This here dog is brown.	That there dog is white.	Them dogs bark a lot.
STANDARD	**This** dog is brown.	**That** dog is white.	**Those** dogs bark a lot.

when* and *where   Do not use *when* to begin a definition unless you are defining a time. Do not use *where* to begin a definition unless you are defining a place.

NONSTANDARD   Roasting is when you cook food in an oven.

Having the flu is where you have chills, fever, and a headache.

STANDARD   Five o'clock is **when** we'll begin roasting our dinner.

Summer camp is **where** she caught the flu.

your*, *you're   *You're* is a contraction of *you* and *are*. *Your* is a possessive form of the pronoun *you*. *Your* means "belonging to you."

EXAMPLES   **You're** the first person who bought a ticket. [*You're* is a contracted form of *you are*.]

You should bring **your** sweater or jacket. [*Your* means "belonging to you."]

EXERCISE B Underline the word in parentheses that is correct according to formal, standard English in each of the following sentences.

Examples 1. Do you know who lives in *(this, this here)* house? [*This here* is nonstandard usage. *This* is the standard form.]

2. Rowing is *(where, how)* people use oars to move a boat. [*Where* means "at that place," and *Rowing* is not a place.]

11. Why do you need all of *(them, those)* pencils? [Is *them* a standard form of a demonstrative adjective?]

12. Las Vegas is *(where, when)* I first went to school. [Is *Las Vegas* a time?]

13. *(That there, That)* couch is really comfortable!

14. *(Those, Them)* flowers were picked this morning.

15. Are you sure that this is *(your, you're)* room?

16. *(Your, You're)* supposed to be at practice this afternoon.

17. I've been trying for an hour to open *(this, this here)* jar of pickles.

18. You can make a call from *(that, that there)* telephone.

19. Tell me *(your, you're)* e-mail address.

20. Tennis is a game *(where, in which)* the players hit a ball back and forth across a net.

Glossary of Usage D
Double Negatives

Using **two** negative words for **one** negative idea is called a *double negative.* Avoid using double negatives. Common negative words are *no, not, never, none, no one, nothing, nowhere, hardly, neither, scarcely* and *barely.*

NONSTANDARD	I couldn't hardly see the movie screen from that seat. [*Couldn't* is a contraction of *could not. Not* and *hardly* are both negative words.]
STANDARD	I could **hardly** see the movie screen from that seat. [The sentence has only one negative word, *hardly.*]
STANDARD	I could**n't** see the movie screen from that seat. [The sentence has only one negative word, *not*, which is found in the contraction *couldn't*.]

EXERCISE A Use proofreading symbols to correct each of the following sentences containing double negatives. Hint: There is more than one way to correct each double negative; show only one correction.

Example 1. The traffic is so heavy that we can't barely get out of the driveway. [*Can't* is a contraction for *can not.* Used together, *not* and *barely* form a double negative. Deleting the apostrophe and *t* in *can't* to form the word *can* corrects the double negative. A second way to correct the sentence would be to delete *barely,* a negative word: *The traffic is so heavy that we can't get out of the driveway.*]

1. I don't hardly know anyone in that class. [Which two words or word parts are negative?]

2. Don't none of you want to eat now?

3. That bus is not going nowhere with that flat tire.

4. There isn't scarcely enough room in here to hold a reception.

5. The dog hasn't never been to the beach.

Nonsexist Language

Gender-specific words apply only to men or only to women. Often these words refer to occupations or professions. Some gender-specific words, like *manpower, mankind,* and *man-made,* are commonly used. Substitute gender-specific words with words that apply to all people.

Indefinite pronouns such as *anybody, anyone, each, either, everybody, everyone, neither, nobody, no one, one, somebody,* and *someone* are singular and do not have a gender. Avoid using masculine singular pronouns, such as *he, him,* and *his,* to refer to one of these words.

Nonsexist language is language that at once applies to both male and female people. Use nonsexist language rather than gender-specific words.

GO ON ➡

GENDER-SPECIFIC	NONSEXIST
stewardess, steward	flight attendant
fireman	firefighter
policeman	police officer
man-made	synthetic, manufactured
manpower	workers
mailman	mail carrier
mankind	humanity, people
he	he or she
him	him or her
his	his or her

EXERCISE B Use proofreading symbols to replace the gender-specific word in each of the following sentences with a nonsexist word that makes sense. Hint: There may be more than one way to replace a gender-specific word; show only one replacement.

Example 1. Some ~~man-made~~ flooring materials look like wood. [*Man-made* means "made by

people." A nonsexist word meaning *man-made* is *synthetic.*]

6. Our mailman, whose name is Susan, is late today. [What word applies only to men? Which

nonsexist word can you substitute for that gender-specific word?]

7. The stewardess served snacks and drinks to the passengers.

8. A policeman was directing traffic in front of the stadium.

9. That huge store needs a lot of manpower.

10. My niece Tina wants to become a fireman.

EXERCISE C Underline the word or word group in parentheses that appropriately completes the sentence without being gender-specific.

Example 1. Anyone who wants a ride should give (*their,* <u>*his or her,*</u> *his*) name to Grace. [*Anyone* is

a singular pronoun. *His or her* is also singular and includes both males and females.]

11. <u>Everybody</u> wants to bring (*their, her, a*) backpack. [*Everybody* is a singular pronoun. Would the

best choice be one of the pronouns or the article *a?*]

12. <u>No one</u> wants to go to that movie (*by themselves, by himself, alone*).

13. Did <u>anybody</u> leave (*his or her, their, her*) notebook on the bus?

14. If <u>someone</u> would move (*their, that, his*) car, I could get by.

15. <u>Everyone</u> introduced (*his or her, their, his*) parents.

Capitalization A

First Words

12a. Capitalize the first word in every sentence.

> **EXAMPLE**   **T**he bluebonnets are blooming. [*The* is the first word of the sentence.]

A quoted sentence also begins with a capital letter, even when the quoted sentence begins in the middle of a longer sentence.

> **EXAMPLES**   Miguel said, "**T**he tennis match is next Saturday." [*The* is capitalized because it is the first word of the sentence that is quoted.]
>
> "**W**e painted my brother's bedroom today," said Maureen. [*We* is the first word of the sentence that is quoted. *We* is also the first word of the longer sentence.]

EXERCISE A Circle the letter that should be capitalized in each of the following sentences.

Examples 1. Richard asked, "(W)hen is your family moving, Eduardo?" [The *w* in *when* should be capitalized because it is the first word of the quoted sentence.]

2. (I)s Olympia or Seattle the capital of Washington? [The *i* in *is* should be capitalized because it is the first word of the sentence.]

1. my neighbor grows the prettiest flowers on the whole block. [Is the first word of the sentence capitalized?]

2. Paul asked, "did you understand last night's homework?" [Is the first word of the quoted sentence capitalized?]

3. "one of the problems was difficult," said Rita.

4. we grilled chicken and made a salad for lunch.

5. the bicycle race begins at noon tomorrow.

6. Mark pointed and said, "that's my house."

7. if the bus doesn't come soon, we'll be late.

8. Anna shouted, "call me at home later!"

9. put the glass bottles in the recycling bin.

10. After a few minutes, Angel whispered loudly, "this door isn't locked!"

GO ON ➡

Salutations and Closings

12b. Capitalize the first word in both the salutation and the closing of a letter.

The salutation is the greeting that begins a letter. The closing is the short line at the end of a letter, right before your signature.

SALUTATIONS Dear Mrs. Bartlett: My dear granddaughter,

CLOSINGS Very truly yours,   Sincerely,

NOTE Except for names and titles, the first word is the only word that is capitalized in a salutation or closing. In the examples, *Mrs.* is capitalized because it is a title. *Bartlett* is capitalized because it is a name.

EXERCISE B Circle the letter that should be capitalized in each salutation or closing.

Example 1. ⓓear Mrs. Lake, [The *d* in *dear* should be capitalized because it is the first letter of the salutation of a letter.]

11. sincerely yours, [Is the first letter of the closing capitalized?]

12. dear Senator McIntyre:

13. dear Officer Hammett:

14. dearest Grandma,

15. regards,

The Pronoun *I*

12c. Capitalize the pronoun *I*.

In English, the pronoun *I* is always capitalized, even if it is not the first word of a sentence.

EXAMPLES Mom and **I** helped with the garage sale.

I'll see you after math class. [The pronoun *I* is always capitalized, even when it appears in a contraction.]

EXERCISE C Circle the letter that should be capitalized in each of the following sentences.

Example 1. ⓘ've finished my algebra homework. [The pronoun *I* should always be capitalized.]

16. i will major in history in college. [Is the pronoun *I* capitalized?]

17. Should i volunteer at the hospital this summer?

18. If you'll cook dinner tonight, i'll wash the dishes.

19. i'd like a glass of water, please.

20. She and i ran two miles yesterday.

Capitalization B

Proper Nouns and Proper Adjectives

12d. Capitalize proper nouns and proper adjectives.

A *proper noun* names a particular person, place, thing, or idea. Proper nouns are capitalized. A *common noun* names a kind or type of person, place, thing, or idea. A common noun generally is not capitalized unless it begins a sentence or is part of a title.

PROPER NOUNS	Chicago	Brentwood Park	Colorado River
COMMON NOUNS	city	park	river

A *proper adjective* is an adjective formed from a proper noun. A proper adjective is capitalized, too. Some proper adjectives are formed by giving the proper noun an ending such as *–ish*, *–ese*, *–ic*, *–ian*, or *–an*. Sometimes the proper adjective is exactly the same as the proper noun.

> **EXAMPLES** Pacific coastline [has the same form as the proper noun]
> Chinese vase [formed from the proper noun *China*]
> Irish ancestry [formed from the proper noun *Ireland*]

EXERCISE A Circle the word or word group in each pair that is capitalized correctly.

Examples 1. a. texas   **b.** (Arizona)

[The name *Arizona* is correctly capitalized. The *t* in *texas* should be capitalized.]

2. a. (the Japanese restaurant)   **b.** a European Vacation

[The proper adjective *Japanese* is correctly capitalized. The *E* in *European* is correctly

capitalized, but *vacation* is a common noun and should not be capitalized.]

1. a. Sears Tower   **b.** eiffel tower

[Which word group is a correctly capitalized proper noun?]

2. a. the Roman ruins   **b.** a greek vase

[Which word group contains a correctly capitalized proper adjective?]

3. a. maya angelou   **b.** Alice Walker

4. a. Mississippi River   **b.** Caribbean sea

5. a. John f. Kennedy   **b.** Lyndon B. Johnson

6. a. Shea Stadium   **b.** mile high stadium

7. a. William Shakespeare   **b.** christopher marlowe

8. a. lake pontchartrain   **b.** Lake Charles

9. a. the Russian language   **b.** the arabic alphabet

10. a. a city in California   **b.** the Mountains in Colorado

GO ON ➡

People, Animals, and Initials

Capitalize the names and initials of people and animals.

PEOPLE	George Eliot	Henri Matisse	S. I. Hayakawa
ANIMALS	Buddy	Babe	Peter Rabbit

NOTE Some proper nouns consist of more than one word. In these names, prepositions of fewer than five letters (*at, in, of, on, over,* and so on), articles (*a, an,* and *the*), and coordinating conjunctions (*and, but, or, nor, for, yet,* and *so*) are generally not capitalized.

> **EXAMPLES** Winnie-the-Pooh [The article *the* is not capitalized.]
>
> Catherine **of** Aragon [The short preposition *of* is not capitalized.]

EXERCISE B Write a name that corresponds to each word group below. Be sure to capitalize the proper nouns that you write. You can make up a name if you don't know a corresponding proper noun.

Examples 1. a president of the United States _____Abraham Lincoln_____ [*Abraham Lincoln* is a

proper noun because it is the name of a specific president.]

2. a famous singer _____Enrico Caruso_____ [*Enrico Caruso* is a proper noun because

it is the name of a specific singer.]

11. the author of a book _____

12. one of my relatives _____

13. a dog _____

14. a teacher _____

15. the leader of another country _____

16. a cat in my neighborhood _____

17. a coach at my school _____

18. a person who has been in the news recently _____

19. the full name of a close friend _____

20. the nickname of someone I know _____

Capitalization C

Geographical Names

Capitalize geographical names, including the names of towns and cities, counties, townships, provinces, states, countries, continents, islands, mountains, bodies of water, parks and forests, other natural landmarks, regions, roads, streets, highways, and other place names.

EXAMPLES	**A**tlanta [city]	**S**pringdale [town]
	Iowa [state]	**B**razil [country]
	Park **A**venue [street name]	**B**luebird **L**ane [street name]
	Atlantic **O**cean [body of water]	**O**ld **F**aithful [natural landmark]

NOTE Some geographical names consist of more than one word. In these names, prepositions of fewer than five letters (*at, in, of, on, over,* and so on), articles (*a, an,* and *the*), and coordinating conjunctions (*and, but, or, nor, for, yet,* and *so*) are generally not capitalized.

EXAMPLES Bay **of** Biscay [The preposition *of* is not capitalized.]

Denali National Park **a**nd Preserve [The conjunction *and* is not capitalized.]

EXERCISE A Circle any letter that should be capitalized in each of the following sentences.

Examples 1. Where is the (S)trait of (m)agellan? [The *s* in *strait* and the *m* in *magellan* should be capitalized because the Strait of Magellan names a specific body of water. The short preposition *of* should not be capitalized.]

    2. We helped paint the house on (r)avenwood (a)venue. [The *r* in *ravenwood* and the *a* in *avenue* should be capitalized because Ravenwood Avenue is the name of a specific street.]

1. australia is in the Southern Hemisphere. [Is the name of a country capitalized?]

2. We floated on a raft down the comal river. [Is each word that names a specific body of water capitalized?]

3. My aunt lives in raleigh, north carolina.

4. kentucky horse park is a beautiful park.

5. Italy is located on the continent of europe.

6. We live in davidson county in Tennessee.

7. We studied india today in geography class.

8. The picture of the alps in the textbook was breathtaking.

9. I have only seen the grand canyon from an airplane window.

10. Is san antonio one of the largest cities in the United States?

GO ON

Planets, Stars, and Constellations

The names of planets, stars, constellations, and other heavenly bodies are capitalized.

> **EXAMPLES** Jupiter [planet]   **H**alley's comet [heavenly body]
>
> **B**ig **D**ipper [constellation]   **O**rion [constellation]

NOTE▶ The words *sun* and *moon* are generally not capitalized. The word *earth* is capitalized only when used with the name of another heavenly body that is capitalized.

> **EXAMPLES** The planet Mercury is smaller than **E**arth. [*Earth* is capitalized because it is used with the name of another planet.]
>
> One of **e**arth's most precious resources is clean water. [The word *earth* is not capitalized because it is not used with the name of any other heavenly body.]

EXERCISE B Circle each letter that should be capitalized in each of the following sentences.

Examples 1. All of the planets, including ⓟluto, revolve around the sun. [*Pluto* should be capitalized because it is the name of a planet, but *sun* is generally not capitalized.]

2. The constellation Ⓛeo is bright this time of year. [*Leo* should be capitalized because it is the name of a constellation.]

11. We studied saturn in astronomy class today. [Is the name of a planet capitalized?]

12. alpha centauri is a very bright star. [Are all the words in the name of a star capitalized?]

13. Isn't mars sometimes called the "Red Planet"?

14. The pleiades is a cluster of stars in the Taurus constellation.

15. Is Jupiter warmer or colder than earth?

16. We are looking for the little dipper tonight.

17. The observatory showed a documentary on neptune.

18. That star is named antares.

19. One of the moons of Jupiter is called io.

20. venus is the second planet from our sun.

Capitalization D

Organizations, Teams, Government Bodies, and Institutions

Capitalize the names of organizations, teams, institutions, and government bodies.

> **EXAMPLES**   American Cancer Society [organization]
> Carson City High School Chargers [team]
> St. Francis Memorial Hospital [institution]
> Congress [government body]

NOTE▶ The names of some organizations and institutions consist of more than one word. In these names, prepositions of fewer than five letters (*at, in, of, on, over,* and so on), articles (*a, an,* and *the*), and coordinating conjunctions (*and, but, or, nor, for, yet,* and *so*) are generally not capitalized.

> **EXAMPLES**   Department **of** Public Safety [The short preposition *of* is not capitalized.]
> Housing **and** Urban Development [The conjunction *and* is not capitalized.]

EXERCISE A Circle each letter that should be capitalized in each of the following sentences.

Example 1. My brother is attending the ⓤniversity of ⓟennsylvania in the fall. [*University* and *Pennsylvania* should be capitalized, but the preposition *of* should not be capitalized.]

1. The students met with the head of the environmental protection agency. [Are all the words in the name of a government body capitalized?]

2. Katie's good grades earned her membership in the national honor society.

3. My brother Ben joined the united states army.

4. Who is the new coach for the carbondale cougars?

5. My mother is a surgeon at frankfurt general hospital.

Businesses and Brand Names

Capitalize the names of businesses and the brand names of business products. Do not capitalize the name of a type of product.

> **EXAMPLES**   Johnson & Johnson [business name]
> Band-Aid [product brand name]
> bandage [product type]

GO ON ▶

EXERCISE B Circle each letter that should be capitalized in each of the following sentences.

Example 1. My grandfather started his own business, the ⓜiller Ⓒorporation. [*Miller Corporation* should be capitalized because it is the name of a specific business.]

6. My mother sold our honda civic this weekend. [Are all the words that name a business or a brand name of a product capitalized?]

7. Does that builder use kohler plumbing fixtures?

8. The computers in the library are made by dell.

9. We bought colgate toothpaste at the supermarket.

10. Karen's uncle owns kelly's deli on Baker Street.

Buildings and Other Structures

Capitalize the names of particular buildings and other structures. Do not capitalize the name of a type of building unless the word is part of the building's name.

    EXAMPLES   Chrysler Building   Golden Gate Bridge
                     Ritz Hotel   Parkfield Zoo

NOTE Unless it is the first word of a sentence, the word *the* is not usually capitalized, even though we often say or write *the* before the name of a building or structure.

    EXAMPLES   Is your family staying at **t**he Ritz Hotel?
                     Isn't **t**he Golden Gate Bridge beautiful at night?

EXERCISE C Circle each letter that should be capitalized in the following sentences.

Example 1. That big building is the Ⓣrump Ⓣower. [*Trump Tower* should be capitalized because it is the name of a particular building. The word *the* is not capitalized.]

11. ridgeway memorial hospital is down the street and on your left. [Are all the words in the name of a particular building capitalized?]

12. lakecrest mall has been in business for ten years.

13. Meet us at 7:00 P.M. at westfield cinema.

14. My little brother is having his birthday party at brownsville children's museum.

15. The new planetarium is called kaspar's cosmos.

         HOLT HANDBOOK | Fifth Course

Capitalization E

Monuments, Memorials, and Awards

Capitalize the names of monuments, memorials, awards, and other special prizes.

> **EXAMPLES** **V**ietnam **V**eterans **M**emorial [name of a memorial]
>
> **C**ongressional **M**edal of **H**onor [name of an award]
>
> **B**ooker **P**rize [name of a prize]

EXERCISE A Circle each letter that should be capitalized in the following sentences.

Example 1. N. Scott Momaday's novel *House Made of Dawn* won a Ⓟulitzer Ⓟrize in 1969.

> [*Pulitzer Prize* names a specific award and should be capitalized.]

1. mount rushmore national memorial features the faces of four former presidents. [Are all the words in the name of a monument capitalized?]

2. Sam won the national essay championship award.

3. Each year, the Academy of Motion Picture Arts and Sciences awards an oscar for the best movie of the year.

4. The rutherford grotto at National Park Cemetery honors the local heroes of foreign wars.

5. Our visit to the civil rights memorial was unforgettable.

Special Events, Holidays, Calendar Items, and Historical Events and Periods

Capitalize the names of special events, holidays, and calendar items including the names of months and days of the week. The names of historical events and historical periods are also capitalized.

> **EXAMPLES** **F**inal **F**our   **L**abor **D**ay   **A**pril
>
>   **S**unday   **I**ce **A**ge   **C**ivil **W**ar

NOTE▶ The names of the seasons are usually not capitalized. Capitalize the name of a season only if the season is personified or used in the name of a special event.

> **EXAMPLES** Are you working this **s**ummer? [The word *summer* is not being personified or used in the name of a special event.]
>
>   I found a job at the **S**ummer Jobs Festival. [*Summer* is part of the name of a special event.]

GO ON ▶

Developmental Language Skills

123

EXERCISE B Circle each letter that should be capitalized in the following sentences.

Example 1. Are you watching the Ⓢuper Ⓑowl today? [*Super Bowl* should be capitalized because it

is the name of a specific sporting event.]

6. The math test is on friday. [Is the name of a day of the week capitalized?]

7. We watched the olympics on television.

8. Is your little sister going to camp in july?

9. Mr. Rodriguez assigned the chapter on the american revolution.

10. Everyone wore green clothing to the st. patrick's day party.

Nationalities, Races, and Peoples

Capitalize the names of nationalities, races, and peoples.

EXAMPLES	**A**sian	a **C**herokee	the **B**razilians	**H**mong
	Tahitians	the **G**ermans	**C**anadians	the **P**ima

NOTE The names of nationalities, races, and peoples are often used as proper adjectives. These names should be capitalized whether they are used as proper nouns or proper adjectives.

> **EXAMPLE** **E**gyptian cotton

EXERCISE C Circle each letter that should be capitalized in each of the following sentences.

Example 1. Many Ⓘrish came to the United States because of the potato famine. [*Irish* should be

capitalized because it is the name of a particular nationality.]

11. My new stepmother is canadian. [Is the name of a nationality capitalized?]

12. My friend Jane is chippewa.

13. Michael wrote an essay about his italian heritage.

14. Maya told me about the african american holiday Kwanzaa.

15. Our town celebrates the mexican holiday Cinco de Mayo.

Capitalization F

Religions, Holy Days, Sacred Writings, and Deities

Capitalize the names of religions, religious followers, holy days and celebrations, sacred writings, and specific deities.

> **EXAMPLES**   **B**uddhism [religion]
> **E**aster [holy day]
> **T**almud [sacred writings]
> **A**llah [deity]

EXERCISE A Circle each letter that should be capitalized in the following sentences.

Example 1. Many scholars study the bible. [*Bible* should be capitalized because it is the name of a

sacred writing.]

1. Janet will be absent on yom kippur. [Are all the words in the name of a holy day capitalized?]

2. The ancient Greek god of the oceans was named poseidon.

3. We read passages from the koran in social studies.

4. Julian attends the presbyterian church on the corner of Rosedale and Pine.

5. I am learning about the history and customs of catholicism.

Ships, Trains, Aircraft, Spacecraft, and Other Vehicles

Capitalize the names of ships, trains, aircraft, spacecraft, and any other vehicle. The names of the make and model of a vehicle are capitalized, but the type or kind of vehicle is not capitalized.

> **EXAMPLES**   USS *Lexington* [ship]
> *Spruce Goose* [aircraft]
> *Columbia* [spacecraft]
> *Mir* space station [space station]

NOTE The names of ships, trains, aircraft, spacecraft, and other vehicles should be italicized (underlined).

EXERCISE B Circle each letter that should be capitalized in the following sentences.

Example 1. The name of that train is the *california zephyr*. [*California Zephyr* should be capitalized

because it is the name of a specific train.]

6. My dad once rode on the *orient express*. [Are all the words in the name of a specific train capitalized?]

7. Many people know that *air force one* is the President's plane.

8. The spacecraft *sojourner* photographed the surface of Mars.

9. He nicknamed his bicycle the *red whirlwind*.

10. One of Christopher Columbus's ships was called the *santa maria*.

School Subjects

Capitalize the names of language classes or course names that include a number. Otherwise, the names of school subjects are not capitalized.

> **EXAMPLES** algebra   Physical Education **II**   **S**panish

NOTE▶ Do not capitalize the class name *senior, junior, sophomore,* or *freshman* unless it is part of a specific event, place, or award.

> **EXAMPLES** **F**reshman **A**rts and **C**rafts **F**air [*Freshman* is capitalized because it is part of the name of a specific event.]
>
> Each **s**enior will mentor one of the new **f**reshmen. [The words *senior* and *freshmen* are not capitalized.]

EXERCISE C Circle each letter that should be capitalized in the following sentences. Draw a slash (/) through any letter that is capitalized but should not be.

Example 1. I am taking ⓖerman next year. [*German* is capitalized because it is the name of a language class.]

11. We learned about sculpture in Art class today. [Is the name of a school subject generally capitalized?]

12. In geography III class, our project is constructing a relief map of Africa.

13. Our school is offering a new course this year, computer science 101.

14. I had a dentist appointment this morning, so I was late to Science class.

15. Bring your book to french class today.

Capitalization G

Titles of Persons

Capitalize professional, military, civil, official, and noble titles of persons when the title comes before the person's name. Even if the title is abbreviated, capitalize it.

EXAMPLES   **S**en. Elizabeth Marco spoke to the school board yesterday. [*Sen.*, an abbreviation for the title *Senator*, is capitalized because it comes before a person's name.]

Is he running for **s**enator? [*Senator* does not come before a person's name and is not capitalized.]

EXERCISE A Circle each letter that should be capitalized in the following sentences. Draw a slash (/) through each letter that is capitalized but should not be.

Example 1. Who will run for G̸overnor in 2004? [*Governor* should not be capitalized because it is not followed by a person's name.]

1. The volunteers at the animal shelter gave mr. Williams an award. [Is a title before a person's name capitalized?]

2. I heard an interesting lecture in prof. Ian McDonald's class.

3. Harold made an appointment to see the Doctor.

4. Did you watch general Powell's speech on television last night?

5. The citizens complained to the County Commissioners.

Family Relationships

Capitalize a word that shows a family relationship when the word comes before a person's name or is used in place of the person's name. Do not capitalize a word that shows a family relationship if the word follows a possessive pronoun (*my, our, your, his, her, their*).

EXAMPLES   When did **A**unt Gail see the new baby? [*Aunt* is capitalized because it is used with the person's name.]

What movie would you like to see, **M**om? [*Mom* is capitalized because it is used in place of the person's name.]

Did your **m**om come to the art exhibition? [*Mom* is not capitalized because it follows the possessive pronoun *your*.]

GO ON

EXERCISE B Circle each letter that should be capitalized in the following sentences. Draw a slash (/) through each letter that is capitalized but should not be.

Example 1. Your A̸unt Sophie is very funny. [*Aunt* should not be capitalized because the possessive pronoun *Your* comes before it.]

6. Ask grandma if she would like some iced tea. [Is a word used in place of a person's name capitalized?]

7. mom, dad, and my little sister Sue went to the art gallery last Friday.

8. Is your Uncle coming with us to the park?

9. I was pleased that your Father won the golf tournament.

10. My Cousin is visiting from Utah.

Titles of Creative Works

Capitalize the titles of books, poems, articles, songs, plays, paintings, movies, and any other creative works. Do not capitalize articles (*a, an,* or *the*), short prepositions (*at, in, of, on, over, with,* and so on), or coordinating conjunctions (*and, but, or, nor, for, yet,* and *so*) unless the article, preposition, or conjunction is the first or last word in the title or subtitle.

EXAMPLES *The Hobbit* [book]
"The Signing of the Declaration of Independence" [chapter of a book]
Newsweek [magazine]
"The Love Song of J. Alfred Prufrock" [poem]
"The Life You Save May Be Your Own" [short story]

EXERCISE C Circle each letter that should be capitalized in the following sentences.

Example 1. Have you finished reading Ⓢilas Ⓜarner? [*Silas Marner* is capitalized because it is the title of a book.]

11. Did you read *the once and future king*? [Which words in the title of a book are capitalized?]

12. My little brother enjoys singing "twinkle, twinkle, little star."

13. We saw the painting *american gothic* in an art history textbook.

14. Phillipa wrote a poem called "thank you."

15. Did you renew your subscription to *national geographic*?

End Marks

13a. A statement (or *declarative sentence*) is followed by a period.

> **EXAMPLE**   Frank studied all week for the history test. [The sentence is a statement, so it is followed by a period.]

13b. A question (or *interrogative sentence*) is followed by a question mark.

> **EXAMPLE**   Does this dog belong to Manuel? [The sentence is a question, so it is followed by a question mark.]

NOTE Sometimes a statement sounds like a question. A statement should be followed by a period.

> **EXAMPLES**   Who won the game? [This sentence asks a question and should be followed by a question mark.]
>
> Roger asked Joy who won the game. [The sentence is a statement and should be followed by a period.]

EXERCISE A Decide whether each of the following sentences is a statement or a question. Then, add the more appropriate end mark where needed.

Examples 1. Are you joining the music club? [The sentence asks a question, so the sentence is *interrogative* and should be followed by a question mark.]

2. Joyce asked for a list of club members. [The sentence makes a statement, so the sentence is *declarative* and should be followed by a period.]

1. I watched a good program about insects [Should a period or a question mark follow this sentence?]

2. Did Carol see the program, too [Should a period or a question mark follow this sentence?]

3. She asked whether I had been practicing the violin

4. I believe I am getting better at the violin every day

5. Are you writing a poem for language arts class

6. I will write an essay about the Civil War for history class

7. Has the children's museum opened yet

8. Did he say whether he would be in French class today

9. Have you finished your homework

10. Our team will win tonight's game

GO ON ▶

13c. An exclamation (or *exclamatory sentence*) is followed by an exclamation point.

> **EXAMPLE**   How beautiful the weather is! [The sentence is an exclamation, so it is followed by an exclamation point.]

13d. A request or command (or *imperative sentence*) is generally followed by either a period or an exclamation point.

A request or a mild command is followed by a period. A strong command is followed by an exclamation point.

> **EXAMPLES**   Please wash the car when you get home from school. [The sentence is a request, so it is followed by a period.]
>
> Wash the car. [The sentence is a mild command, so it is followed by a period.]
>
> Look out for that ball! [The sentence is a strong command, so it is followed by an exclamation point.]

EXERCISE B Decide whether each of the following sentences is a statement, a question, an exclamation, or a command or request. Then, add the most appropriate end mark where needed.

Examples 1. That is a great song you wrote! [or .] [The sentence can be either an exclamation or a statement. Either a period or an exclamation point should follow the sentence.]

2. Maria told us when the meeting would take place. [The sentence is a statement, so it should be followed by a period.]

11. Cathy asked whether I had walked the dog [Is the sentence a statement or a question?]

12. Watch out for that broken glass [Is the sentence a request or a strong command?]

13. This birthday party was a real surprise

14. Wait for me

15. Our guests would like some iced tea

16. Wow! What a great concert

17. When did Michael get his license

18. Please water the plants while I am gone

19. Do you think that I should rewrite this essay

20. Those are the most beautiful flowers I have ever seen

Abbreviations A

Personal Names and Titles

13e. Use a period after certain abbreviations.

Abbreviations in the names of people should be followed by a period. Do not abbreviate any part of a person's name unless the person is commonly known by the abbreviation.

> **EXAMPLES** Ulysses S. Grant   W.E.B. DuBois   Arthur C. Clarke

Social titles (*Dr., Mr., Mrs., Ms., Sr., Sra.*) are always abbreviated before full names or last names used alone. Civil and military titles are generally abbreviated before full names or before initials and last names. Spell out a civil or military title if only the last name is used.

> **EXAMPLES** **Mrs.** Martin [social title before last name only]
>
> **Sr.** (Señor) Ricardo Martinez [social title before full name]
>
> **Col.** K.S. Jones [military title before initials and last name]
>
> **Colonel** Jones [military title before last name only]
>
> **Sen.** Mary Davidson [civil title before full name]

Titles and academic degrees that follow proper names are always abbreviated. Don't include social titles (*Mrs., Dr.,* and so on) when the name is followed by a professional title or degree.

> **EXAMPLES** **Dr.** Charles Franklin, **Jr.** [*Dr.* is a social title. *Jr.* is a part of the name, not a professional title or degree. Both titles should be abbreviated.]
>
> Charles Franklin, **Jr., M.D.** [*M.D.* is a professional title that follows the name, so the social title *Dr.* is not used. *Jr.* is a part of the name.]

EXERCISE A Underline the item that is correctly abbreviated in each of the following pairs.

Examples 1. a. Doctor Allen   **b.** <u>Dr. Allen</u>

> [*Dr.* is a social title and should be abbreviated before a last name.]

2. a. <u>Sergeant Clayton</u>   **b.** Sgt. Clayton

> [*Sergeant* is a military title and should be spelled out before a last name.]

1. a. Daniel T Hernandez   **b.** Daniel T. Hernandez

[Does an initial in a name need a period?]

2. a. Mr. Martin Badachape, B.A.   **b.** Martin Badachape, B.A.

[Is a social title used when an academic title follows the name?]

3. a. General Jameson   **b.** Gen. Jameson

4. a. Prof. Anderson   **b.** Professor Anderson

5. a. JoAnne P. Riley   **b.** JoAnne P Riley

6. a. Sen. Joseph Lieberman   **b.** Sen Joseph Lieberman

GO ON ➡

Developmental Language Skills

7. a. Walter Winkelmann, M.D.   **b.** Dr. Walter Winkelmann, M.D.

8. a. Phillip Rosetti, Jr.   **b.** Phillip Rosetti, Jr

9. a. Sen. Carol Newman   **b.** Sen Carol Newman

10. a. Sr Ochoa   **b.** Sr. Ochoa

Agencies, Organizations, and Acronyms

An *acronym* is a word formed from the first letters of a group of words. Acronyms are written without periods. Many agencies and organizations are commonly known by their acronyms. In writing, spell out the first use of the name of an agency or organization. After that, use the common abbreviation or acronym.

> **EXAMPLES**   **MADD**   **M**others **A**gainst **D**runk **D**riving
>   **AMA**   **A**merican **M**edical **A**ssociation

EXERCISE B First, look at the full name of the agency or organization. Then, underline the correct abbreviation for the name of the agency or organization.

Example 1. World Health Organization

     a. <u>WHO</u>   **b.** W.H.O.

     [Acronyms should be written without periods.]

11. National Aeronautics and Space Administration

     a. NASA   **b.** NA and SA

     [How should this common acronym be spelled?]

12. Parent-Teacher Association

     a. PTA   **b.** PT Assoc.

13. Environment Protection Agency

     a. Env. P.A.   **b.** EPA

14. National Football League

     a. NFL   **b.** Nat. Football Lg.

15. Public Broadcasting Service

     a. PBS   **b.** P.B.S

Abbreviations B

Geographical Terms

13e. Use a period after certain abbreviations.

Spell out the names of states and geographical terms in regular text. Abbreviate them in tables, footnotes, and bibliographies.

> **TEXT** My family is originally from Atlanta, **Georgia.**
>
> **TABLE** Atlanta, **Ga.**   Albuquerque, **N. Mex.**
>
> **FOOTNOTE** [4]The University of Memphis is located in Memphis, **Tenn.**

Spell out all words in an address in regular text. Abbreviate the words in letter and envelope addresses and in tables. Two-letter state abbreviations without periods are used only when the ZIP Code is included.

> **TEXT** The study groups will meet at 32 **West Broad Street.**
>
> **ENVELOPE** 32 **W.** Broad **St.**
>
> Phoenix, **AZ** 85027
>
> **TABLE** 32 **W.** Broad **St.,** Phoenix, **Ariz.**

EXERCISE A Underline the correct item in each of the following pairs.

Example 1. a. <u>My aunt spent two weeks in London, England.</u>

 b. My aunt spent two weeks in London, Eng.

 [*England* is the name of a country and should be spelled out in regular text.]

1. a. [5]James Andrews is currently an attorney in Austin, Tex.

 b. [5]James Andrews is currently an attorney in Austin, Texas.

 [Should the name of a state be abbreviated in a footnote?]

2. a. 1920 Euclid Ave.

 Nashville, Tennessee 37245

 b. 1920 Euclid Ave.

 Nashville, TN 37245

3. a. My uncle lives at 24 West Auburndale Avenue.

 b. My uncle lives at 24 W. Auburndale Ave.

4. a. Send the letter to the following address: 75 East Lansing Avenue, Lexington, KY 40596.

 b. Send the letter to the following address: 75 E. Lansing Ave., Lexington, Ky. 40596.

5. a. I mailed the package to my sister in Memphis, Tenn., not Memphis, Miss.

 b. I mailed the package to my sister in Memphis, Tennessee, not Memphis, Mississippi.

GO ON ➡

Units of Measurement

Spell out the names of units of measurement in regular text. Abbreviate units of measurement in tables and notes when the unit name follows a numeral. Write the abbreviations for measurements without periods, except for the abbreviation for *inch*. Use *in.* to avoid confusing it with the word *in*.

> **TEXT**   The recipe called for four **pounds** of spinach. [*Pounds* should be spelled out in regular text.]
>
> **TABLE**   6 **ft** 5 **in.** [The abbreviation for *feet* is written without a period, but the abbreviation for *inches* uses a period.]

EXERCISE B Underline the item that is abbreviated correctly in each of the following pairs.

Example   1. a. <u>8 oz of milk</u>   **b.** 8 oz. of milk

[The abbreviations for units of measurement are generally written without periods.]

6. a. Place four tbsp of thyme in the bowl.

  b. Place four tablespoons of thyme in the bowl. [Should measurements be spelled out in regular text?]

7. a. Isn't the table in the dining room about five feet long?

  b. Isn't the table in the dining room about five ft long?

8. a. We could make the casserole, but we don't have three c of rice.

  b. We could make the casserole, but we don't have three cups of rice.

9. a. This scooter doesn't go over fifteen mph.

  b. This scooter doesn't go over fifteen miles per hour.

10. a. The baby grew three inches in two months.

  b. The baby grew three in in two months.

Commas with Items in a Series

13f.   Use commas to separate items in a series.

> **EXAMPLES**   The squirrel ran up the tree, across the power line, and down the shed. [Each phrase is a separate item, so commas separate the phrases.]
>
> Jonathan ate, studied, and napped. [Each verb is a separate item, so commas separate the verbs.]
>
> Please wear your coat, gloves, boots, and a scarf. [Each noun in the list is a separate item, so commas separate the nouns.]
>
> Sit down, put your books away, and take out a pencil. [Three independent clauses are separated by commas.]

If all the items in a series are joined by *and, or,* or *nor,* do not use commas to separate them.

> **EXAMPLES**   We washed the car **and** raked the lawn **and** watered the plants. [The items in the series are joined by *and,* so they don't need commas between them.]
>
> We could go to the park **or** ride our bikes **or** have a picnic. [The items in the series are joined by *or,* so they don't need commas between them.]

EXERCISE A Insert commas where they are needed in each of the following sentences. If a sentence is already correct, write *C* before the item number.

Examples   **1.** Joseph, Calvin, and Evan formed a softball team. [The names are items in a series and should be separated by commas.]

   C   **2.** My sister wants to be a veterinarian or a lawyer or a clown when she grows up. [The items in the list are all joined by *or,* so the sentence is correct without commas.]

1. Julie and Philip and Michael made the best grades on the algebra test. [Should commas separate items in a series that are joined by *and*?]

2. My mom jogged down the street across Main Street and toward the park. [Should commas separate items in a series of phrases?]

3. We could join the glee club the math club or the drama club.

4. I could practice the piano or write my essay or take a nap.

5. For healthy teeth, you should brush floss and see your dentist regularly.

6. We stretched jogged and cooled down.

7. The baby cried and ate and slept.

8. The governor promised to raise taxes build new roads and improve schools.

GO ON

9. We could build a model of a volcano the sea or a mountain.

10. My aunt is visiting Italy or Germany or France.

| **13g.** | Use commas to separate two or more adjectives before a noun. |

> **EXAMPLES**   That calm, affectionate, intelligent dog is a beagle. [Commas separate each
> item in the series of adjectives before *dog*.]
>
> Judith is a kind, thoughtful girl. [Two adjectives precede *girl* and are
> separated by commas.]

NOTE Do not use a comma between an adverb and the adjective it modifies.

> **EXAMPLES**   You should wear a **light,** warm jacket. [In this sentence, *light* is an
> adjective that means "lightweight." It modifies the noun *jacket*, so a
> comma is needed to separate the two adjectives, *light* and *warm*.]
>
> I like your **light** blue sweater. [In this sentence, *light* is an adverb that
> modifies the adjective *blue*. No comma should separate *light* and *blue*.]

EXERCISE B Underline the sentence that is punctuated correctly in each of the following pairs.

Example   **1. a.** That was a long dull movie.

   b. <u>That was a long, dull movie.</u>

   [Two adjectives precede the noun *movie*, so a comma should come after *long*.]

11. a. We couldn't find pale pink balloons for my sister's birthday party.

   b. We couldn't find pale, pink balloons for my sister's birthday party.

   [Should a comma separate an adverb and the adjective it modifies?]

12. a. The cute fuzzy rabbit finally hopped away.

   b. The cute, fuzzy rabbit finally hopped away.

13. a. The mayor praised the hardworking dedicated teachers.

   b. The mayor praised the hardworking, dedicated teachers.

14. a. She has long, curly, very dark hair.

   b. She has long, curly, very, dark hair.

15. a. We bought the most, dependable, efficient, economical, car we could afford.

   b. We bought the most dependable, efficient, economical car we could afford.

Commas with Independent Clauses

13h. Use a comma before a coordinating conjunction (*and, but, for, nor, or, so,* or *yet*) when it joins independent clauses.

REMINDER An *independent clause* is a group of words that has a subject and a verb, expresses a complete thought, and can stand alone as a sentence.

EXAMPLES We missed the parade, so we went back home. [A comma and the coordinating conjunction *so* join the two independent clauses.]

We took a train to visit Grandma, but we took an airplane to visit Aunt Sue. [A comma and the coordinating conjunction *but* join the two independent clauses.]

EXERCISE A Insert commas where they are needed in each of the following sentences.

Examples 1. The algebra test is on Tuesday, and the history test is on Wednesday. [The coordinating conjunction *and* joins two independent clauses, so a comma should separate the clauses.]

2. Gary studied for the algebra test, but he forgot about the history test. [The coordinating conjunction *but* joins two independent clauses, so a comma should separate the clauses.]

1. Michael filled the bicycle tire with air and then we went on a bike ride. [Should a comma separate the two independent clauses?]

2. We could rent a movie or we could go out for dinner. [Should a comma separate the two independent clauses?]

3. Joshua fed the baby her supper and Maya played pat-a-cake with her.

4. Mark planned the project yet Ethan presented it to the class.

5. She walked the dog and I gave it a bath.

6. We planted trees and Jacob pulled weeds from the garden.

7. Shamika washed the car and Chi dried it.

8. The mayor spoke to the city council on Tuesday and he met with parents on Thursday.

9. The clown made a balloon animal and the magician performed a magic trick.

10. We cancelled the picnic for the weather was terrible.

GO ON

A compound sentence has two or more independent clauses. Each independent clause can stand alone as a complete sentence. Do not confuse a compound sentence with a simple sentence that has a compound verb. A compound verb is made up of two or more verbs that are joined by a conjunction and that share a subject.

>   **S** **V**   **V**
> **EXAMPLES** We went to the movies and walked around the mall. [This simple sentence has one subject and a compound verb. The sentence is one independent clause. No comma is needed.]
>
>   **S** **V**   **S** **V**
> We went to the movies, and later we walked around the mall. [This sentence has two independent clauses. Each clause has a subject and a verb. A comma before the coordinating conjunction *and* separates the two clauses.]

EXERCISE B Decide whether each of the following sentences is a compound sentence or a simple sentence with a compound verb. Then, insert a comma if needed to separate independent clauses. If a sentence is already correct, write C on the line provided.

Examples __C__ **1.** I volunteered at the hospital and worked at the animal shelter this summer. [This sentence is a simple sentence with a compound verb, so no comma is needed.]

_____ **2.** The kitten leapt at the window, and the bird flew up to the trees. [The sentence has two independent clauses that should be separated by a comma.]

_____ **11.** Mom picked us up after school and Dad drove us to soccer practice. [Does the sentence have two independent clauses?]

_____ **12.** Rosita blocked the shot and scored the winning point. [Does the sentence have two independent clauses?]

_____ **13.** Eli made an excellent grade on the test for he had studied hard.

_____ **14.** The dog barked and the opossum ran across the yard.

_____ **15.** We visited the Empire State Building but the Museum of Modern Art was closed.

_____ **16.** Everyone knew the material so no one worried when the teacher gave us a quiz.

_____ **17.** Kristin traveled to Canada and stayed at her grandmother's house.

_____ **18.** When did you wash and wax the car?

_____ **19.** David will fold all the clothes and Cindy will straighten up the living room.

_____ **20.** The children played hopscotch and the parents sat and talked.

Commas with Nonessential Clauses and Phrases
Subordinate Clauses

13i.   Use commas to set off nonessential subordinate clauses and nonessential participial phrases.

A *nonessential* subordinate clause adds extra information to a sentence but is not necessary for understanding the meaning of the sentence. A nonessential clause can be removed from the sentence without changing the basic meaning of the sentence.

An *essential* subordinate clause contains important information that cannot be left out without changing the basic meaning of the sentence.

> **EXAMPLES**   My brother**, who is a great teacher,** enjoys his job. [The subordinate
> clause *who is a great teacher* is nonessential. Commas separate the clause
> from the basic information in the sentence.]
>
> The girls **who are standing by the lockers** are members of the school band.
> [The subordinate clause *who are standing by the lockers* is essential, so it is
> not set off with commas. The information in the clause tells the reader
> *which* girls are members of the band.]

REMINDER▶ A *subordinate clause* has a subject and a verb but does not express a complete
thought and cannot stand by itself as a sentence.

EXERCISE A The subordinate clause in each of the following sentences is underlined. If the clause is nonessential, insert commas to set off the clause. If the clause is essential and does not need commas, write *C* on the line provided.

Examples   _____C_____   **1.** The trees <u>that my grandfather planted many years ago</u> are still bearing

fruit. [The information in the clause is essential to understand *which* trees, so

no commas are needed.]

_____   **2.** This jacket, <u>which I bought at a sale last winter,</u> still fits me. [The

information in the clause is nonessential to the basic meaning of the sentence.

The clause should be set off with commas.]

_____   **1.** My piano teacher <u>who is an accomplished musician</u> is giving a recital Friday. [Is the

information in the subordinate clause essential to the basic meaning of the sentence?]

_____   **2.** The dog <u>that ran away yesterday</u> has been found. [Is the information in the clause

essential to the basic meaning of the sentence?]

_____   **3.** Our house <u>which was once painted brown</u> is now light green.

_____   **4.** The senator <u>who introduced the bill</u> made a good speech.

_____   **5.** Mario <u>who came in third in the last race</u> is determined to win today.

_____   **6.** Some of the children <u>who were in the play</u> live in my neighborhood.

GO ON ▶

_____ 7. Even stars that appear very bright are extremely far away.

_____ 8. The flowers that were blooming yesterday have all wilted today.

_____ 9. The yard which is overgrown and full of weeds needs a lot of work.

_____ 10. The duck quacked angrily at the children who were swimming in the pond.

Participial Phrases

A *nonessential* participial phrase adds extra information to a sentence but is not necessary for understanding the meaning of the sentence. A nonessential phrase can be removed from the sentence without changing the basic meaning of the sentence.

An *essential* participial phrase contains important information that cannot be left out without changing the basic meaning of the sentence.

REMINDER▶ A *participial phrase* is a group of words that begins with a present or past *participle* (*–ing* and *–ed* forms) of a verb. The whole participial phrase is used as an adjective.

   EXAMPLES My father, **carrying a bag of groceries in each arm,** asked us to open the door. [The participial phrase *carrying a bag of groceries in each arm* is nonessential. Commas separate the phrase from the basic information in the sentence.]

   A pasta sauce **made with fresh tomatoes** tastes delicious. [The participial phrase *made with fresh tomatoes* is essential to understand the meaning of the sentence. *Which* or *what kind of* pasta sauce tastes delicious? No commas are needed.]

EXERCISE B The participial phrase in each of the following sentences is underlined. If the phrase is nonessential, insert commas to set off the phrase. If the phrase is essential and does not need commas, write *C* on the line provided.

Example _____ 1. The captain, faced with a difficult decision, paced back and forth on the

   deck. [The participial phrase *faced with a difficult decision* is nonessential to the

   basic meaning of the sentence. The phrase should be set off with commas.]

_____ 11. This photograph taken at my uncle's house is one of my favorites. [Is the participial

   phrase essential to understanding the basic meaning of the sentence?]

_____ 12. The book lying on the table is John's lost science book.

_____ 13. The dog wearing a red collar belongs to my neighbor.

_____ 14. The dentist smiling and telling jokes made me feel at ease.

_____ 15. The woman wearing glasses is the best speaker.

Commas with Introductory Elements

13j. Use a comma after certain introductory elements.

Use a comma to set off words such as *well, oh, why, yes,* and *no.*

> **EXAMPLES** Oh, you came to the party.
>
> Yes, I am feeling better now.

Use a comma after an introductory participle or participial phrase.

REMINDER A participle is a verb form (*–ing* and *–ed* forms) that is used as an adjective. A *participial phrase* is a group of words that begins with a participle and is used as an adjective.

> **EXAMPLES** **Laughing,** the little girl swung higher into the air. [The introductory participle *Laughing* is followed by a comma.]
>
> **Fascinated by the twinkling lights,** the children ran toward the carnival rides. [The introductory participial phrase is followed by a comma.]
>
> **Shining brightly,** the car gleamed after its wash. [*Shining brightly* is an introductory participial phrase.]

EXERCISE A Insert commas where they are needed in each of the following sentences.

Examples 1. Driven by the wind, the snow piled up against the barn. [*Driven by the wind* is an introductory participial phrase and should be followed by a comma.]

2. Well, I think you need more practice. [An introductory word such as *Well* should be followed by a comma.]

1. Frowning the doctor looked at my broken leg. [Should a participle that introduces a sentence be followed by a comma?]

2. Blown gently by the breeze the paper finally fluttered to the ground. [Should an introductory participial phrase be followed by a comma?]

3. Grinning broadly Fred led Jane into the living room for her surprise party.

4. Oh you can pay me back tomorrow.

5. Snarling the lion rolled over, yawned, and refused to look at the camera.

6. Yes I do enjoy art class.

7. Wagging its tail happily the puppy ran inside.

8. Delighted with my new haircut I rushed home to show it off.

9. No I don't care for more soup, thank you.

10. Buzzing angrily the bees chased the bear.

Use a comma after two or more introductory prepositional phrases or after one long phrase.

> **EXAMPLES**   **Under the patio table on the deck,** the dog settled down for a nap. [*Under the patio table* and *on the deck* are both prepositional phrases. Two or more introductory prepositional phrases are followed by a comma.]
>
> **After dinner and playtime outside,** the father gave the baby a bath. [The long introductory prepositional phrase is followed by a comma.]

Use a comma after an introductory adverb clause. An *adverb clause* is a group of words that has a subject and a verb, cannot stand alone as a sentence, and is used as an adverb. Adverb clauses begin with a subordinating conjunction (*although, after, because, if, since, when, whenever, where, while*).

> **EXAMPLES**   **Although we weren't really thirsty,** we couldn't resist sampling the lemonade. [The introductory adverb clause is followed by a comma.]
>
> **After we eat lunch,** we will take the dog for a walk. [The introductory adverb clause is followed by a comma.]

EXERCISE B   Insert commas where they are needed in each of the following sentences.

Examples   **1.** Under the bench on the back porch, the cat settled down for a nap. [A comma should follow two or more introductory prepositional phrases.]

       2. After we see Mount Rainier and the Space Needle, what other sights should we see in Seattle? [A comma should follow an introductory adverb clause.]

11. Near the door leading downstairs David hid the key. [Should a long introductory prepositional phrase be followed by a comma?]

12. In the shade of the branches of the old oak tree we studied for the test. [Should more than one introductory prepositional phrase be followed by a comma?]

13. When you visit your brother at college this year get some information about enrollment.

14. Next to the rake and the shovel in the shed you'll find the potting soil.

15. In about two or three months we will be ready for a vacation.

16. If you like tuna salad you're welcome to share my sandwich.

17. Because I woke up late I missed the bus.

18. From the top of the mountain the hikers could see the whole valley.

19. Behind the book with the red cover you will see a secret compartment.

20. When the batteries ran out we were sitting in total darkness.

for **CHAPTER 13: PUNCTUATION** | *pages 311–13*

Commas with Interrupters

13k. Use commas to set off an expression that interrupts a sentence.

Nonessential appositives and appositive phrases are set off by commas. An *appositive* is a noun or pronoun that is placed beside another noun or pronoun to explain or describe it. An *appositive phrase* is a group of words that includes an appositive and any words that modify it.

Nonessential appositives and appositive phrases can be removed from the sentence without changing the basic meaning or sense of the sentence.

> **EXAMPLE** Riley**,** **my cousin from South Dakota,** is visiting this weekend. [The appositive phrase *my cousin from South Dakota* describes Riley but is not needed to understand the basic information in the sentence. It is set off by commas.]

An essential appositive or appositive phrase is not set off by commas. When an essential appositive or appositive phrase is removed from a sentence, the remaining words don't make sense alone.

> **EXAMPLE** The book ***The Wind in the Willows*** was my favorite when I was younger. [*The Wind in the Willows* is essential because it tells *which* book was the favorite. It is not set off by commas.]

EXERCISE A The appositives and appositive phrases in the following sentences are underlined. If the appositive is nonessential, insert commas where they are needed in the sentence. If the appositive is essential and is correct without commas, write *C* on the line provided.

Examples _____C_____ **1.** The movie *The Princess Bride* is very good. [The appositive *The Princess Bride* gives information that is essential to the meaning of the sentence. No commas are needed.]

_____ **2.** That car, the blue one on the corner, is for sale. [The appositive *the blue one on the corner* is a nonessential appositive phrase, so it should be set off by commas.]

_____ **1.** Jacob <u>the youngest child in our family</u> is starting first grade next year. [Is the appositive phrase nonessential?]

_____ **2.** Sally <u>my only aunt</u> lives in Australia. [Is the appositive phrase nonessential?]

_____ **3.** Frederick <u>my little sister's favorite teddy bear</u> needs a bath.

_____ **4.** My friend <u>Rosita</u> invited me to her family's barbecue.

_____ **5.** One of my teachers <u>Ms. Goldberg</u> encouraged me to enter the science fair.

_____ **6.** That store <u>Kelly's Collectibles</u> has a large selection of dolls.

_____ **7.** My favorite cousin <u>Maria</u> is a talented dancer.

GO ON ➡

_____ **8.** The flowers that we bought <u>pansies, daisies, and roses</u> are being planted today.

_____ **9.** The assignment <u>Chapter 13</u> is due tomorrow.

_____**10.** My classmate <u>Simon</u> is studying to become a chef.

Words used in direct address are set off by commas. A word is in direct address when it names the person or persons spoken to.

    EXAMPLES Do you know the answer to the question**, Monique**? [*Monique* names the person being spoken to and is set off by a comma.]

                 I will wash the dishes**, Mom,** after we eat dinner. [*Mom* names the person being spoken to and is set off by commas.]

Parenthetical expressions are set off by commas. A *parenthetical expression* is a side remark that adds information or shows a relationship between ideas in the sentence. (Despite their name, parenthetical expressions are not set off by parentheses.) Some common parenthetical expressions are *by the way, for example, however, in fact, nevertheless, of course,* and *therefore.*

    EXAMPLE We realized**, however,** that the game would soon be rained out. [*However* is a parenthetical expression and is set off by commas.]

EXERCISE B Insert commas where they are needed in each of the following sentences.

Examples 1. He was on his way to the gym, I believe. [The parenthetical expression *I believe* should be set off by a comma.]

         2. Raymond, are you listening to me? [*Raymond* is a word used in direct address and should be set off by a comma.]

11. This poem Paul is quite good. [Should a word that is used in direct address be set off with commas?]

12. As a matter of fact the movie was better than the book. [Should a parenthetical expression be set off with a comma?]

13. Don't forget Dad that I have guitar practice after school today.

14. Are you going to the concert tonight Luis?

15. The essay on the other hand took longer to write than the poem.

16. The application form however was not in the packet.

17. Naturally she was concerned about her grandfather's health.

18. Your barking Rover is driving me crazy!

19. Cindy by the way came in first in the race.

20. At any rate no one was injured when the tree fell on the house.

Commas in Conventional Situations

| **13l.** | Use commas in certain conventional situations. |

Use a comma to separate items in dates. Use a comma to separate the last item in a date from the words that come after it. Do not use commas to set off the month from the day or the month from the year when no day is given.

> **EXAMPLES** Last Thursday, April 30, 2003, I took my first tuba lesson. [Commas separate the day of the week from the month, the day of the month from the year, and the last item in the date from the rest of the sentence. No comma separates the month and the day of the month.]
>
> We moved in **November 1996.** [No comma separates the month from the year when no day is given.]

EXERCISE A Insert commas where they are needed in each of the following sentences. If the punctuation is already correct, write *C* on the line provided.

Example _____ **1.** On Friday, April 24, 2003, I decided which college I will attend. [Use commas to separate items in dates.]

_____ **1.** My parents' anniversary is February 17 1982. [Should a comma separate the date from the year?]

_____ **2.** On July 4 1776 the American colonies declared independence.

_____ **3.** In May 2004 Uncle José will be a college graduate.

_____ **4.** On Tuesday December 25 2001 I began writing in a journal.

_____ **5.** My nephew will be eighteen years old on January 30 2018.

Use a comma to separate items in addresses. Use a comma to separate the last item in an address from the words that come after it. Do not use commas to set off a house number from a street name, a state abbreviation from a ZIP Code, or address items joined by prepositions.

> **EXAMPLES** Please send the package to me at 1510 Woodrow Avenue, Cleveland, OH 44199. [Commas separate the street name from the city and the city from the state. No comma separates the house number and the street name or the state abbreviation and the ZIP Code.]
>
> The new supermarket will be **on** the corner of Koenig Street **in** Midtown. [No commas separate address items joined by prepositions.]

GO ON

EXERCISE B Insert commas where they are needed in each of the following sentences. If the punctuation is already correct, write *C* on the line provided.

Example _____ **1.** I mailed my application to University of Michigan, University Park Drive, Ann Arbor, MI 48109. [Use commas to separate items in addresses.]

_____ **6.** The new museum is located on Finley Avenue on the west side of town. [Are commas used to separate items joined by prepositions?]

_____ **7.** Send your contribution to 575 Charity Blvd. Memphis TN 38747.

_____ **8.** Dana is staying at a hotel on Memory Lane in downtown Smithfield.

_____ **9.** My uncle visited the Donmar Warehouse Theatre in the West End London, England.

_____ **10.** You should address a letter to the President as follows: The President The White House Washington DC 20500.

Use a comma after the salutation of a personal letter and after the closing of any letter.

Use a colon after the salutation of a business letter.

REMINDER▶ The salutation is the greeting that begins a letter. The closing is the short line at the end of a letter, right before the signature.

      EXAMPLES Dear James,   Yours truly,

                  Dear Professor Jameson: [A business letter salutation is followed by a colon.]

Use commas to set off a title, such as *Jr., Sr.,* or *M.D.,* that follows a person's name.

      EXAMPLES Maria Angelo, M.D.

                  Dr. Martin Luther King, Jr.

EXERCISE C Insert commas or colons where they are needed in each of the following items.

Example 1. Dear Jamie, [A salutation in a personal letter is followed by a comma.]

11. Paul Andrew Thomas Jr. [Should a comma be used to set off a title that follows a person's name?]

12. Sincerely yours

13. Dear Dr. Morris

14. Dear Aunt Frances

15. Mario Alan Rodriguez Sr.

Semicolons

Use a semicolon between independent clauses that are closely related in thought and that are not joined by a coordinating conjunction (*and, but, for, nor, or, so,* or *yet*), and between independent clauses joined by a conjunctive adverb or transitional expression.

EXAMPLES   We were going across the desert; we packed hats, sunscreen, and a lot of water. [A semicolon joins two closely related independent clauses.]

I will tighten that screw; otherwise, it might fall out. [A semicolon appears between two independent clauses joined by the conjunctive adverb *otherwise.*]

The flowers pleased me; in fact, they made my whole day special. [A semicolon appears between two independent clauses joined by the transitional expression *in fact.*]

REMINDER Conjunctive adverbs and transitional expressions show readers how linked independent clauses are related to each other.

EXERCISE A Each of the following sentences contains two independent clauses. Use proofreading marks to insert a semicolon where needed in each sentence.

Examples 1. The map Ed had was very old; his grandfather had bought it in 1918. [A semicolon should join the two closely related independent clauses.]

2. Glenda is an artist; therefore, she agreed to make the posters. [A semicolon should come before the conjunctive adverb *therefore.*]

1. I took the leash from the hook my dog Ginger wagged her tail happily. [Should the independent clauses be joined by a semicolon?]

2. The electricity came on again, as a result, we were finally able to cook supper. [Should a semicolon precede the transitional expression in this sentence?]

3. Pete skipped rope nonstop for two hours consequently, he set a new school record.

4. The park ranger pointed to the sign, he explained that owls nested nearby.

5. My watch ticked away the minutes the grandfather clock chimed away the hours.

6. The projects were very creative, for instance, one student brought a real honeycomb to class.

7. Mrs. Kim's class toured the train museum, meanwhile, our class explored the old depot.

8. The ball whooshed through the net, the crowd burst into cheers.

9. Karo's joke really made me laugh in fact, I could not stop laughing.

10. Grace promised to bring me a special treat she arrived with homemade bread.

GO ON

Use a semicolon between items in a series if the items contain commas. A semicolon, rather than a comma, also may be needed before a coordinating conjunction to join independent clauses that contain commas.

 EXAMPLES The student candidates included Sue Long, for president; Craig Shaw, for vice-president; and Mick Parks, for treasurer. [The items in this series contain commas, so semicolons separate all the items.]

      I wanted thin brushes, oil paints, and a sturdy easel; **but** thick brushes, water-colors, and a flimsy easel were all I found. [The two independent clauses contain commas that may be confusing, so they are joined by a semicolon and the coordinating conjunction *but*.]

EXERCISE B Each of the following sentences contains either two independent clauses or a list of items. Use proofreading marks to place a semicolon where needed in each sentence.

Example 1. Mrs. Fuller had not forgotten the plates for sandwiches, glasses for water, and forks for salad; nor had she missed the tablecloth and napkins for the picnic. [One of the two independent clauses contains commas that could be confusing, so the clauses should be separated by a semicolon in addition to the coordinating conjunction.]

11. This year's horse show contestants were Alice Jones, riding Lady, Ben Toth, riding Silver, and Lin Yang, riding Spirit. [Should items that contain commas be separated by semicolons?]

12. Marco brought pencils, lots of paper, and a calculator, but only a good breakfast, a good night's sleep, and intense study could really prepare him for the test.

13. Gentlemen once sent ladies rosemary, for remembrance, red roses, for love, and French marigold, for jealousy.

14. A tour guide led us through the library, into the kitchen, and back into the bedrooms and then, after lunch, we were shown the garden and shed.

15. This summer I read the stories "Liberty," by Julia Alvarez, "Two Kinds," by Amy Tan, "The First Seven Years," by Bernard Malamud, and "Son," by John Updike.

Colons

14e. Use a colon to mean "note what follows."

Use a colon before a list of items, especially after expressions such as *as follows* and *the following*. A colon is also used before a long, formal statement or quotation and between independent clauses when the second clause explains or restates the idea of the first.

EXAMPLES   The cook bought several fruits**:** apples, oranges, peaches, and pears. [The colon announces that a list follows.]

The cook used **the following** items**:** apples, oranges, peaches, and mint. [The words *the following* and the colon announce that a list is included.]

The Chinese sage Tzu-Gung offers this wisdom**:** "**H**e who does his work like a machine grows a heart like a machine, and he who carries the heart of a machine in his breast loses his simplicity." [The colon precedes a long, formal quotation. Because the quotation is a complete sentence, it begins with a capital letter.]

Griffin had a reason to smile**:** **H**e had gotten the job. [The second independent clause explains the first clause. Because the second clause is a complete sentence, it begins with a capital letter.]

EXERCISE A   Use proofreading marks to insert colons where needed in each of the following sentences. Remember to change capitalization where needed.

Examples 1. The restaurant has a strict policy**:** **N**o separate checks are accepted. [A colon should separate two independent clauses when the second clause explains or restates the first clause. The first word of the second clause should be capitalized because the clause is a complete sentence.]

2. Don't forget to buy supplies for the picnic**:** bread, mustard, pickles, cheese, and grapes. [A colon should be used to announce that a list follows.]

1. The jeweler used the following gems diamonds, rubies, and opals. [Should a colon follow *the following gems* before the list of gems?]

2. My grandmother has a saying about life, "riches are not what you hold in your hand, but what you hold in your heart." [Should a colon precede a long, formal quote? Should the first word of a quotation that is a sentence be capitalized?]

3. I planned the following activities, Reading, skating, swimming, and drawing.

4. The kids invented a new song "Rain, rain, come today. In the rain we wish to play."

5. The baby likes noisy toys, rattles, bells, and whistles are his favorite playthings.

GO ON ▶

6. The old trunk contained many interesting items, love letters, a diary, and dried flowers.

7. Autumn makes me think of the following things apples, bright leaves, and pumpkins.

8. The contestant picked three numbers two, six, and twelve.

9. The application asks for the usual information, name, address, telephone number, date of birth, and previous experience.

10. Mr. Long saved the day, he found the key under a rock.

14f.   Use a colon in certain conventional situations.

Use a colon between the hour and the minute, between chapter and verse in Biblical references, between titles and subtitles, and after the salutation of a business letter.

>   **EXAMPLES** 10:30 A.M. [A colon separates hours from minutes.]
>   Psalms 144:1–3 [A colon separates chapter and verse in a Biblical reference.]
>   *Paw Prints:* The Life of a Clever Cat [A colon separates title and subtitle.]
>   Dear Sir or Madam: [A colon is used after the salutation of a business letter.]

EXERCISE B Use proofreading marks to insert colons where needed in the following items.

 Examples 1. Carrie's letter began, "Dear Mrs. Camp: Enclosed is my application." [A colon should follow the salutation of a business letter.]

    2. We leave at 6:30 in the morning. [A colon should separate the hour and the minutes.]

11. Mr. Clark asked us to read Mark 4 1–10 in the Bible. [Should a colon separate chapter and verse in a Biblical reference?]

12. I wanted to see the exhibition *Monet's Garden The Artist and Nature* at the gallery. [Should a colon separate title and subtitle?]

13. My pastor read John 3 16–18 at today's service.

14. Aunt Maria served dinner at exactly 500 P.M. each day.

15. Did you know that *Shabanu Daughter of the Wind* is her favorite book?

16. I hope "Dear Sir or Madam" was the right way to start my letter.

17. Buses will leave for the game every fifteen minutes between 430 and 700.

18. Did I capitalize "To Whom It May Concern" correctly?

19. This guidebook is called *New Mexico Your Guide to the Land of Enchantment.*

20. My alarm clock started buzzing at 600 this morning.

Parentheses, Dashes, and Brackets

Parentheses

14g. Use parentheses to enclose informative or explanatory material of minor importance.

> **EXAMPLE**   Florence Griffith Joyner **(**called "FloJo"**)** won four medals in the 1988 Olympics. [The information in parentheses is interesting additional information, but it is not important to the sentence's main idea.]

Sometimes a complete sentence appears in parentheses.

> **EXAMPLES**   Call Mary **(h**er number is on the list**)** about the party. [The sentence in parentheses does not begin with a capital letter and is not followed by a period.]
>
> Zelda Gunn **(d**o you know her**?)** was the guest of honor. [The sentence in parentheses does not begin with a capital letter but is followed by a question mark.]
>
> The judges chose Kevin's project as the winner. **(H**e made a model rocket.**)** [The sentence in parentheses stands alone. It begins with a capital letter and ends with a period.]

EXERCISE A Determine the main idea of each of the following sentences. Then, set off any additional or unimportant material by inserting parentheses where needed. Do not add commas.

Example 1. The U.S. golden dollar (the one issued in 2000) features the image of an American

Indian woman. [The words *the one issued in 2000* add extra information that is not nec-

essary to the sentence's basic meaning, so they should appear within parentheses.]

1. This recipe calls for 40 grams 1.5 ounces of cornstarch. [Which information is additional to the

main information in the sentence?]

2. Vancouver Island is part of British Columbia. See the map on page 100.

3. That full-length wool coat there's no way I could afford one! is certainly beautiful.

4. The actor James Stewart from the movie *It's a Wonderful Life* stars in the movie *Mr. Smith Goes

to Washington.*

5. Dr. Martin's new office it's in the Professional Building on Second Street will be open

tomorrow.

Dashes

14h. Use a dash to indicate an abrupt break in thought or speech.

> **EXAMPLE**   You must be at home Friday because**—**well, I can't tell you why. [The dash indicates that the statement was unfinished.]

GO ON ▶

14i. Use a dash to mean *namely, in other words,* or *that is* before an explanation.

> **EXAMPLE** Cindy felt more than happy—she felt on top of the world! [The dash indicates *that is,* she felt on top of the world!]

EXERCISE B Use proofreading marks to insert dashes where needed in the following sentences.

Example 1. That kind man I never got his name found my wallet. [Dashes should set off an abrupt break in thought or speech.]

6. Then the patient opens her eyes and but I won't spoil the book's ending for you. [Should a dash be used to indicate an unfinished statement?]

7. The mosquitoes had a grand feast look at my legs!

8. The ranger said that bears have one favorite food whatever you're eating!

9. We left on Monday or maybe it was Tuesday for Florida.

10. Someone I won't tell you the name is coming with a surprise.

Brackets

14j. Use brackets to enclose an explanation within quoted or parenthetical material.

> **EXAMPLE** The book reviewer wrote, "Beccah King's new book **[Lone Star]** is her best yet." [Brackets surround the title of the book because that information was not part of the original quotation.]

EXERCISE C Each of the following sentences is followed by information in brackets. Draw an arrow to show where the bracketed information should be inserted in the sentence.

Example 1. Halley's Comet (named after astronomer Edmond Halley) will return in 2061. [1656–1742] [The dates in brackets are the dates of Halley's life. Such dates are often in parentheses following a person's name. In this sentence the dates must be in brackets because the dates will be inserted within parenthetical material.]

11. The St. Louis Cardinals (once called the St. Louis Perfectos for a short time) are my favorite team. [1899–1900] [Where should the bracketed information be inserted?]

12. The Great Pyramid in Egypt (481 feet high) was completed around 2600 B.C. [147 meters]

13. "Most of Caral is buried, but what has been unearthed is impressive." [an ancient city in Peru]

14. "The book *Ahab's Wife* was inspired by a brief passage in Melville's *Moby-Dick*." [Herman]

15. The description in the catalog said, "Australians are fond of wearing their 'Blunnies' everywhere—from backyards to Bondi Beach." [Blundstone boots]

Italics (Underlining)

Titles and Subtitles

14k. Use italics (underlining) for the titles and subtitles of books, plays, long poems, periodicals, works of art, movies, radio and TV series, videos, video games, long musical works and recordings, computer games, and comic strips.

BOOK	*Silas Marner*	**WORK OF ART**	*The Favorite Cat*
PLAY	*Hamlet*	**MOVIE**	*Field of Dreams*
LONG POEM	*The Odyssey*	**TV SERIES**	*Earthpulse*
PERIODICAL	*Seventeen*	**LONG MUSICAL WORK**	*The Phantom of the Opera*

EXERCISE A Underline the word or words that should be italicized in each of the following sentences.

Examples 1. The novel <u>To Kill a Mockingbird</u> was made into an award-winning movie. [The title of a book should be italicized (underlined).]

2. That movie got a great review in <u>The New York Times</u>. [The title of a newspaper or periodical should be italicized (underlined).]

1. Our guests hoped to see the opera Carmen tonight. [Should the title of a long musical work be italicized (underlined)?]

2. I listen to the series Weather Vane on the radio every morning. [Should the title of a radio series be italicized (underlined)?]

3. The newspaper USA Today is available in many places in the country.

4. My niece improves her math skills with the computer game Math Blaster.

5. The class is reading Shakespeare's play As You Like It.

6. My parents always read Sally Forth in the comics section.

7. The book Pinocchio was originally written in Italian.

8. Kim reads The Wall Street Journal for business tips.

9. I kept my program from the play Death of a Salesman.

10. Jill feels inspired by Georgia O'Keeffe's painting Dark Mesa.

Names

14l. Use italics (underlining) for the names of trains, ships, aircraft, and spacecraft.

SHIP	*Titanic*	**AIRCRAFT**	*Spirit of St. Louis*
TRAIN	*Rocky Mountaineer*	**SPACECRAFT**	*Viking 2*

GO ON

EXERCISE B Underline the word or words that should be italicized in each of the following sentences.

Example 1. More than six thousand people helped investigate the explosion of the space shuttle

<u>Challenger</u>. [The name of a spacecraft should be italicized (underlined).]

11. Why did the Mary Celeste disappear during a sea voyage in 1872? [Are the names of ships

italicized (underlined)?]

12. We watched the orbiter Endeavour pass overhead last night.

13. The miniature train in the park is called the Houston Hornet.

14. The German airship Hindenburg exploded as it was landing at Lakehurst, New Jersey, in 1937.

15. In 1947, Thor Heyerdahl sailed a raft named Kon-Tiki from the Pacific coast of South America

to Polynesia.

Words, Letters, Symbols, and Numerals

14m. Use italics (underlining) for words, letters, symbols, and numerals referred to as such, and for foreign words that have not been adopted into English.

EXAMPLES My report came back with a large **A** at the top! [The letter *A* is italicized because it is referred to as a letter.]

I wrote **16,** but I meant to write **19.** [The numbers *16* and *19* are italicized because they are referred to as numbers.]

Lyla answered with the word **merci,** which means "thanks" in French. [*Merci* is not part of English vocabulary, so it is italicized (underlined).]

EXERCISE C Underline the words, symbols, letters, or numerals that should be italicized in each of the following sentences.

Example 1. Is that a <u>7</u> or a <u>1</u> with a hook on it? [The numerals *7* and *1* should be italicized (underlined) because they are referred to as numbers.]

16. Place an A on the page that comes first. [Should a letter that is referred to as a letter be italicized

(underlined)?]

17. Maria uses the German word nein when she means "no."

18. I know what the C stands for in C. J.'s name.

19. I wrote 20, not 40, on the order form.

20. Mick looked up the definition of the word stoic.

Quotation Marks A

Direct Quotations

14n. Use quotation marks to enclose a ***direct quotation***—a person's exact words.

Capitalize the first word of a direct quotation that is a complete sentence. A quotation that is a fragment or only a few words of the original quotation generally begins with a lowercase letter.

If words that identify the speaker or another interrupting expression divide a quoted sentence into two parts, the second part of the quoted sentence begins with a lowercase letter.

> **EXAMPLES** Tracy said, **"Here, let me do those dishes."** [Quotation marks begin and end Tracy's exact words. The quotation is a complete sentence, so it begins with a capital letter.]
>
> **"Here,"** Tracy kindly said, **"let me do those dishes."** [Tracy's exact words are divided into two parts, and each part begins and ends with quotation marks. The second part of the quoted sentence begins with a lowercase letter.]
>
> Marsha agreed to let her do the dishes **"just this one time."** [The quotation is a fragment and begins with a lowercase letter.]

EXERCISE A Insert quotation marks where needed, and draw three lines under any letters that should be capitalized in each of the following sentences.

Examples 1. "Barbara," called Lou, "I need the flashlight." [Lou's exact words are divided into two parts. Each part should begin and end with quotation marks.]

2. Barbara replied, "the flashlight is in the top drawer." [Quotation marks begin and end Barbara's exact words. *The* should be capitalized because it is the first word of a quoted sentence.]

1. Mr. Bradley said, now put on your safety glasses. [Should Mr. Bradley's exact words begin and end with quotation marks? Should the first word of the quoted sentence be capitalized?]

2. I trained very hard, said the champion, and I had a lot of luck. [Should quotation marks begin and end each part of a sentence divided by words that identify the speaker?]

3. Tom took a train to Tulsa tonight, crooned the singer.

4. Amy suggested, try some of this salad.

5. A polar bear's body is designed to keep it warm, explained the biologist.

6. That dog, said the neighbor, brings my paper to me.

7. The compass needle points south, our guide told us.

GO ON ▶

8. The queen commanded, the ships will sail tomorrow!

9. Get your program right here, cried the usher.

10. Do me a favor, Ginny requested, and sweep up those leaves.

A direct quotation can be set off from the rest of the sentence by a comma, a question mark, or an exclamation point, but not by a period. Commas are placed outside opening quotation marks but inside closing quotation marks. A period that ends both the sentence and the quotation is placed inside the closing quotation marks. Question marks and exclamation points are placed inside the closing quotation marks if the quotation itself is a question or an exclamation.

EXAMPLES   Dan said, "This restaurant's soup is really delicious." [The quoted sentence is set off by a comma that comes before the quotation starts. The quotation ends with a period inside the closing quotation marks.]

"I want chicken soup," Dan told the waitress. [The quoted sentence is set off from the rest of the sentence by a comma inside the quotation marks.]

"Do you have chicken soup today?" asked Dan. [The quoted question is set off from the rest of the sentence by a question mark inside the quotation marks.]

Did she say, "No soup today"? [The sentence asks a question, but the quotation is not a question, so the question mark is placed outside the quotation marks.]

EXERCISE B Use proofreading marks to correct any errors in punctuation and capitalization in the sentences below.

Example 1. Mom ordered, "quit yawning"! [The quoted sentence should begin with a capital letter. The quotation itself is an exclamation, so the exclamation point should be placed inside the closing quotation marks.]

11. "The leaves in autumn", Anna wrote, "Look like flames." [Should a comma be placed inside the closing quotation marks? Should the second part of a divided quotation begin with a lowercase letter?]

12. "Do fish have ears"? Yolanda wondered.

13. "The solar sail will be the size of a soccer field." said the scientist.

14. Does that ad say, "All couches are on sale today?"

15. "Hey, you!" called the driver. "you forgot your books"!

Quotation Marks B

Titles

14o. Use quotation marks to enclose titles (including subtitles) of short works such as short stories, poems, essays, articles and other parts of periodicals, songs, episodes of radio and TV series, and chapters and other parts of books.

SHORT STORY	"Everyday Use"
ESSAY	"The Death of the Moth"
ARTICLE	"This Year's Election"
SONG	"My Heart Will Go On"
TV EPISODE	"Blue Moon"
BOOK CHAPTER	"Getting to Know Your Pet"

NOTE When you use the title of a short work within another quotation, use single quotation marks around the title.

EXAMPLE   Maya asked, "Have you heard the song 'Lazy Days' by Enya?" [The song title *'Lazy Days'* is enclosed in single quotation marks because it is within another quotation.]

EXERCISE A Insert quotation marks around titles of short works in each of the following sentences.

Examples 1. Please read the chapter "Introduction to Sonar" in your textbook. [The title of a book chapter should be enclosed by quotation marks.]

2. Let's check the "Movies Today" section of the newspaper. [The title of a part of a periodical should be enclosed by quotation marks.]

1. I enjoyed the Pet Tricks episode on the *Tyler Tonight* show. [Should the title of an episode of a television series be enclosed by quotation marks?]

2. My grandmother said, "In the 1940's, the song Blues in the Night was a big hit." [Should a short title that appears inside another quotation be enclosed by single quotation marks?]

3. Did you see the article When the Greeks Went West in *National Geographic*?

4. Our teacher taped the episode To the Moon when it appeared on *Nova*.

5. Kirk was inspired by the essay Walking in Summer.

6. You can find that number in the Quick Reference section of the phone book.

7. Mrs. King assigned Frost's poem The Road Not Taken.

8. In Laura's story A Cat's Skills, a cat is the main character.

9. I read the chapter From Lemonade Stand to Boardroom twice.

10. Jill's song Moon Howl might make her famous.

GO ON ➡

Slang, Invented Words, Technical Terms, and Definitions

14p. Use quotation marks to enclose slang words, invented words, technical terms, dictionary definitions of words, and any expressions that are unusual in standard English.

> **EXAMPLES** We sure had a **"gully washer"** last night! [*Gully washer,* an expression that means "heavy storm," is an unusual or slang word.]
>
> Mom jokingly calls herself a **"domestic engineer."** [*Domestic engineer* is an invented word that means "homemaker."]
>
> I never knew that a group of kangaroos is called a **"mob."** [*Mob* is the technical term for a group of kangaroos.]
>
> According to the dictionary, *persevere* means **"to persist in spite of discouragement."** [The definition of *persevere* is enclosed by quotation marks.]
>
> This board game includes **"bones"** (dice). [*Bones* is an unusual term for *dice* in standard English.]

EXERCISE B Insert quotation marks around slang words, invented words, technical terms, dictionary definitions of words, and unusual expressions in each of the following sentences.

Examples 1. My cousin prefers "snail mail" to e-mail. [*Snail mail* should be enclosed in quotation marks because it is an invented term for postal mail.]

2. I was so thin when I was a child that my grandmother called me a "beanpole." [*Beanpole* should be enclosed in quotation marks because it is a nonstandard term meaning "very thin."]

11. How long should I zap this popcorn in the microwave? [Is the word *zap* a standard term for cooking something in a microwave?]

12. In this country, legal tender refers to both coins and paper money. [Is the term *legal tender* a technical term in the banking industry?]

13. A tom is a male cat.

14. The gardener uses black gold (compost) to grow her flowers.

15. Pilots radio Mayday when they need help.

16. I made lots of dough this summer by mowing lawns.

17. A buckyball is a ball-shaped group of carbon atoms.

18. The player in the lead made a bogey on that hole.

19. Some people say that he's a real live wire.

20. The captain pointed out the growler, a small iceberg.

Ellipsis Points

Quotations

14q. Use ellipsis points (. . .) to mark omissions from quoted material.

Ellipsis points are used to show where words were left out at the beginning, middle, or end of a quoted sentence. Do not begin a quotation with ellipsis points.

ORIGINAL	The writer said, "I started out writing a column for my school newspaper. Then, the *Dayton Chronicle* offered me a job. Now I write mystery novels because I love suspense." [The original quotation is three complete sentences.]
BEGINNING	The writer said, "I started out writing a column for my school newspaper. . . . [T]he *Dayton Chronicle* offered me a job. Now I write mystery novels because I love suspense." [The word *Then* was omitted from the beginning of the second sentence and replaced by ellipsis points that follow the period at the end of the second sentence. The *T* is in brackets to show that it was not capitalized in the original quotation.]
MIDDLE	The writer said, "I started out writing . . . for my school newspaper. Then, the *Dayton Chronicle* offered me a job. Now I write mystery novels because I love suspense." [The words *a column* were omitted from the middle of the first sentence and replaced by ellipsis points.]
END	The writer said, "I started out writing a column for my school newspaper. Then, the *Dayton Chronicle* offered me a job. Now I write mystery novels. . . ." [The ellipsis points show that words were omitted at the end of a sentence. The shortened sentence ends with a period that comes before the ellipsis points.]

EXERCISE A Rewrite the following sentences by replacing the underlined words with ellipsis points. You may need to add a capital letter in brackets at the beginning of a new sentence.

Example 1. The chemist explained, "Our sense of taste is complex. The process of tasting a food

produces chemical reactions in your mouth." [The period at the end of the first

sentence should be followed by three ellipsis points. The *t* should be capitalized and

placed in brackets because *tasting* is the new first word of the sentence.]

The chemist explained, "Our sense of taste is complex. . . . [T]asting a food produces

chemical reactions in your mouth."

1. The scout said, "I think I've found a shortcut to our camp." [Should a period end a sentence

when words are omitted from the end of the sentence?]

_____

GO ON ►

2. Paolo murmured, "I need to add one more bird to my bird-watcher's list. <u>So far I've written</u> <u>down jays, robins, and sparrows.</u> I would love to see a hawk."

_____

3. As we approached the rapids, I thought, "Okay. This is it. I can do this <u>because I trained for it.</u>"

_____

4. "I saw an incredible, <u>amazing, unbelievable, spectacular</u> coral reef down there!" sputtered the diver.

_____

5. The speaker said, "Today's graduates will face many new challenges, <u>challenges that no one</u> <u>can even imagine yet.</u> "

_____

Dialogue

14r. Use three ellipsis points (. . .) to indicate a pause in dialogue.

Speakers sometimes hesitate or pause for dramatic effect. Ellipsis points help readers know to make a dramatic or hesitant pause in the sentence.

> **EXAMPLE** "So . . . you want to be a rock star?" Aunt Fran asked. [The ellipsis points show that Aunt Fran is hesitating in her speech.]

EXERCISE B Use proofreading marks to insert ellipsis points in the most appropriate place for a pause in each of the following sentences.

Example 1. "It's a whirlwind, a tornado, a newᵃbaby brother," joked my friend. [Ellipsis points

should show where the speaker pauses for dramatic effect.]

11. "I think your dress is nice," Carlos carefully answered. [Ellipsis points should be inserted where a speaker would pause for effect or hesitate.]

12. The party guest commented, "Well at least the food was good."

13. Jan looked at the skunk and gasped, "That is your pet?"

14. After listening to all of the reports, the teacher said, "My I must admit that I was very impressed with everyone's report."

15. "Well I'm really not supposed to tell you that," teased Joseph.

Apostrophes in Possessive Case
Nouns

| **14s.** | Use an apostrophe to form the possessive forms of nouns and indefinite pronouns. |

The *possessive case* of a noun shows ownership or possession. To form the possessive case of most singular nouns, add an apostrophe and an *s*. When a singular noun already ends in *s*, and the word has two or more syllables, add only an apostrophe if an apostrophe and an *s* would make the word awkward to pronounce.

> **EXAMPLES** Some of that peacock**'s** feathers are three feet long. [*Peacock* is a singular noun that does not end in *s*. An apostrophe and an *s* form the possessive.]
>
> Uncle Ulysses**'** parakeet makes a lot of noise. [*Ulysses* is a singular proper noun. It has three syllables and already ends in *s*. An apostrophe forms the possessive because adding another *s* would make the word awkward to pronounce.]

To form the possessive case of a plural noun that ends in *s*, add only the apostrophe. If the plural noun does not end in *s*, add an apostrophe and an *s*.

> **EXAMPLES** Someone saw two mice in the boys**'** locker room. [*Boys* is a plural noun that ends in *s*, so an apostrophe alone is added to make the noun possessive.]
>
> The women**'s** shoe department is on the second floor. [*Women* is a plural noun that does not end in *s*, so an apostrophe and an *s* are added to make the noun possessive.]

EXERCISE A Use proofreading marks to add an apostrophe or an apostrophe and an *s* to form the possessive case of each underlined noun in the following sentences.

Examples 1. The trail᾽ˢsurface was rocky. [The possessive of the singular noun *trail* is formed by adding an apostrophe and an *s*.]

2. The boys᾽locker room is to the left. [The plural noun *boys* ends in an *s*, so the possessive is formed by adding an apostrophe.]

1. Did you ever read the myth about Theseus battle with the Minotaur? [*Theseus* is a singular proper noun that ends in *s* and has three syllables. Would the word be awkward to pronounce if an apostrophe and an *s* were added?]

2. I want to photograph those birds nests. [Is only an apostrophe used to form the possessive of a plural noun that ends in *s*?]

3. The skillet surface began to sizzle.

4. That pattern reminds me of a moth wings.

5. Would you like to see Hannah drawings?

6. The <u>women</u> basketball team practices on Thursday now.

7. My cousin <u>Moses</u> sand castle was huge!

8. Across the prairie, the <u>grasses</u> seeds scattered in the wind.

9. The alarm <u>clock</u> buzz woke me up this morning.

10. Friday is <u>children</u> day at the museum.

Pronouns

Never add an apostrophe to form the possessive case of a personal pronoun. Personal pronouns already have possessive forms. To form the possessive of an indefinite pronoun, add an apostrophe and an *s*.

> **EXAMPLES** That car is missing **its** license plate. [The pronoun *its* is the possessive formed of the pronoun *it*.]
>
> Is this anybody**'s** towel? [The possessive case of the indefinite pronoun *anybody* is formed by adding an apostrophe and an *s*.]

EXERCISE B Each of the following sentences is followed by a pronoun in brackets. Complete each sentence by writing the possessive form of the pronoun on the blank in the sentence.

Examples 1. Bob found the ring in _____his_____ car. *[he]* [The possessive form of the personal pronoun *he* is *his*.]

2. ___Someone's___ lab kit is still on the table. *[Someone]* [The possessive case of the indefinite pronoun *someone* is formed by adding an apostrophe and an *s*.]

11. The carnival set up _____ booths in the park. *[it]* [What is the possessive form of the pronoun *it*?]

12. One twin always finishes the _____ sentences. *[other]* [How is the possessive case of an indefinite pronoun formed?]

13. The rafters were soaked after _____ adventure on the river. *[they]*

14. We must arrive at the station before _____ friends arrive. *[we]*

15. The horse will take treats from _____ hand. *[anybody]*

16. Kendra will need _____ umbrella today. *[she]*

17. _____ car could get through that mud. *[No one]*

18. I am looking for _____ book. *[I]*

19. May I have _____ attention, please? *[everyone]*

20. _____ stomach just growled. *[Somebody]*

Apostrophes in Contractions and Plurals

Contractions

14t. Use an apostrophe to show where letters, numerals, or words have been omitted in a contraction.

Contractions are shortened forms of words, word groups, or numerals. The apostrophe generally takes the place of all the letters, words, or numbers that have been left out.

EXAMPLES

they are = they're	1998 = '98	of the clock = o'clock
we had = we'd	where is = where's	would not = wouldn't
will not = **won't**	cannot = **can't**	he is (*or* he has) = he's

TIP Do not confuse contractions with possessive pronouns.

EXAMPLES **It's** time we gave the dog **its** bath. [*It's* is a contraction for *It is*. *Its* is a possessive pronoun meaning *belonging to it*.]
Who's going to decide **whose** turn it is? [*Who's* is a contraction for *who is*. *Whose* is a possessive pronoun meaning *belonging to whom*.]

EXERCISE A On the blanks provided, write the contraction for the words or numerals in brackets that follow each sentence.

Examples 1. This letter was written in _____'53_____, the year my mother was born. *[1953]* [In a contraction for a year, the apostrophe takes the place of the first two numerals, so *'53* is correct.]

2. Laura _____can't_____ go to the beach today. [cannot] [The contraction for *cannot* is *can't*.]

1. _____ Jolleyville on this map? *[Where is]* [What letter does the apostrophe replace in the contraction?]

2. In May, the class of _____ will graduate. *[2004]* [How is the contraction for a year written?]

3. _____ training for the race. *[Jennifer is]*

4. _____ better hurry to catch the train on time. *[They had]*

5. By eleven _____ I was hungry. *[of the clock]*

6. _____ go to the stadium on the bus. *[Let us]*

7. I _____ get through that maze. *[could not]*

8. The children _____ want to play outside in the rain. *[do not]*

9. _____ so glad you liked my plan. *[I am]*

10. One jar _____ got a lid. *[has not]*

GO ON ▶

Plurals

14u. Use an apostrophe and an *s* to form plurals of lowercase letters, symbols, numerals, some upper-case letters, and some words referred to as words.

> **EXAMPLES** The word *Mississippi* has four *i*'s in it. [Without the apostrophe, the plural of *i* would look like the word *is*.]
>
> The child practiced writing cursive *U*'s. [U is not a lowercase letter, but without the apostrophe it would look like *Us*.]
>
> The address has three *8*'s in it. [The plural of the numeral *8* is written by adding an apostrophe and an *s*.]
>
> The final vote included three *no*'s. [The plural of the word *no* is formed by adding an apostrophe and an *s*.]

EXERCISE B Use proofreading marks to insert apostrophes where needed to form the plurals of letters, numerals, symbols, and words referred to as words in each of the following sentences.

Examples 1. Rebekka spells her name with two *k*'s. [An apostrophe should be used to form the plural of a lowercase letter.]

2. After three *achoo*'s, Sam got a tissue. [An apostrophe should be used to form the plural of a word referred to as a word.]

11. Please add $s to all the prices on that list. [Should an apostrophe be used to form the plural of a symbol?]

12. How many *A*s did she get? [Should the plural of a capital letter be formed with an apostrophe to avoid confusion?]

13. Cindy rolls her *r*s when she speaks German.

14. The crew answered the captain with loud *aye*s.

15. We counted six *yes*s on that vote.

16. Do all Web addresses begin with *www*s?

17. That price sure has lots of *0*s in it.

18. Please cross out the *3*s on that sign.

19. Mrs. Carr wrote ✓s by the items on her list.

20. *Vacuum* has two *u*s, I believe.

Hyphens

14v. Use a hyphen to divide a word at the end of a line.

> **EXAMPLES** Mark unwrapped the package and took out the glasses care-
> fully. [A hyphen is used to divide the word *carefully* at the end of the
> line.]
>
> Near the horizon, the dark, billowy storm clouds were thin-
> ning. [A hyphen between the doubled consonant *n* divides the word
> *thinning*.]

NOTE Divide words between syllables, between prefixes and base words, and between
suffixes and base words. Divide hyphenated words only at the hyphen, and do not
divide a word so that one letter stands alone. Single-syllable words are not divided.

> **EXAMPLES** agi-tate [between syllables]   depend-able [between base and
>   suffix]
>
> in-spect [between prefix and base]   two-way [already hyphenated
>   word]

EXERCISE A Draw a slash (/) to show where the underlined words in each of the following sentences
might be divided. If a word cannot be hyphenated, write *C* on the line provided. Use a dictionary if you
are not sure about how to divide a word.

Examples _____ **1.** After class, my mind was spin/ning with ideas. [The word *spinning* should

be divided between the doubled consonant *n*.]

_____C_____ **2.** One of my ancestors signed the Declaration of Independence. [The word

signed should not be hyphenated because it has only one syllable.]

_____ **1.** I decided to go alone to the pool. [Should a word be hyphenated if only one letter will

stand alone?]

_____ **2.** Each runner in the city marathon must wear a number. [Where could this three-syllable

word be hyphenated?]

_____ **3.** Spurs and a saddle hang in the tack room.

_____ **4.** Call a plumber to repair the sink as soon as possible.

_____ **5.** Aunt Keisha keeps a scrapbook of her travels.

_____ **6.** Won't you climb aboard the airport shuttle?

_____ **7.** This morning, a cottontail rabbit appeared on the lawn.

_____ **8.** The Layton Farmers' Market offered seeds, fruits, and vegetables.

_____ **9.** Lee signed up for soccer rather than baseball.

_____ **10.** I hope we can prepare for the party in time.

GO ON

Some words are always hyphenated. Use hyphens with the following: compound numbers from *twenty-one* to *ninety-nine;* fractions used as modifiers; the prefixes *ex–, self–, all–,* and *great–;* the suffixes *–elect* and *–free;* prefixes before proper nouns and adjectives; and compound adjectives that precede the nouns they modify.

> **EXAMPLES**   Otis needs **twenty-six** coins for the copier. [*Twenty-six* is a compound number from *twenty-one* to *ninety-nine.*]
>
> Two laps of the pool is **one-quarter** mile. [The fraction *one-quarter* is used to modify *mile.*]
>
> **Two thirds** of the coins would not work. [The fraction *two thirds* is not hyphenated because it is not used as a modifier.]
>
> My **great-aunt** is the **president-elect** of her gardening club. [Use a hyphen with the prefix *great–* and with the suffix *–elect.*]
>
> The style of furniture is certainly **mid-Victorian.** [The prefix *mid–* is hyphenated before a proper adjective.]
>
> That park has comfortable, **well-built** cabins. [The compound adjective is hyphenated because it comes before the word it modifies.]
>
> The cabins in that park are **well built** and comfortable. [The compound adjective is not hyphenated because it does not precede *cabins.*]

EXERCISE B Use proofreading marks to insert hyphens where needed in each of the following sentences. If no hyphens are needed, write *C* on the line provided.

Examples _____ **1.** Tom's great͜grandfather owned a dairy. [The prefix *great–* should be used

with a hyphen.]

_____ **2.** The club needs a two-thirds majority to approve the dress code. [The

fraction *two-thirds* modifies *majority,* so a hyphen should be used.]

_____**11.** Three fourths of the tulips are red. [Should a fraction be hyphenated when it is not used as

a modifier?]

_____**12.** The stylist said my hairstyle is up to date. [Is *up to date* hyphenated?]

_____**13.** That book was written by an expresident.

_____**14.** Fifty three sailboats entered the race.

_____**15.** Are you going to the all school talent show?

_____**16.** I read an article about creating a dust free bedroom.

_____**17.** My great uncle grew up in pre World War II Los Angeles.

_____**18.** Paula had to make a split second decision.

_____**19.** That song has become world famous.

_____**20.** The commercial claims that this is a well built car.

Words with *ie* and *ei*

15a. Write *ie* when the sound is long *e*, except after *c*.

The long *e* sound is what you hear in words such as *speed*, *thief*, and *bead*.

EXAMPLES	*i* before *e:*	*ei* after *c:*
	relief	deceive
	field	perceive
	niece	conceit
	pier	ceiling
	yield	receipt

15b. Write *ei* when the sound is not long *e*.

Choose *ei* especially when the sound is a long *a*. The long *a* sound is what you hear in words such as *plate*, *afraid*, *weight*, and *okay*.

EXAMPLES	*ei:*	*ei* pronounced *ay:*
	foreign	rein
	height	weight
	forfeit	sleigh

TIP If you have trouble with the above guidelines, remember the old rhyme: **i** *before* **e,** *except after* **c** *(or when sounded as* **ay,** *as in* neighbor *and* weigh*).*

EXERCISE A Underline the word in parentheses that is spelled correctly in each of the following sentences.

Examples 1. Do you (*beleive*, *believe*) that really happened? [The letters make a long e sound, but they do not follow c. The correct spelling is *believe*.]

    2. The rider held the (*reins*, *riens*) of the horse. [The letters are pronounced *ay*. The correct spelling is *reins*.]

1. Cathy saw a large spider web in the corner of the (*ceiling*, *cieling*). [Do the letters make a long e sound? Do they follow c?]

2. Mark's (*neice*, *niece*) and nephew are visiting this summer. [Do the letters make a long e sound? Do they follow c?]

3. The team (*forfeited*, *forfieted*) the game because four players were ill.

4. A good rain would provide some (*releif*, *relief*) from this heat.

5. One of our (*neighbors*, *nieghbors*) has a new dog.

6. Kim has been elected editor-in-(*cheif*, *chief*) of the newspaper.

7. This package makes (*eight*, *ieght*) servings of pasta.

GO ON

8. She was named as an *(heir, hier)* in her uncle's will.

9. The *(casheir, cashier)* demonstrated the cash register for the new employee.

10. Did you *(receive, recieve)* an invitation to the party?

Most words will follow the rules for *ie* and *ei*, but some common words are exceptions. It is always a good idea to use a dictionary if you are unsure of the spelling of a word.

> **EXAMPLES**   e**i**ther   n**ei**ther   prot**ei**n   s**ei**ze
> [Most Americans pronounce these words with a long *e* sound, as in *feet*, but they are spelled with *ei*.]
> v**ie**w   fr**ie**nd   anc**ie**nt   misch**ie**f
> [These words have a vowel sound that is not long *e*, but they are spelled with *ie*.]

EXERCISE B Underline the word in parentheses that is spelled correctly in each of the following sentences. Hint: Some of the words follow the *ie/ei* spelling rules, but others do not.

Examples 1. (<u>Neither</u>, Niether) of the rooms is unlocked. [Most Americans pronounce *neither* with a long *e*, but the word does not follow the *ie* rule.]

      2. Does that room have a good (*veiw*, <u>view</u>) of the park? [*View* is not pronounced with a long *e*, and the letters do not follow *c*. *View* does not follow the *ei* rule.]

11. He's really very shy, but everyone thinks he's *(conceited, concieted)*. [Do the letters make a long *e* sound? Do the letters follow *c*?]

12. The children got into *(mischeif, mischief)* while you were gone. [Do the *ie/ei* rules apply to the word?]

13. I usually eat *(either, iether)* an apple or a banana after lunch.

14. Her *(consceince, conscience)* told her that she should apologize.

15. One of my *(freinds, friends)* works in that building.

16. She *(seized, siezed)* the rope tightly and swung out over the water.

17. The students were ready for *(their, thier)* exams.

18. Would you like a *(peice, piece)* of fruit?

19. I would prefer a slice of that apple *(pei, pie)*.

20. How much does that sack of potatoes *(weigh, wiegh)*?

Prefixes and Suffixes

Prefixes

A *prefix* is a letter or a group of letters added to the beginning of a word to change its meaning.

15d. When adding a prefix, do not change the spelling of the original word.

> **EXAMPLES** im + possible = im**possible**   mis + understand = mis**understand**

EXERCISE A Add the prefix to the word for each of the following items.

Example 1. re + mark = _____remark_____ [Adding the prefix *re–* does not change the

spelling of *mark*.]

1. dis + charge = _____ [Does adding a prefix change the spelling of *charge*?]

2. hemi + sphere = _____

3. un + happy = _____

4. mis + spell = _____

5. il + literate = _____

Suffixes

A *suffix* is a letter or a group of letters added to the end of a word to change its meaning.

15e. When adding the suffix *–ness* or *–ly*, do not change the spelling of the original word.

> **EXAMPLES** lone + ly = **lone**ly   whole + ness = **whole**ness

If a word ends in *y*, change the *y* to *i* before adding *–ness* or *–ly*.

> **EXAMPLES** merry + ly = **merri**ly   happy + ness = **happi**ness

EXERCISE B Add the suffix to the word for each of the following items.

Example 1. tardy + ness = _____tardiness_____ [*Tardy* ends in *y*, so the *y* must change to *i*

before *–ness* is added.]

6. love + ly _____ [Does the word end in *y*?]

7. dizzy + ness _____

8. part + ly _____

9. kind + ness _____

10. happy + ly _____

GO ON ➡

Drop the final silent *e* before adding a suffix that begins with a vowel. A silent *e* is not pronounced when you say the word.

EXAMPLES   ride + ing = **rid**ing   desire + able = **desir**able

Keep the final silent *e* before adding a suffix that begins with a consonant.

EXAMPLES   hope + ful = **hope**ful   loathe + some = **loathe**some

EXERCISE C Add the suffix to the word for each of the following items.

Example 1. spite + ful = _____*spiteful*_____ [The suffix begins with the consonant *f,* so the

final silent *e* is kept.]

11. write + ing = _____ [Does the prefix begin with a vowel or a consonant?]

12. excite + ment = _____

13. file + ed _____

14. remove + al = _____

15. same + ness = _____

When a word ends in *y* and the *y* follows a consonant, change the *y* to *i* before adding any suffix that does not begin with *i*. If the suffix begins with *i*, keep the *y*.

EXAMPLES   happy + ly = **happi**ly [The suffix –*ly* does not begin with *i*.]
multiply + ing = **multiply**ing [The suffix –*ing* begins with *i*.]

When a word ends in *y* and the *y* follows a vowel, keep the *y* when adding a suffix.

EXAMPLES   enjoy + ment = **enjoy**ment [The *y* follows the vowel *o*.]
play + ed = **play**ed [The *y* follows the vowel *a*.]

EXERCISE D Add the suffix to the word for each of the following items.

Example 1. body + ly = _____*bodily*_____ [*Body* ends in y. The letter before *y* is the

consonant *d*. The suffix does not begin with *i*. The *y* changes to *i*.]

16. say + ing = _____ [Is the letter before *y* a consonant or a vowel?]

17. fry + ed = _____

18. defy + ant = _____

19. decoy + ing = _____

20. mercy + less = _____

Plurals of Nouns

Most nouns can be made plural simply by adding –s to the end of the word.

SINGULAR	table	duo	key	Johnson
PLURAL	tables	duos	keys	Johnsons

Some nouns are made plural by adding –es to the end of the word. Most nouns that end in s, x, z, ch, or sh form their plurals this way.

SINGULAR	lunch	cross	box	Cortez
PLURAL	lunches	crosses	boxes	Cortezes

TIP If the plural form of a word has one more syllable than the singular word has, the plural word is probably spelled with –es. A syllable is a word part that can be pronounced as one uninterrupted sound.

EXAMPLE The singular word *ranch* has one syllable. The plural word *ranches* has two syllables: *ranch • es*. The plural word *ranches* is formed by adding –es to the singular word *ranch*.

EXERCISE A Write the plural form of each of the following words.

Examples 1. dinner _____dinners_____ [The plural *dinners* has the same number of syllables as the singular *dinner*. The plural is formed by adding –s.]

2. fox _____foxes_____ [The plural *foxes* has one more syllable than the singular *fox*. The plural is formed by adding –es.]

1. mix _____ [Does the plural form have the same number of syllables as the singular, or does the plural form have one more syllable?]

2. trumpet _____ [Does the plural form have the same number of syllables as the singular, or does the plural form have one more syllable?]

3. lunch _____

4. automobile _____

5. flower _____

6. miss _____

7. action _____

8. buzz _____

9. boss _____

10. camera _____

GO ON

Many words that end in *–y* form the plural by changing the *y* to *i* before adding *–es*. If the final *y* follows a vowel, keep the *y* and add *–s*.

SINGULAR	fly	destiny	courtesy	bay	decoy
PLURAL	fl**ies**	destin**ies**	courtes**ies**	ba**ys**	deco**ys**

Many words that end in *–f* or *–fe* form the plural by changing the *f* to *v*. In some words, the *f* does not change.

SINGULAR	thie**f**	wi**fe**	lea**f**	roo**f**	sa**fe**
PLURAL	thie**ves**	wi**ves**	lea**ves**	roo**fs**	sa**fes**

EXERCISE B Write the plural form of each of the following words.

Examples 1. guy _____*guys*_____ [The letter before *y* is a vowel, so the plural is formed by adding *s*.]

2. knife _____*knives*_____ [The *f* in *knife* changes to *v* in the plural form.]

11. army _____ [Is the letter before *y* a consonant or a vowel?]

12. half _____ [Does the *f* change to *v* in the plural?]

13. loaf _____   **17.** party _____

14. buoy _____   **18.** giraffe _____

15. candy _____   **19.** chef _____

16. life _____   **20.** donkey _____

The plurals of some nouns are formed in irregular ways. A few nouns do not change at all to form the plural.

SINGULAR	child	mouse	louse	pliers	sheep
PLURAL	children	mice	lice	pliers	sheep

EXERCISE C Each of the following words is a plural form. On the line provided, write the singular form of each word.

Example 1. women _____*woman*_____ [The *a* in *woman* changes to *e* in the plural.]

21. geese _____ [Were any letters changed to make this plural?]

22. deer _____

23. oxen _____

24. children _____

25. swine _____

Writing Numbers

15l. Spell out a ***cardinal number***—a number that shows how many—if it can be expressed in one or two words. Otherwise, use numerals.

Cardinal numbers are the numbers used for counting: *1, 2, 3*, and so on. When a cardinal number is used as an adjective, it tells *how many* persons, places, things, or ideas.

> **EXAMPLES** **sixteen** horses
>
> **fifty-two** cards [These numbers are one or two words.]
>
> **597** voters
>
> **1,440** minutes [These numbers are more than two words.]

Be consistent when using two or more cardinal numbers in the same sentence. Do not spell out one number and use numerals for the other.

> **AWKWARD** We sold **292** drinks but only **thirty** sandwiches.
>
> **BETTER** We sold **292** drinks but only **30** sandwiches.

EXERCISE A In the following sentences, underline any number that should be spelled out. If all the numbers in a sentence are written correctly, write *C* on the line provided.

Example _____ **1.** Only <u>65</u> students are going on the field trip. [The number can be written in two words, so it should be spelled out.]

_____ **1.** I counted 547 books in these 14 boxes. [Can these numbers be written in one or two words? What if one number can be, but the other can't be?]

_____ **2.** Sharon bought 2 pairs of sunglasses, one for herself and one for her sister.

_____ **3.** Neil stopped counting birds after he got to three hundred.

_____ **4.** If 70 children are going to the zoo, we'll need more than 1 bus.

_____ **5.** The stadium has seats for over fifty thousand people.

15m. Spell out a number that begins a sentence.

A long number at the beginning of a sentence is difficult to read. Revise the sentence if the spelled-out number is longer than two or three words.

> **EXAMPLES** **Four thousand** is the answer. [The spelled-out number is only two words.]
>
> **Four thousand six hundred forty-two** is the answer. [The spelled-out number is longer than the rest of the sentence.]
>
> The answer is **4,642**. [The sentence was revised so that numerals could be used.]

GO ON

EXERCISE B Underline any number that should be spelled out in each of the following sentences. If all the numbers in a sentence are written correctly, write *C* on the line provided.

Example _____ **1.** <u>12</u> schools participate in the competition. [The numeral *12* should be spelled out because the number begins the sentence.]

_____ **6.** Seven hundred seventy-five students registered for classes. [Does the number begin a sentence? Is the spelled-out number longer than two or three words?]

_____ **7.** Dan prepared 1,550 registration packets, 25 for each homeroom.

_____ **8.** Twenty-eight teachers picked up the packets.

_____ **9.** 32 dollars for one book is a lot of money!

_____ **10.** You'll get a dollar or 2 in change from that bill.

15n. Spell out *ordinal numbers*—numbers that express order.

Ordinal numbers are the numbers used when describing the position or order of something: *first, second, third,* and so on.

> **EXAMPLES** He came in **first** in his age category.
> That must be the **tenth** time the phone has rung this morning.

EXERCISE C Underline any number that should be spelled out in the following sentences. If all the numbers in a sentence are written correctly, write *C* on the line provided.

Example _____ **1.** The <u>6th</u> person in line was my brother. [The ordinal number *sixth* should be spelled out.]

_____ **11.** We'll eat some lunch 1st.

_____ **12.** The eighteenth problem has an error in it.

_____ **13.** My fourth and 5th paragraphs are too long.

_____ **14.** Rick won 2nd place in his division at the science fair.

_____ **15.** The 3rd item on the agenda is a discussion of the budget.

Words Often Confused A

People often confuse the following words. Some of these words are *homonyms*—that is, their pronunciations are the same. However, these words have different meanings and spellings. Other words in the following groups have the same or similar spellings yet have different meanings.

already [adverb] *previously; something accomplished by or before the specified time*
Have you **already** sent your application?

all ready [adjective] *all prepared; in readiness*
The campers were **all ready** for the hike.

altogether [adverb] *entirely; everything included; everything being considered*
The movie is **altogether** too violent for children.

all together [adjective] *in the same place*
The supplies are **all together** on one shelf.
[adverb] *at the same time*
The woodwinds did not start **all together.**

EXERCISE A Underline the word or words in parentheses that will complete the sentence correctly.

Examples 1. The gymnasium is decorated and (*all ready*, *already*) for the dance. [The meaning is "prepared," so *all ready* is correct.]

2. By the time we arrive, the dance will (*all ready*, *already*) have started. [The meaning is "previously," so *already* is correct.]

1. The plot of the novel is (*altogether*, *all together*) too confusing. [Which word means "entirely"?]

2. The team was huddled (*altogether*, *all together*) on the field. [Which word means "in the same place"?]

3. If you want to cook now, the kitchen is clean and (*already*, *all ready*) for you.

4. The imaginative drawings in the book are (*altogether*, *all together*) delightful.

5. When my family is (*all together*, *altogether*), we always have a good time.

6. I've (*all ready*, *already*) finished the laundry and folded the clothes.

7. I don't know when we will be (*all together*, *altogether*) again.

8. The hardware store had (*already*, *all ready*) closed by the time we got there.

9. Although we were (*already*, *all ready*) to eat, we had to wait for James.

10. Let's try the music (*all together*, *altogether*) this time.

GO ON

    brake   [noun] *a device to stop a machine*
             Did you have the **brakes** checked?

    break   [verb] *to fracture; to shatter*
             That runner will **break** a world record some day.

    capital   [noun] *a city that is the seat of government of a state or country*
             The **capital** of Montana is Helena.
             [noun] *money or property*
             The investors expect a return on the **capital** they have invested.
             [adjective] *punishable by death; important or serious; an uppercase letter*
             In some societies, theft was a **capital** crime.
             The name of a month begins with a **capital** letter.

    capitol   [noun] *a building where a legislature meets*
             The **capitol** was built during the 1930s.
             The dome of the **Capitol** is white. [The U.S. Capitol is always capitalized.]

    coarse   [adjective] *rough; crude; not fine*
             The cloth was **coarse** and scratchy.

    course   [noun] *path of action; unit of study; route* [also used in the phrase *of course*]
             The navigator will plot the **course** of the ship.
             Of **course** you may have a glass of water.

EXERCISE B Underline the word in parentheses that will complete the sentence correctly.

Example 1. Parts of the *(coarse, course)* are steep, but the runners are well trained. [The meaning

            is "a route," so *course* is correct.]

11. The heat may *(break, brake)* that test tube. [Which word means "to fracture" or "to shatter"?]

12. The truck dumped *(coarse, course)* gravel in the driveway. [Which word means "rough"?]

13. *(Capital, Capitol)* punishment is a controversial subject.

14. Rick will take that *(coarse, course)* after he finishes chemistry.

15. The *(break, brake)* on that old wagon is just a piece of wood.

16. You won't make any money, and you risk losing your *(capital, capitol)*.

17. I can't *(break, brake)* a promise to a friend.

18. Does Mrs. McReynolds spell her name with two *(capital, capitol)* letters or one?

19. The road follows the *(coarse, course)* of the river.

20. Can anyone tell me the name of the *(capital, capitol)* of Austria?

Words Often Confused B

People often confuse the following words. Some of these words are *homonyms*—that is, their pronunciations are the same. However, these words have different meanings and spellings. Other words have the same or similar spellings yet have different meanings.

complement   [noun] *something that makes whole or complete*
Which angle is the **complement** of angle QRS?
[verb] *to make whole or complete*
Asparagus would perfectly **complement** the rest of the meal.

compliment   [noun] *praise; respect*
He has never learned how to accept a **compliment.**
[verb] *to express praise, appreciation, or respect*
Mr. Fallows **complimented** her on her achievement.

desert   [noun, pronounced *des'•ert*] *a dry, barren, sandy region; a wilderness*
Is the Sahara the world's largest **desert**?

desert   [verb, pronounced *de•sert'*] *to abandon; to leave*
The defenders did not **desert** the fort.

dessert   [noun, pronounced *des•sert'*] *a sweet, final course of a meal*
The **desserts** on the menu sound tempting.

formally   [adverb] *in a strict or dignified manner*
Mark knew her, but they had not been **formally** introduced.

formerly   [adverb] *previously*
Our guest speaker was **formerly** a state representative.

EXERCISE A Underline the word in parentheses that will complete the sentence correctly.

Example 1. Nick *(formally, formerly)* taught school in Japan. [The meaning is "previously," so

formerly is the correct word.]

1. A good drummer is a necessary *(complement, compliment)* for the band. [Which word means "something that makes whole or complete"?]

2. The students *(desert, dessert)* the campus every Friday. [Which word means "to abandon"?]

3. I meant that comment as a *(complement, compliment)*.

4. Everyone at the awards banquet was *(formally, formerly)* dressed.

5. The words of the song are a perfect *(complement, compliment)* to the music.

6. After a big dinner, I have no room for *(desert, dessert)*.

7. The new stadium will be *(formerly, formally)* opened tomorrow.

8. At sunrise, the air in the *(desert, dessert)* was dry but cool.

9. She was *(formerly, formally)* employed as an aerospace engineer.

10. I doubt his *(complements, compliments)* were sincere.

> **its** [possessive form of the pronoun *it*] *belonging to it*
> The bird spread **its** wings and flew away.
>
> **it's** [contraction of *it is* or *it has*]
> **It's** not a common bird in this part of the country.
>
> **lead** [verb, rhymes with *feed*] *to go first; to guide or direct*
> Who will **lead** the singing of the national anthem?
>
> **led** [verb, past tense of *lead*] *went first*
> The clues **led** the explorers to the treasure.
>
> **lead** [noun, rhymes with *red*] *a heavy metal; graphite used in a pencil*
> As he climbed, his tired legs felt like **lead.**
>
> **loose** [adjective, rhymes with *goose*] *not tight; free; not confined*
> One of the legs on the chair is **loose.**
>
> **lose** [verb, rhymes with *snooze*] *to suffer loss*
> The team was determined not to **lose** this game.

EXERCISE B Underline the word in parentheses that will complete the sentence correctly.

Example 1. *(Its, It's)* been a long time since we've had a day off. [The meaning is "it has," so *It's* is
the correct word.]

11. The cat twitched *(its, it's)* tail and left the couch. [Which word means "belonging to it"?]

12. The cowboys rounded up all the *(loose, lose)* horses. [Which word means "free" or "not confined"?]

13. *(Led, Lead)* poisoning from old paint still occurs, especially in young children.

14. Do you want go to the movie if *(its, it's)* still showing tomorrow?

15. The *(led, lead)* in this mechanical pencil keeps breaking.

16. She simply couldn't afford to *(loose, lose)* the job.

17. As the ship approached, he could see *(its, it's)* flag waving from the mast.

18. The candidates will *(led, lead)* their party to victory in November.

19. We may *(loose, lose)* this game, but we should play our best.

20. The squirrel removed the walnut from *(its, it's)* shell.

Words Often Confused C

People often confuse the following words. Some of these words are *homonyms*—that is, their pronunciations are the same. However, these words have different meanings and spellings. Other words have the same or similar spellings yet have different meanings.

> **passed**   [verb, past tense of *pass*] *went by; successfully completed a course of study*
> She barely **passed** the exam.
>
> **past**   [noun] *time gone by*
> At the history museum, the **past** almost comes alive.
> [preposition] *beyond; farther than*
> Don't go **past** that fence on the edge of the cliff.
> [adjective] *ended; gone by*
> I've been looking for you for the **past** half-hour.
>
> **quiet**   [adjective] *still; silent*
> Our street is usually **quiet** at night.
>
> **quite**   [adverb] *completely; rather; very*
> We didn't **quite** finish watching the video.

EXERCISE A Underline the word in parentheses that will complete the sentence correctly.

Example 1. Each lazy summer day (*past, passed*) slowly. [The meaning is "went by," so *passed* is

correct]

1. Their visit was (*quiet, quite*) a surprise. [Which word means "completely" or "rather"?]

2. In the early hours of the morning, even a busy city seems (*quiet, quite*).

3. Go (*past, passed*) the museum, and turn right.

4. The man told us interesting stories about his colorful (*past, passed*).

5. Teresa (*past, passed*) her driving test last week.

> **than**   [conjunction used for comparisons]
> The dog wakes up earlier **than** I do.
>
> **then**   [adverb] *at that time; next*
> What did you do **then?**
>
> **their**   [possessive form of the pronoun *they*] *belonging to them*
> Two children have forgotten **their** jackets.
>
> **there**   [adverb] *at that place*
> Please plan to meet us **there** at five o'clock.
> [expletive, used to begin a sentence]
> **There** are three primary colors.

GO ON ➡

they're [contraction of *they are*]
They're best friends.

weather [noun] *atmospheric conditions*
I hope the **weather** is better tomorrow.

whether [conjunction, indicates an alternative or doubt]
She doesn't care **whether** we go tomorrow or the next day.

who's [contraction of *who is* or *who has*]
Who's in charge of the refreshments?

whose [possessive form of *who*] *belonging to whom*
Whose job is to put up the decorations?

EXERCISE B Underline the word in parentheses that will complete the sentence correctly.

Examples 1. The neighbors have painted (*their*, *there*, *they're*) house bright green. [The meaning is "belonging to them," so *their* is correct.]

2. Do you know (*who's*, *whose*) book this is? [The meaning is "belonging to whom," so *whose* is correct.]

6. I would rather stay home tonight (*then*, *than*) go to the game. [Which word is used for comparisons?]

7. Gordon isn't sure (*weather*, *whether*) he will have time to work this weekend. [Which word describes an alternative or doubt?]

8. (*Who's*, *Whose*) making all that noise outside?

9. My father always checks the (*weather*, *whether*) report before he goes to bed.

10. Rita scored four more points (*than*, *then*) I did.

11. Everyone (*who's*, *whose*) name begins with the letters *A* through *M* should line up.

12. (*Their*, *There*, *They're*) are three cars parked in front of the house.

13. We should eat lunch now, and (*than*, *then*) we can finish shopping.

14. Can you tell me what time (*their*, *there*, *they're*) meeting?

15. The army marched more (*than*, *then*) twenty miles in a day.

Common Errors Review

Common Usage Errors

Be sure to proofread each writing assignment before you turn it in. Errors in writing can confuse and distract readers, and careless mistakes may even lead readers to form poor impressions of a writer. Look for errors by asking yourself these questions:

Are subjects and verbs in agreement?   Are modifiers correct and placed correctly?
Are verb tenses and forms correct?   Are troublesome words correct?
Are pronoun references clear?   Is usage appropriate to audience and purpose?

After you make any corrections or changes to your writing, read your writing again. Sometimes a change you make will create the need to adjust another part of your writing.

The following exercises will help you recognize and correct common errors in usage and mechanics.

EXERCISE A Use the list of questions above to help you find and correct the common errors in usage found in the following sentences. Use proofreading marks to make your corrections.

Example 1. Everyone must listen carefully and choose the candidates ~~they like~~ best. [The
                                                                          he or she likes

antecedent of the pronoun *they* is *Everyone,* a singular indefinite pronoun. *They* should

be changed to the singular personal pronoun *he or she.* The singular pronoun *he or she*

takes a singular verb, *likes.*]

1. You had ought to vote for me for class president because I am the better of all the candidates.

[Are all the usages standard? Is there an incorrect form of a modifier?]

2. Everyone agree that the sophomore dance I planned was great fun, and just between you and

I, nobody's fundraisers are as successful as mine are. [Is there a singular indefinite pronoun used

with a plural verb? Is there a personal pronoun that is in the wrong case?]

3. My can-do attitude has a positive affect on everyone I work with, and I promise that this class

will have less problems than any other junior class!

4. Working with teachers, parents, students, and etc., a great class trip will be planned.

5. We could choose between the beach, the mountains, or a theme park for our trip, but I think a

theme park would be more fun.

6. Us students also have to plan the junior prom, and we have to work real hard to make that the

best event of the whole year.

7. Hopefully I can count on your vote, but the most important thing are to get involved.

GO ON

8. If somebody says that they would make a better class president, don't believe it.

9. I already do good in my classes, so the extra work won't be no problem.

10. Whom will get you're vote for class president?

Common Mechanics Errors

Be sure to check your capitalization, punctuation, and spelling when you write. Use a dictionary if you're not sure of a spelling or of how to divide a word. Make sure you haven't confused two words that sound alike but are spelled differently. Attention to these details will make a big difference in your writing! Ask yourself these questions as you proofread your work:

Does every sentence begin with a capital letter?
Are all proper nouns capitalized?
Does every sentence end with an appropriate end mark?
Are words spelled and divided correctly?
Are commas and apostrophes placed where they are needed?
Are direct quotations and titles capitalized and punctuated correctly?

EXERCISE B Correct errors in capitalization, punctuation, and spelling in the following sentences. Use proofreading marks to make your corrections.

                December
Example 1. On ~~Dec.~~ 2 three american history classes will visit the Aviation Museum at 212

Westside drive. [The name of a month shouldn't be abbreviated in running text. Proper

nouns and adjectives should be capitalized. Declarative sentences should end with peri-

ods.]

11. The classes will leave at 10.30 A.M. in the morning, accompanied by 8 teachers and Principle

Hernandez. [Is the time written and punctuated correctly? Should numbers be spelled out or

written in numerals? Is there a misspelled word in the sentence?]

12. Students should bring a sack lunch and a drink, everyone should wear comfortable walking

shoes and nice clothes—no cutoffs!

13. before the field trip, students should review Chapter 7, *America at War*, in their history textbook.

14. At the Museum, students will learn about womens' role as pilots during world war II and

they will hear the story of the African American pilots from Tuskegee Alabama.

15. We will also see the types of aircraft used during the war, fighters, bombers, and reconnaissance

planes!

Using Parallel Structure

In a sentence, *parallel structure* is balanced structure. Similar items in a series should take the same form. Nouns balance nouns, phrases balance phrases, and clauses balance clauses.

NOT PARALLEL Marshall's hobbies are running and to play the violin. [The items in the series are not parallel. One is a gerund, and the other is an infinitive phrase.]

PARALLEL Marshall's hobbies are **running** and **playing** the violin. [The items are now parallel. Both are gerunds.]

NOT PARALLEL We looked under the desk, behind the cabinet, and the shelves. [The items in the series are not parallel. The first two are prepositional phrases, and the third is a noun.]

PARALLEL We looked **under the desk, behind the cabinet,** and **between the shelves.** [The items are now parallel. All three are prepositional phrases.]

EXERCISE A Decide whether the underlined items in the following sentences have parallel structure. Then, on the line provided, write *P* for *parallel structure* or *N* for *not parallel structure*.

Example ___N___ **1.** The landscape designer recommended native plants, grasses, and to plant trees. [The series of items contains two nouns and one infinitive phrase, so the structure is not parallel.]

_____ **1.** As we sat near the water, we saw turtles, fish, and there were ducks. [Is each underlined item a noun?]

_____ **2.** Liz hopes to learn more about health and to become a physical therapist.

_____ **3.** The room seemed very gloomy because the carpet was gray, the walls were gray, and gray upholstery on the furniture.

_____ **4.** To help others and growing personally are two good reasons to do volunteer work.

_____ **5.** I enjoy sitting outside, looking at the stars, and listening to the crickets.

Use parallel structure when you compare or contrast ideas.

NOT PARALLEL To arrive safely is as important as getting there on time. [The items being compared are not parallel. One is an infinitive phrase, and the other is a gerund phrase.]

PARALLEL **Arriving safely** is as important as **getting there on time.** [Now the items being compared are parallel. Both are gerund phrases.]

NOT PARALLEL Jeff certainly enjoys eating home-cooked meals more than fast food. [The items being contrasted are not parallel. One is a gerund phrase, and the other is a noun.]

GO ON ➡

> **PARALLEL** Jeff certainly enjoys **home-cooked meals** more than **fast food.** [Now the items being contrasted are parallel. Both are nouns.]

EXERCISE B Decide whether the underlined items in the following sentences have parallel structure. Then, on the line provided, write *P* for *parallel structure* or *N* for *not parallel structure.*

Example ___P___ **1.** Did Lori say she liked dancing or singing more? [The two underlined items are both gerunds, so the sentence is parallel.]

_____ **6.** Matt enjoys taking pictures of people more than to photograph landscapes. [Is each underlined item an infinitive phrase?]

_____ **7.** To know her facts is as crucial to the attorney as to understand the client's story.

_____ **8.** Being courteous to customers is more important than being the fastest checker.

_____ **9.** Would you prefer to write the report or researching it?

_____ **10.** Listening to my grandparents' stories is more entertaining than to watch television.

Use parallel structure when you link ideas with correlative conjunctions: *both . . . and, either . . . or, neither . . . nor,* and *not only . . . but also.*

> **NOT PARALLEL** Not only to teach but also for learning is why Jan works with young children. [The ideas linked by the correlative conjunction *not only . . . but also* are not parallel. One is an infinitive, and the other is a prepositional phrase.]
>
> **PARALLEL** **Not only to teach but also to learn** is why Jan works with young children. [Now the ideas are parallel. Both are infinitives.]

EXERCISE C Decide whether the underlined items in the following sentences have parallel structure. Then, on the line provided, write *P* for *parallel structure* or *N* for *not parallel structure.*

Example ___N___ **1.** Both knowing basic math skills and to have problem-solving skills are necessary to succeed in math. [The two ideas linked by the correlative conjunction *both . . . and* are not parallel. One is a gerund phrase, and the other is an infinitive phrase.]

_____ **11.** Roland enjoys woodworking, so he plans either to become a master carpenter or he may open a custom furniture store. [Is each underlined item an infinitive phrase?]

_____ **12.** Have you looked for the skillet both in the dishwasher and in the cabinets?

_____ **13.** Because I get seasick easily, neither sailing nor deep-sea fishing appears enjoyable.

_____ **14.** Not only sleeping but also to wake up is easier if you go to bed early.

_____ **15.** Both swimming and to snorkel are exciting watersports.

Complete Sentences and Sentence Fragments

A *complete sentence* has a subject and a verb, and it expresses a complete thought. A *sentence fragment* lacks a subject, a verb, or both a subject and a verb; or it may not express a complete thought.

FRAGMENT	Forty miles east of Flagstaff, Arizona. [no subject or verb]
FRAGMENT	Lives forty miles east of Flagstaff, Arizona. [no subject]
FRAGMENT	Aunt Sarah forty miles east of Flagstaff, Arizona. [no verb]
FRAGMENT	After we left the Grand Canyon. [not a complete thought]
SENTENCE	After we left the Grand Canyon, we visited Aunt Sarah, who lives forty miles east of Flagstaff, Arizona. [complete sentence]

EXERCISE A Decide whether each of the following items is a sentence fragment. Then, on the line provided, write *F* for *sentence fragment* or *S* for *complete sentence*.

Example _____F_____ **1.** A reel mower better for the environment. [The word group does not contain a verb, and it does not express a complete thought. It is a sentence fragment.]

_____ **1.** If the red light on the phone is blinking. [Does the word group have both a subject and a verb? Does it express a complete thought?]

_____ **2.** The leaves a loud crackling sound.

_____ **3.** Did you see any hummingbirds eating out of the hummingbird feeder today?

_____ **4.** Ruth opened the closet to hang up the freshly washed clothes.

_____ **5.** Because the temperature dropped so suddenly and no one had brought a coat.

Phrase Fragments

A *phrase* is a word group that lacks a subject and a verb. A phrase that is not part of a complete sentence is a *phrase fragment.* Four types of phrases that are often mistaken for sentences are *prepositional phrases, verbal phrases, appositive phrases,* and *absolute phrases.*

FRAGMENT	On the morning of my birthday. [prepositional phrase]
SENTENCE	My family made my favorite breakfast **on the morning of my birthday.** [The prepositional phrase is added to a complete sentence.]
FRAGMENT	Locally owned and operated since 1980. [verbal phrase]
SENTENCE	**Locally owned and operated since 1980,** The Native and Natural Nursery has the best selection of native and organically grown plants and vegetables. [The verbal phrase is added to a complete sentence.]

GO ON ➡

	FRAGMENT	A piece of granite. [appositive phrase]

FRAGMENT A piece of granite. [appositive phrase]

SENTENCE He put the paperweight, **a piece of granite,** on top of the papers before he opened the window. [The appositive phrase is added to a complete sentence.]

FRAGMENT Candles shining in the darkness. [absolute phrase]

SENTENCE **Candles shining in the darkness,** the carolers made their way down Main Street. [The absolute phrase is added to a complete sentence.]

Subordinate Clause Fragments

A *clause* is a word group that has a subject and a verb. An *independent clause* expresses a complete thought and can stand alone as a sentence. A *subordinate clause* does not express a complete thought and cannot stand alone as a sentence. A subordinate clause that is not part of a complete sentence is a *subordinate clause fragment.*

FRAGMENT Whenever the doorbell rings. [The clause has a subject and a verb, but it does not express a complete thought.]

SENTENCE **Whenever the doorbell rings,** our dogs bark and run to the front door. [The subordinate clause is joined to a complete sentence.]

EXERCISE B Each of the following word groups is a fragment. Revise each fragment to make it a complete sentence by adding a subject, a verb, or both a subject and a verb; or attach the fragment to a complete sentence. Write the revised sentences on the lines provided.

Example 1. Swayed and raised their arms gracefully. [This word group has two verbs but no subject. Without a subject, it cannot express a complete thought.]

The dancers swayed and raised their arms gracefully.

6. A postcard with a short message. [Is the word group missing a subject, a verb, or both a subject and a verb? Does it express a complete thought?]

_____

7. Hanging on the clothesline.

_____

8. My favorite color.

_____

9. From several area schools.

_____

10. As long as the cool breeze was blowing.

_____

Run-on Sentences

Two or more complete sentences joined without correct punctuation or connecting words form a **_run-on sentence._**

RUN-ON	A marathon is a long-distance race for runners the runners must cover slightly more than twenty-six miles to complete the race. [Two sentences have been joined without any punctuation.]
CORRECT	A marathon is a long-distance race for runners**.** **T**he runners must cover slightly more than twenty-six miles to complete the race. [The sentences have been separated with a period and a capital letter.]
RUN-ON	The mail carrier has already delivered the mail, we didn't get any mail today. [Two sentences have been joined with only a comma. A comma by itself cannot join two sentences.]
CORRECT	The mail carrier has already delivered the mail**, but** we didn't get any mail today. [The coordinating conjunction *but* is used with the comma to join the sentences.]

NOTE▶ There are two types of run-on sentences. *Fused sentences* have no punctuation at all between complete thoughts. *Comma splices* have only a comma between complete thoughts.

EXERCISE A Decide whether each of the following items is a run-on sentence. Then, on the line provided, write *R* for *run-on sentence* or *C* for *correct sentence*.

Example ___R___ **1.** Call a taxi, it's time to go to the airport. [A comma by itself cannot join two sentences.]

_____ **1.** It's so hot, let's go inside. [Can a comma join two sentences?]

_____ **2.** Algae has grown all over the fish tank walls Kay needs to clean the tank soon.

_____ **3.** Do you prefer a pencil, or would you rather write with a pen?

_____ **4.** Gillian reported to the committee on the project, it will be finished next week.

_____ **5.** Most young men wear tuxedos to the prom they look distinguished in them.

Revising Run-on Sentences

There are several ways to revise a run-on sentence.

(1) Make two sentences by adding punctuation and a capital letter.
(2) Make a compound sentence by using a comma and a coordinating conjunction. The coordinating conjunctions are *and, but, or, nor, for, so,* and *yet.*
(3) Change one of the independent clauses into a subordinate clause.
(4) Make a compound sentence by using a semicolon.
(5) Make a compound sentence by using a semicolon, a conjunctive adverb, and a comma. Common conjunctive adverbs include *also, however, nevertheless,* and *therefore.*

GO ON ▶

RUN-ON	The roof of the doghouse leaked, we repaired it.
CORRECT	The roof of the doghouse leaked**.** **W**e repaired it. [A period and a capital letter make these two complete sentences.]
CORRECT	The roof of the doghouse leaked**,** **so** we repaired it. [A comma and the coordinating conjunction *so* make this a compound sentence.]
CORRECT	**Because** the roof of the doghouse leaked**,** we repaired it. [The first independent clause was changed into a subordinate clause.]
CORRECT	The roof of the doghouse leaked**;** we repaired it. [A semicolon makes this a compound sentence.]
CORRECT	The roof of the doghouse leaked**; therefore,** we repaired it. [A semicolon, a conjunctive adverb, and a comma make this a compound sentence.]

NOTE▶ A compound sentence consists of two or more closely related sentences. If the sentences are not closely related, make two or more sentences.

      EXAMPLES   The library is having a book sale this weekend**, and** I want to go. [closely related]

                       The library is having a book sale this weekend**. T**here is a bus stop at the library. [not closely related]

EXERCISE B Using the methods listed on this worksheet, revise the following run-on sentences. Write your revised sentences on the lines provided. Hint: Some sentences can be revised in more than one way, but you need to give only one revision for each sentence.

Example 1. I volunteer at the humane society, I love animals. [A comma by itself cannot join two sentences.]

        I volunteer at the humane society because I love animals.

6. The remote control is missing again have you seen it? [Where does one sentence end and the other begin?]

_____

7. Elands are the largest type of antelope, they live in Africa.

_____

8. Zach saw the lightning flash nearby, he heard the thunder rumble.

_____

9. We've ordered more copies of the book it may take several days for the shipment to arrive.

_____

10. After the long hike, we were tired and hungry we stopped to rest and eat lunch.

_____

            HOLT HANDBOOK | Fifth Course

Combining Sentences by Inserting Words and Phrases

Inserting Words

Combining sentences can add variety and interest to your writing. One way to combine sentences is to take important words from one sentence and add them to another sentence.

> **ORIGINAL**   Jon told his family the news. The news was good. [The only new information in the second sentence is the adjective *good*.]
>
> **COMBINED**   Jon told his family the **good** news. [The adjective *good* is added to the first sentence. *Good* describes *news*.]
>
> **ORIGINAL**   The breeze flowed around us. It flowed in a steady way. [The only new information in the second sentence is the adjective *steady*.]
>
> **COMBINED**   The breeze flowed **steadily** around us. [The adjective *steady* has been changed to the adverb *steadily*. *Steadily* describes the verb *flowed*.]

EXERCISE A Combine the following pairs of sentences by inserting the underlined word of one sentence into the other sentence. The directions in parentheses will tell you whether to change the underlined word as you combine the sentences. Write your new sentences on the lines provided.

Example 1. He carved the wooden block. His carving was <u>careful</u>. (Add *–ly* to *careful*.)

> He carefully carved the wooden block.

[The adverb *carefully* modifies the verb *carved*.]

1. The tracks were <u>wet</u>. The freight train struggled up the steep tracks. (no change to *wet*) [What word in the second sentence should the adjective *wet* modify?]

2. Autumn leaves blanketed the sidewalk. The leaves <u>rustle</u>. (Add *–ing* to *rustle*.)

3. The carpenters hammered the nails into the boards. Their hammering was <u>noisy</u>. (Add *–ly* to *noisy*.)

4. Are the children sharing their toys? Are they <u>cheerful</u> about sharing them? (Add *–ly* to *cheerful*.)

5. What a <u>thoughtful</u> gift! How generous of you to give us this gift! (no change to *thoughtful*)

GO ON

Inserting Phrases

An entire *phrase* from one sentence sometimes can be inserted into another sentence. A phrase is a word group that functions as one part of speech and does not have both a subject and verb. Types of phrases commonly used to combine sentences are *prepositional phrases, participial phrases,* and *appositive phrases.*

ORIGINAL	Please bring me the sponge. Bring it from the sink.
COMBINED	Please bring me the sponge **from the sink.** [The prepositional phrase *from the sink* is inserted after *sponge* and tells which sponge.]
ORIGINAL	The sponge soaks up water. It becomes heavy.
COMBINED	**Soaking up water,** the sponge becomes heavy. [The participial phrase *Soaking up water* is inserted at the beginning of the sentence and is set off from the main clause by a comma.]
ORIGINAL	The sponge's skeleton is made of mesh. This mesh is called spongin.
COMBINED	The sponge's skeleton is made of mesh **called spongin.** [The participial phrase *called spongin* is added to the sentence.]
ORIGINAL	There are natural and synthetic sponges. Sponges hold water.
COMBINED	Sponges, **natural and synthetic ones,** hold water. [The appositive phrase describes *Sponges* and is set off by commas.]

EXERCISE B Combine the following pairs of sentences by inserting the underlined words of one sentence into the other sentence. Add commas where they are needed. Write your sentences on the lines provided.

Example 1. The harbor was crowded with boats. The boats were <u>trying to dock.</u>

> The harbor was crowded with boats trying to dock.
> _____

[The participial phrase *trying to dock* describes *boats.*]

6. The mud came <u>from the overflowing creek.</u> The truck's tires spun in the thick mud. [Which noun

in the second sentence can be described with the underlined prepositional phrase?]

_____

7. Basil is a popular seasoning. It is <u>an herb that comes in several varieties.</u>

_____

8. Jon turned the television off. He was <u>annoyed by the noise.</u>

_____

9. Michelle took good notes. She was <u>preparing for her presentation.</u>

_____

10. Swimming is Ned's favorite activity. He especially enjoys swimming <u>for the school team.</u>

_____

Combining Sentences by Coordinating Ideas

Using Compound Subjects and Verbs

A *compound subject* consists of two or more nouns or pronouns that have the same verb and are joined by a conjunction. A *compound verb* consists of two or more verbs that have the same subject and are joined by a conjunction. The coordinating conjunctions *and, but, for, or, nor, so,* and *yet* can be used to create compound subjects and verbs.

ORIGINAL	A skunk was out in the rain. An opossum was out in the rain, too. [The same verb, *was,* has two subjects, *skunk* and *opossum.*]
COMBINED	A **skunk and** an **opossum** were out in the rain. [The coordinating conjunction *and* links the two subjects in a compound subject, *skunk* and *opossum.*]
ORIGINAL	Kevin reads detective novels. Kevin watches detective movies, too. [The two verbs, *reads* and *watches,* have the same subject, *Kevin.*]
COMBINED	Kevin **reads** detective novels **and watches** detective movies. [The coordinating conjunction *and* links the two actions in a compound verb, *reads* and *watches.*]

EXERCISE A Combine each of the following sets of sentences into a single sentence. The directions in parentheses tell you whether to make a compound subject, a compound verb, or a compound subject and a compound verb. Write the new sentences on the lines provided.

Example 1. The driver boarded the bus. The passengers boarded it, too. They drove to Atlanta.

(compound subject and verb)

<u>The driver and the passengers boarded the bus and drove to Atlanta.</u>

[The first two sentences have the same verb, *boarded.* The subject of the last sentence,

They, refers to the subjects of the first two sentences. The compound subject is *driver* and

passengers. The verb in the last sentence is *drove.* The compound verb is *boarded* and

drove.]

1. Do you drive a car to work? Do you ride your bike to work? *(compound verb)* [Which

coordinating conjunction can be used to combine the two verbs?] _____

_____

2. Drivers should wear seatbelts. Passengers should wear them, too. *(compound subject)*

_____

3. The car's seatbelts prevent certain types of injury. The airbags also prevent certain types of

injury. *(compound subject)* _____

_____

GO ON

4. Drive carefully. Watch for playing children. *(compound verb)*

_____

5. Luisa checked the spare tire. Julian checked it, too. They stowed it securely in the trunk.

(compound subject and verb) _____

_____

Creating Compound Sentences

Closely related sentences can be combined to form a *compound sentence.* A compound sentence is two or more independent clauses linked together by (1) a comma and coordinating conjunction such as *and, but, or, nor, for, so,* or *yet;* (2) a semicolon; or (3) a semicolon, a conjunctive adverb, such as *however, nevertheless,* or *therefore,* and a comma.

> **ORIGINAL**   Those birds migrate to warmer places in the winter. They return when the weather warms up again. [The two sentences are closely related.]
>
> **COMBINED**   Those birds migrate to warmer places in the winter; **however,** they return when the weather warms up again. [A semicolon and a conjunctive adverb followed by a comma join the two independent clauses.]

EXERCISE B Combine each of the following pairs of sentences into a compound sentence. Add commas, conjunctions, semicolons, and conjunctive adverbs where they are needed. Write the new sentences on the lines provided.

Example 1. Students may choose to attend the pep rally. They may prefer to work in study hall.

> Students may choose to attend the pep rally, or they may prefer to work in study hall.

[A comma and the coordinating conjunction *or* are used to join these two sentences.]

6. Dad does not feel like cooking tonight. Mom says she'd be willing to grill some chicken.

[Which coordinating conjunction can be used to combine these two sentences?] _____

_____

7. The foxes heard the sound of footsteps. They hid in the brush right away. _____

_____

8. I'll spend the afternoon either working on the lawn or the car. I'll enjoy myself. _____

_____

9. "Surprise!" yelled Roland's friends. Then they jumped out from behind the furniture. _____

_____

10. These ladybugs will keep aphids off the cabbages. They will protect the beans, too.

_____

Combining Sentences by Subordinating Ideas

Creating Complex Sentences

One way to combine sentences is to create a complex sentence. A *complex sentence* contains one independent clause and one or more subordinate clauses.

REMINDER An *independent clause* expresses a complete thought and can stand alone as a sentence. A *subordinate clause* does not express a complete thought and cannot stand alone as a sentence.

Adjective Clauses

An *adjective clause* is a subordinate clause that functions as an adjective. An adjective clause tells *which one, what kind,* or *how many*. Adjective clauses begin with relative pronouns like *who, which,* or *that* and generally follow the nouns or pronouns they modify.

ORIGINAL   Is this the newspaper? It is supposed to contain information about the festival. [The second sentence tells what kind of newspaper.]

COMBINED   Is this the newspaper **that is supposed to contain information about the festival**? [The relative pronoun *that* replaces the subject *It* from the second sentence to form an adjective clause modifying *newspaper*.]

EXERCISE A Combine each of the following pairs of sentences into a complex sentence. Use the word in parentheses to make one of the sentences into an adjective clause. Then, insert the new adjective clause into the remaining sentence. Write the new sentence on the line provided.

Example 1. Pay attention to the park ranger. He knows the park's terrain well. *(who)*

         Pay attention to the park ranger, who knows the park's terrain well.

         [*Who* replaces *He* to form an adjective clause describing *park ranger.*]

1. Where is Colleen? She knows how to set up this tent. *(who)* [What part of the second sentence can be replaced with *who*?] _____

   _____

2. Walter can tell a good campfire story. We all want to listen to him. *(who)* _____

   _____

3. Here are the bass. They were caught this morning. *(that)* _____

   _____

4. It has strong currents and cold water. Stay out of the creek! *(that)* _____

   _____

5. Has anyone gathered small twigs? They help to get a fire going. *(which)* _____

   _____

GO ON ▶

Adverb Clauses

An *adverb clause* is a subordinate clause that functions as an adverb. Adverb clauses modify verbs, adjectives, or adverbs. Adverb clauses often begin with a subordinating conjunction, such as *after, although, when, while, where,* or *so that,* and often tell *when, where,* or *under what conditions* the action of the sentence occurs. An adverb clause may appear at the beginning, middle, or end of a sentence.

ORIGINAL	The coyotes howled across the prairie. The moon began to rise. [The second independent clause explains *when* the coyotes howled.]
COMBINED	The coyotes howled across the prairie **as the moon began to rise.** [*As* is placed before the second independent clause. The new adverb clause is inserted into the remaining sentence.]
	As the moon began to rise, the coyotes howled across the prairie. [The new adverb clause begins the sentence and is followed by a comma.]

EXERCISE B Combine the following pairs of sentences into a complex sentence. Use the subordinating conjunction in parentheses to make one sentence into an adverb clause. Write the new sentence on the line provided. Hint: Be sure to include a comma after an adverb clause that begins a sentence.

Example 1. Julie's father said, "Good job!" She had finished cleaning the garage. *(when)*

When she had finished cleaning the garage, Julie's father said, "Good job!"

[*When* is used to make the second independent clause an adverb clause describing *when* Julie's father spoke. The adverb clause is followed by a comma.]

6. Nicole waved hello. She wasn't sure who was waving at her. *(even though)* [Where can you place *even though* in the second sentence to make it an adverb clause?] _____

_____

7. It's a good thing tomorrow is recycling pick-up day. The recycling bin is full. *(because)* _____

_____

8. The movie finally started. The theater owner managed to get the sound turned on. *(after)*

_____

9. The bird had not grown all of its feathers. It was learning to fly. *(although)* _____

_____

10. The wind died down. The birds began to chatter again. *(when)* _____

_____

Varying Sentence Beginnings

One way to bring variety to your writing is to begin sentences in different ways. Many English sentences start with a subject followed by a verb and often include modifiers. So beginning a sentence with a word that is not a subject adds variety to your sentence structure. Here are three ways to vary the beginnings of sentences.

(1) Begin the sentence with a one-word modifier. The word might be a participle (an *–ing* or *–ed* form of a verb used as an adjective) or an adverb telling *when, where, how,* or *to what extent.* Use a comma to set off the modifier from the main clause.

> **PARTICIPLE** **Startled,** the birds flew away. [The participle *Startled* describes *birds.*]
>
> **ADVERB** **Earlier,** the showers had lowered the temperature by ten degrees. [The adverb *Earlier* modifies the verb *had lowered* by telling when the action in the sentence occurred.]

EXERCISE A Begin each of the following sentences by writing a meaningful one-word modifier on the line at the beginning of the sentence. Remember to set off the modifier with a comma.

Example 1. _____*Luckily,*_____ the math quiz was easier than I thought it would be. [Many

words could go in the blank, most of them adverbs. A comma sets off *Luckily* from the rest

of the sentence.]

1. _____ the extra time we spent studying really paid off. [What word can

meaningfully begin the sentence? What mark of punctuation should follow it?]

2. _____ the teacher allowed us a few extra minutes to complete the last item.

3. _____ Tom commented that the classroom was warm in the afternoon.

4. _____ these math skills will be useful later in life.

5. _____ let's compare the notes we took in class.

(2) Begin sentences with an introductory phrase. An introductory phrase is often set off from the rest of the sentence by a comma. Sometimes, you can move a phrase from another part of the sentence to the beginning of the sentence.

> **PREPOSITIONAL PHRASE** **At the aquarium,** the students observed rays and sharks. [The prepositional phrase acts as an adverb telling where the action of the sentence occurred.]
>
> **PARTICIPIAL PHRASE** **Swinging confidently,** the batter smacked the ball, dropped his bat, and ran for first base. [The participial phrase acts as an adjective describing the subject, *batter.*]
>
> **INFINITIVE PHRASE** **To travel safely,** always wear a seatbelt and drive carefully. [The infinitive phrase acts as an adverb telling why the action of the sentence occurs.]

GO ON

EXERCISE B Begin each of the following sentences by writing a meaningful phrase on the line provided. Remember to set off the the phrase with a comma.

Example 1. _____*Early on Saturday morning,*_____ Juan brought the paint supplies from

the garage. [A phrase modifying the verb *brought* tells when the action occurred.]

6. _____ the house's exterior needed repainting badly.

[Which sort of phrase would make sense to begin this sentence, adjective or adverb?]

7. _____ the day was a little too humid for painting.

8. _____ paint doesn't dry quickly or smoothly.

9. _____ Juan removed the last flakes of old paint.

10. _____ we can finish the job in a day.

---

(3) Another way to begin sentences is with an adverb clause. An introductory adverb clause is set off from the rest of the sentence by a comma. Sometimes, you can move an adverb clause from another part of the sentence to the beginning of the sentence. An adverb clause begins with a subordinating conjunction such as *because, as soon as,* or *although.*

> **ADVERB CLAUSE** **As soon as Chad gets home,** he makes a healthy snack and rests for half an hour. [The adverb clause begins with the subordinating conjunction *As soon as* and modifies the verb *makes* by telling when the action of the sentence occurs.]

EXERCISE C Begin each of the following sentences by writing a meaningful adverb clause on the line provided. Begin the adverb clause with the subordinating conjunction given in the parentheses after each sentence. Remember to set off the clause with a comma.

Example 1. ____*Since the vacant lot has finally been sold,*____ a new building is going up downtown.

(*Since*) [The introductory adverb clause tells why the action occurs.]

11. _____ the building will be a high-rise. (*Because*) [What

adverb clause would tell why the action occurs?]

12. _____ this building will hold apartments. (*Although*)

13. _____ inspectors will check over every step of the

building process. (*Because*)

14. _____ construction will begin. (*As soon as*)

15. _____ the building should be finished in just under two

years. (*Provided that*)

Varying Sentence Structure

One way to hold your readers' attention is to vary your sentence structure. After you complete a first draft, revise your writing for a balance of the four basic sentence structures; these are formed using independent clauses and subordinate clauses.

SIMPLE SENTENCE   That quiet music makes Kendra feel relaxed. [Only one independent clause is used in a simple sentence.]

COMPOUND SENTENCE   That quiet music makes Kendra feel relaxed, but she must complete her homework. [Two independent clauses are joined by a comma and the coordinating conjunction *but* to make a compound sentence.]

COMPLEX SENTENCE   That quiet music makes Kendra feel relaxed, although she seldom listens to it. [One independent clause—*That quiet music makes Kendra feel relaxed*—combines with a subordinate clause—*although she seldom listens to it*—to make a complex sentence.]

COMPOUND-COMPLEX SENTENCE   That quiet music makes Kendra feel relaxed, but she must complete her homework; why don't you turn it off for a while? [In this sentence structure, two independent clauses and one subordinate clause are combined.]

EXERCISE A Identify the structure of each of the following sentences by writing *S* for *simple, CD* for *compound, CX* for *complex,* or *CD-CX* for *compound-complex* on the line provided.

Example ___*S*___ **1.** Lane and his father entered the old house cautiously. [This simple sentence expresses only one thought.]

_____ **1.** The door creaked on its hinges, and the wind whistled eerily through a broken window. [How many independent clauses are in this sentence? Are there any subordinate clauses?]

_____ **2.** As the men wiped dust off, they wondered how long the house had been empty.

_____ **3.** Now a realtor was going to offer it for sale.

_____ **4.** As he examined the old, carved mantelpiece over the fireplace, Lane knew that it would take a lot of work to fix up the house.

_____ **5.** Although the old house was a mess, the men could imagine what it would be like restored; it could one day be the town's pride if someone fixed it up carefully.

When you revise your writing to vary sentence structure, remember the ways you have learned to combine sentences.

(1) Make an important word or phrase from one clause part of another clause.

ORIGINAL   Hang the picture on the wall, and hang it straight. [Compound sentence]
COMBINED   Hang the picture on the wall **straight**. [The word *straight* is taken from the second independent clause and used in the first clause.]

GO ON ➡

Developmental Language Skills

(2) Use coordination to express related ideas.

> **ORIGINAL** The frame doesn't match the others. The shape is nice. [Two sentences]
>
> **COMBINED** The frame doesn't match the others**, but the shape is nice**. [The second sentence is combined with the first sentence with a comma and the coordinating conjunction *but* to make one compound sentence.]

(3) Use subordination to combine a less important idea with a more important idea.

> **ORIGINAL** It's good to have pictures on the wall. They show how the family has grown and changed. [Two sentences]
>
> **COMBINED** It's good to have pictures on the wall **because they show how the family has grown and changed**. [The second sentence is changed to a subordinate clause by adding the subordinating conjunction *because* and adding the clause to the first sentence.]

EXERCISE B Revise each of the following pairs of sentences, using the structure given in the parentheses. Hint: Make any necessary changes to punctuation and capitalization when you combine sentences.

Example 1. The plane had not yet lifted off. The flight attendants distributed snacks. *(Complex)*

[The first sentence can be changed into a subordinate clause and added to the second sentence.]

Although the plane had not yet lifted off, the flight attendants distributed snacks.

6. The pilot was concerned about the weather. A front was blowing in. *(Complex)* [Which sentence is less important and can be subordinated? Will you need to add any punctuation?]

_____

7. Hadn't the crew recently completed a training session? Wasn't it about severe weather? *(Simple)*

_____

8. Because the storm was so strong, the ride was bumpy. The crew was not nervous. *(Compound-Complex)*

_____

9. The flight went smoothly. It arrived right on time. *(Compound)*

_____

10. The geography of our country is varied. Seeing the variety from the air is wonderful. *(Simple)*

_____

Revising to Reduce Wordiness

Choppy sentences may cause readers to become bored with your writing, and long, wordy sentences may have the same effect. There is no minimum number of words needed to write a good sentence, so write clearly and concisely. Here are three strategies for revising wordy sentences.

(1) Sometimes you can replace a phrase with a single word, making the sentence more readable without losing meaning.

> **WORDY**   With a lot of pride, the runner crossed the finish line.
>
> **REVISED**   **Proudly**, the runner crossed the finish line. [The two prepositional phrases *With a lot* and *of pride* can be replaced with the single word *Proudly*.]

EXERCISE A On the line provided, write a single word that could replace the underlined word group in each of the following sentences. Do not change the sentence's meaning.

Example ___*Gently*___ **1.** With much gentleness, the father put the sleepy baby in her crib. [The prepositional phrase can be replaced with the single word *Gently*.

_____ **1.** Due to the fact that the weather was cold and chilly, the cyclists wore warm windbreakers. [What single word can replace the underlined section of the sentence?]

_____ **2.** With great bravery the firefighter entered the warehouse.

_____ **3.** Actors usually aren't the kind of people who are shy.

_____ **4.** Did the students complete the project with success?

_____ **5.** Some people experience a lot of nervous feelings when they speak in public.

(2) Sometimes you can replace a clause with a phrase without changing the meaning of the sentence.

> **WORDY**   Because we were planning to leave early, we packed the night before.
>
> **REVISED**   **Planning to leave early**, we packed the night before. [Replacing the subordinate clause with a participial phrase makes the sentence more compact without changing its meaning.]

EXERCISE B Write a phrase that more concisely expresses the meaning of the underlined clause in each of the following sentences.

Example 1. My aunt, who is the family member who knows the most about gardening, will show us where to plant the peppers. [A short appositive phrase can carry the same meaning as the longer clause.]

___the family gardener___

GO ON ➡

6. Because he had an eye on the weather, Dad warned us about the approaching storm. [Which

kind of phrase—prepositional, participial, or appositive—could replace the clause? Will any word

forms need to change? Will any punctuation need to be added or deleted?]

_____

7. Ask Marcelle, who is a trusted confidante, for her advice.

_____

8. Carmen wants to see only movies that have happy endings.

_____

9. While they were singing softly, the choir filed onto the stage.

_____

10. The game was not canceled despite the fact that it began to rain.

_____

---

(3) Sometimes you can take out an unnecessary word or even a whole group of unnecessary
words. This word group may simply repeat information already given in the sentence.

> **WORDY**   Yvonne sighed dreamily and sighed happily as she thought of summer
> vacation. [There is no need to repeat the verb *sighed*.]
>
> **REVISED**   Yvonne **sighed dreamily and happily** as she thought of summer vacation.
>
> **WORDY**   Brian wants to go to a restaurant that serves all kinds of food and that has a
> lot of variety. [The clause *that has a lot of variety* repeats information con-
> tained in the first subordinate clause.]
>
> **REVISED**   Brian wants to go to a restaurant **that serves all kinds of food**.

EXERCISE C Underline the unnecessary word or word group in each of the following sentences.

Example 1. Take the books that you checked out of the library back to the library. [The

prepositional phrases *of the library* and *to the library* repeat information. Taking out one of

them reduces wordiness without changing meaning.]

11. The beavers built and built until they finished the dam. [What words repeat information given

elsewhere in the sentence?]

12. The enormous boulder, which is really quite large, marks the trailhead.

13. Randa is trying to say that she wants jazzy music playing in the background.

14. My best friend, who is my favorite of all my friends, will go with me.

15. The timid deer, which was shy around people, hid in the woods.

Manuscript Form

When writing a paper for school, it is important to follow a manuscript style in order to present information in a neat and organized way. Here is one common manuscript style.

Margins

Leave a one-inch margin on the top, sides, and bottom of each page.

Pagination

One half inch from the top of each page, include a header in the upper right-hand corner. The header should include your last name followed by the page number.

Indention

Paragraphs should be indented half an inch; set-off quotations should be indented an inch from the left margin (five spaces and ten spaces, respectively, on standard typewriters).

Heading

On the title page of your paper, include a heading one inch from the top of the page. The heading should include your full name, your teacher's name, the course name, and the date (day, month, year). Double-space between each line of your heading.

Title

On the title page of your paper, include the title of your paper. Double-space between the heading and the title. Center the title and capitalize the appropriate letters. Double-space between the title and body of your paper.

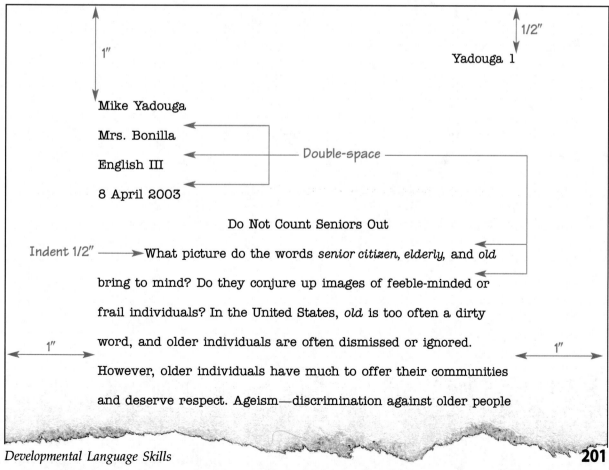

EXERCISE The following passage is excerpted from a research paper written on March 12, 2003, by Suzi Kreici, a student in Mr. Escamilla's English III class. Fill in the blanks with the appropriate information to complete the title page according to the guidelines on the previous page.

Title: Documentary Scores High

First Paragraph: On one level, *Hoop Dreams* is about poverty, social injustice, the sports machine, and basketball. On another, however, it is the story of William Gates and Arthur Agee, two African American boys from inner-city Chicago. Director Steve James's three-hour documentary records their incredible odyssey from ragged neighborhood courts to polished college floorboards in pursuit of NBA stardom. Although the film contains important social commentary, the moving, intimate portrait of two boys' struggle to fulfill their individual potential makes *Hoop Dreams* a compelling documentary.

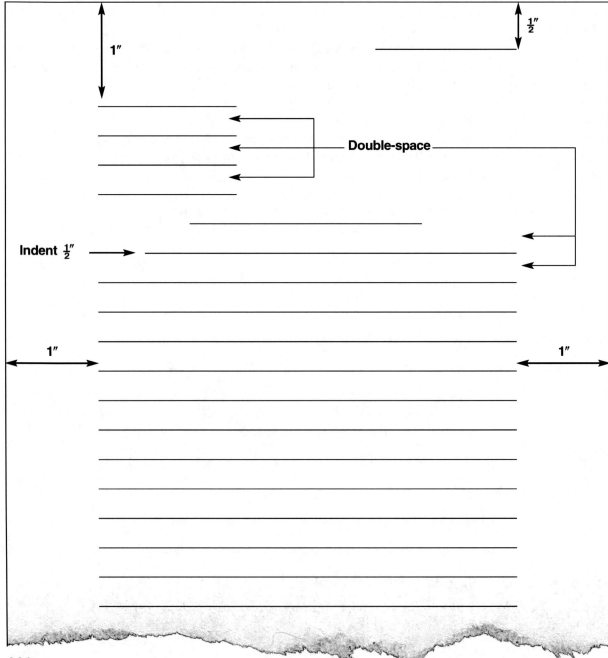

HOLT HANDBOOK | Fifth Course